SS
75¢

UNWIN UNIVERSITY BOOKS

23

HISTORY OF EUROPE

IN THE

NINETEENTH CENTURY

D1564763

by the same author

HISTORY AS A STORY OF LIBERTY

MY PHILOSOPHY

POLITICS AND MORALS

CROCE, THE KING AND THE ALLIES

UNWIN UNIVERSITY BOOKS

HISTORY OF EUROPE

IN THE

NINETEENTH CENTURY

by

BENEDETTO CROCE

Translated from the Italian

by

HENRY FURST

LONDON
UNWIN UNIVERSITY BOOKS

Published in Italian as "Storia d'Europa
nel secolo decimononono"

First Published in Great Britain in 1934
Second Impression 1939
Third Impression 1953
Fourth Impression 1965

2,216

PRINTED IN GREAT BRITAIN
BY JOHN DICKENS AND CO LTD, NORTHAMPTON

TO THOMAS MANN

Pur mo venian li tuoi pensier tra i miei
con simile atto e con simile faccia,
sí che d'entrambi un sol consiglio fei.

Dante, *Inf.*, XXIII, 28-30

TRANSLATOR'S PREFACE

THIS volume is the elaboration of lectures delivered before the Accademia di Scienze morali e politiche of the Società Reale of Naples in the year 1931. The present translation has been made from the third Italian edition (Bari, Laterza, 1932), substantially the same as the first two editions, except for a few minor corrections made by the author. In view of certain false statements which have found credence concerning omissions in the German version, the translator wishes to forestall all such fantasies by affirming that he has adhered as closely as possible to the text. A few words have been omitted here and there where the author, quoting an English expression (such as "Disestablishment Bill") goes on to explain its meaning in Italian. It has been obviously necessary to omit such explanations; otherwise the version is literal and verbatim. In short, the criterion has been followed of *tradurre senza tradire*. Croce employs long sentences and very long paragraphs which it would often be impossible to break up without materially altering his meaning. That is after all the tradition of Italian prose.

The translator wishes to thank Dr. Mario Einaudi, of the University of Turin, and Dr. Gaudence Megaro, of New York, for many valuable suggestions. The latter also kindly read the proof.

HENRY FURST

Camogli, 1933.

CONTENTS

I. THE RELIGION OF LIBERTY

WHEN the Napoleonic adventure was at an end and that extraordinary despot had disappeared from the stage where he had reigned supreme; while his conquerors were agreeing or trying to agree among themselves so that they could unite in giving to Europe, by the restoration of old régimes and the timely manipulation of frontiers, a stable organization to replace the strongly held yet always precarious empire of the French nation—then among all the peoples hopes were flaming up and demands were being made for independence and liberty. These demands grew louder and more insistent the more they met repulse and repression; and in disappointment and defeat hopes went on springing up afresh, purposes were strengthened.

In Germany, in Italy, in Poland, in Belgium, in Greece, and in the distant colonies of Latin America oppressed nations were beginning to attempt some opposition to foreign rulers and governors. There were similar attempts in nations and amputated parts of nations that had been forced into political union with states owing their origin and their form to conquests, treaties, or the property rights of princely families; and in nations that had been cut up into small states, which felt that because they were so broken up they were hampered, weakened, rendered impotent for the part they should be playing in the life of the world, and humiliated as to their dignity before other nations that were united and great. In these nations, and in others, there were longings for many things: for juridical guarantees; for participation in administration and government by means of new or revised representative systems; for various associations of citizens for special economic, social, and political purposes; for open discussion of ideas and interests in the press; and for "constitutions," as people said at the time. And in the nations, like France, to which these constitutions had been granted in the form of "charters," there was urgent demand that these be safeguarded and made broader. In yet other nations, like England, where after a long and gradual growth the representative system was now in force, there was pressure for the removal of the restrictions and inequalities that still existed, and for a general modernization and rationalization of the system that would ensure a freer and more generous way of life and of progress.

Since the historical antecedents and the existing conditions, the spirit and the customs, of the various nations were diverse, these demands differed in the several countries, as to order of appearance, as to magnitude, as to details, and as to their general tone. In one country precedence was given to liberation from a foreign domination or to national unity, and in another to the change from absolutism in government to constitutionalism. Here it was simply a question of reform of the franchise and the extension of political power, while there it was a question of establishing a representative system for the first time, or on new foundations. In one country, which through the efforts of the preceding generations—especially during the French Revolution and the Empire—already enjoyed civil equality and religious tolerance, the people began to call for the participation in government of new social strata. In another country it was necessary to delay first to battle with the political privileges of the feudal classes and persistent forms of servitude, and to shake off the yoke of ecclesiastical oppression. But though these demands were different in importance and in order of appearance, they were all linked in a single chain, and sooner or later one drew another along after itself, and brought to light still others that could be seen in the distance. And over all of them rose one word that summed them all up and expressed the spirit which had given them life—the word *liberty*.

To be sure, it was not a new word in history, as it was not a new word in prose and poetry, or in the rhetoric of prose and poetry. Greece and Rome had handed down the memory of innumerable champions of liberty, and of sublime deeds and tragedies in which men had given their lives magnanimously for liberty, "which is so dear." Christians and their churches had invoked liberty for centuries. Liberty was the cry of the communes against emperors and kings, and of the feudal lords and barons against those same kings and emperors, and these in turn invoked liberty against the barons and the great vassals and against communities that had usurped sovereign rights. It was liberty that the kingdoms, the provinces, the cities, solicitous for their parliaments and chapters and privileges, invoked against the absolute monarchies that were ridding themselves or trying to rid themselves of those obstacles and limits to their activities. The loss of liberty had always been looked upon as the cause or the sign of decadence in the arts, in science, in economics, in morality, whether one looked at the Rome of the Caesars or the Italy of the Spaniards and the Popes. Now of late "liberty," together with "equality" and "fraternity," had shaken to pieces and scattered in ruins, as if by the force of a great earthquake, the whole edifice of old France and almost all of that of old Europe, and the terrifying impression of that deed still lingered. It seemed as though this destruction had snatched from that name the halo of beauty and the lure of the new. And indeed the trinity of which it had made one—the "fixed and immortal triangle of Reason," as the poet Vincenzo Monti called it—fell into disrepute and was well-nigh abhorred. But once more liberty rose above the horizon, this time alone, and men gave it their admiration as a star of incomparable splendour. And the word was spoken by the younger generation with the emotional emphasis of those who have just discovered an idea of vital importance, one illuminating the past and the present, a guide for the future.

The novelty of the idea with which that old, old word was filled did not escape either the feeling or the thought of the people of the time, as may be seen from the problem to which it soon gave rise. This concerned the difference in character between the liberty suited to the modern world and that of the ancient Greeks and Romans and the Jacobins of yesterday. This problem was propounded and discussed for the first time—or almost the first—by Benjamin Constant, in an address he gave in 1819 before the Athénée of Paris, and it has been discussed many times from that day to ours. But though the problem had its kernel of reality, it was not presented correctly when a contrast was made between the ancient and the modern, in which Greece, Rome, and the French Revolution (as following the Graeco-Roman ideals) stood on one side, and on the other the modern world—as if the present were not the point where all the streams of history flow together and history's last act, and as if a single continuous development could be broken by a static opposition. In consequence, the investigation that was based on the supposed contrast ran the risk of being lost in abstractions, separating state and individual, civil liberty and political liberty, the liberty of one man and that liberty of all other men which limits his own. It ran the risk of assigning political but not civil liberty to the ancients, and to the moderns civil but not political liberty (or political liberty of only a low degree), or the risk of reversing these judgments and attributing to the ancients greater liberty for the individual in his relations to the state than that found among modern nations. This error of abstraction always reappears when the attempt is made to define the idea of liberty by juridical distinctions, which are practical in character and concern single and transitory institutions rather than the superior and supreme idea that embraces them all and transcends them all.

If we look for the content of that concept in the history to which it belongs, which we call sometimes the history of thought, sometimes the history of philosophy, we find the consciousness of its novelty which existed at that time to be nothing more than the consciousness of the new thing that had entered thought and through it life, the new concept of man and the vision of the road that was opening before him, broad and well lighted as it had never been before. Men had not attained that concept by chance or suddenly, had not reached the entrance to that road in one leap or one flight; they had been brought there by all the experiences and solutions of philosophy as it laboured for centuries, experiences and solutions that were always lessening the distance and calming the dissension between heaven and earth, God and the world, the ideal and the real. By giving ideality to reality and reality to ideality, philosophy had recognized and understood their indivisible unity, which is identity.

In speaking of the history of thought or philosophy, we mean at the same time all history, whether it be called civil or political or economic or moral, since each of these feeds the first and is fed by it. Therefore we mean not only the philosophy of Plato, Aristotle, Galileo, Descartes, and Kant, but also that of the Greek world which set itself against the barbarians and that of the Rome which civilized those same barbarians by making them Roman citizens. We include the

philosophy of the Christian redemption, that of the Church
which fought against the Empire, that of the Italian and Flem-
ish communes in the Middle Ages, and above all that of the
Renaissance and the Reformation, which vindicated individuality once more in its double value for action and for morality. We mean the philosophy of the religious wars, that of
the English Long Parliament, that of the liberty of conscience
proclaimed by the religious sects of England and Holland
and the American colonies, that of the declaration of the
rights of man made in these countries as well as the one to
which the French Revolution gave special efficacy. We include also the philosophy of technical discoveries and the
revolutionary consequences of these in industry, and all the
events and creations which helped to form that conception,
and to put law and order back into all things, and God back
into the world.

But the latest advance that had been made at the end of
the eighteenth century and the beginning of the nineteenth
had disentangled the problem more clearly and almost con-
clusively, because it had criticized the opposition—acute in
eighteenth-century rationalism and the French Revolution—
between reason and history, in which history had been de-
graded and condemned by the light of reason. It had criticized the opposition, and had healed it by means of dialectics,
which does not separate the finite and the infinite, nor the
positive and the negative. It had made one the rationality and
the reality of the new idea of history, rediscovering the saying of the philosopher Giovanni Battista Vico that the republic sought for by Plato was nothing but the course of
human events. Man, then, no longer looked on himself as belittled by history or as vindicating himself against it and
pushing the past away from him as a shameful memory.
Instead, a true and tireless creator, he looked on himself in
the history of the world as he looked on himself in his own

life. No longer did history appear destitute of spirituality and abandoned to blind forces, or sustained and constantly directed by alien forces. Now it was seen to be the work and the activity of the spirit, and so, since spirit is liberty, the work of liberty. It was all the work of liberty, its unique and eternal positive moment, which alone is made effective in the series of its forms and gives them their significance, and which alone explains and justifies the function fulfilled by the negative moment of subjection, with its constraints, its oppressions, its reactions, and its tyrannies, which (to quote Vico once more) seem to be "untoward events" and are really "opportunities."

Such was the thought, the philosophy, of the age that was at its beginning, a philosophy that was springing up everywhere, spreading everywhere, that was found on the lips of everyone, appearing in the stanzas of poetry and in the words of men of action no less than in the formulas of those who were philosophers by profession. This philosophy dragged along with it the dross of the past, sometimes put on clothes that no longer fitted, was tangled in and struggled with contradictions—and yet always went on its way, and kept ahead of everything else. Traces of it are to be found even among its adversaries: the retarded, the reactionaries, the priests and the Jesuits. And there is no little irony in the fact that the new spiritual attitude received its baptismal name from the least likely sponsor, the country that more than any other in Europe had been tight shut against philosophy and modern culture, a country pre-eminently mediaeval and scholastic—Spain, which at that time coined the word *liberal*, together with its exact antonym *servil*. It is therefore well to note (in order to avoid a reef on which many run aground) that the philosophy of an age must not be sought only among its philosophers or even among its great philosophers, but must instead be dug out of all the manifestations of that age. It cannot be found, or can be found but scantily, among the special philosophers, even the greatest of them. For the latter are always single individuals, and if in addition to the problems of their time they, looking forward to later times, set and solve other problems that their own age does not yet feel, does not apprehend, or does not comprehend clearly, it sometimes happens—since every man has his limitations—that in his day and generation some of the problems set and solved by a given philosopher cannot be made to fit into his system, and outworn and erroneous conceptions take their place. The great philosophers, like the rest of men of every kind, have no fixed and destined place in either the vanguard or the rearguard or the middle ranks of their contemporaries, but are found now in one, now in another, of those positions. Even the great philosophers of free Athens, the most splendid flowers of her liberty, amid the democratic turbulence that offended their sense of harmony and tied as they were to their naturalistic logic, in their theories failed to prove equal to the reality of the life that they lived. But an example fitting our case better is that of the supreme philosopher of the age of which we are speaking, Hegel. More profoundly than any other man he thought about and treated of dialectics and history, defining spirit in terms of liberty and liberty in terms of spirit. Yet because of certain of his political tendencies and theories he deserved to be called *servil* rather than *liberal*. Far above him in this respect, and far better representatives of the thought of the new age, stand minds that are philosophically inferior to his or that are not usually considered in the least philosophical— for example, a woman, Madame de Staël.

The concept of history as the history of liberty had as its necessary practical complement that same liberty as a moral ideal, an ideal that had in fact grown side by side with all the thought and the movement of civilization, and which in

modern times had passed from liberty as a complex of privileges to liberty as a natural right, and from that abstract
natural right to the spiritual liberty of the historically concrete personality. And it had become gradually more coherent
and more solid, strengthened by the corresponding philosophy, according to which that which is the law of being is the
law of what must be. It could be denied only by those who,
following the stale philosophies of transcendence, in some
way separated what must be from what is, or by those who
did not see that they were separating the two, yet did so in
their arguments. Thus, for example, there was the objection
that the moral ideal of liberty neither allows nor promises
the expulsion of evil from the world, and therefore is not
truly moral. Those who said this did not take into consideration that if morality should destroy the idea of evil, it would
itself vanish, that only in the struggle against evil does morality have reality and life, that thanks to the struggle only is it
lauded.

Again some lamented that the very affirmation and acceptance of the struggle that was always beginning anew shut
man out from peace, from happiness, from that state of
blessedness for which he always yearns. These did not take
into consideration that the grandeur of the modern conception lay precisely in having changed the sense of life from
the idyllic (and in consequence the elegiac) to the dramatic,
from the hedonistic (and in consequence the pessimistic) to
the active and creative, and that it had made liberty a continual reacquisition, a continual liberation, a continual battle, one in which a last and final victory is impossible, because it would mean the death of all the combatants, that is,
of all then living.

In view of all this, it is easy to see what value should be
given to the other objections that were propounded at the time
and have been repeated many times and are still repeated,

such as this: The ideal of liberty, just because it is excellent, should be for the few and not for the common people, who need coercion from above, coercion by authority and the lash. This objection would find its exact counterpart in the statement—whose absurdity is obvious—that truth should be for the few and non-truth and error are suited to the many; as if truth were not such because of its intrinsic power of expansion and vitalization and transformation in every way that opens to it. There are other objections that are even more extravagant, for example: Liberty belongs properly to certain nations that have achieved it under unusual conditions, as insular England has done; or to generous-blooded nations like the Germanic, which have cultivated it in the wilds of their forests. This objection in its turn humbles spirit before matter and subjects it to mechanistic determinism. Moreover, facts give it the lie, for these show that though England taught the Continental nations much concerning liberal conceptions, she also learned not a little from them; and that for a long time Germany amid her forests forgot liberty and set up the idols of authority and subjection.

It was, then, quite obvious that to the question, What is the ideal of the new generation? the answer must be that word *liberty* without any qualification, since any addition would cloud the concept. And those cold and superficial observers were wrong who wondered at it or made it a jest and, accusing the concept of empty formalism, asked in irony or sarcasm: "What is liberty anyway? Liberty of whom or of what? Liberty to do what?" Liberty could not accept adjectives or empiric delimitations because of its intrinsic infinity; but none the less it set its own limits from time to time, by free acts, and so it became particularized and acquired content. The distinction, made many times, of two liberties—the singular and the plural, liberty and liberties—is a contradiction of two abstractions, since liberty in the singular exists only in liberties in the plural. But it never coincides with or is exhausted by these or those of its particularizations in the institutions it has created, and therefore, as has been noted, not only can it not be defined in terms of its institutions, that is, juridically, but also there is no need to connect the one with the other by the bond of conceptual necessity, since the institutions, being historical facts, are bound to and unbound from liberty by historical necessity.

The political demands that we have enumerated above under their main headings formed at this time, more or less, its historical body, and in a certain sense, its body flourishing in beauty and renewed youthful vigour, combined with the audacity and recklessness that belong to youth. Incarnate spirituality, and because of that fact, spiritualized corporality, its significance lay solely in the goal at which it aimed—that human life should draw breath more freely, should grow deeper and broader. In opposition to the humanitarianism of the preceding century and the blindness even of men like Lessing, Schiller, and Goethe to the idea of nation and fatherland, in opposition to the scant (where there was any at all) repugnance felt for foreign intervention, the promotion of nationalism strove to promote humanity in its concrete form, that of personality: individuals as well as the human groups bound together by common origin and common memories, by customs and attitudes, nations already existing and active or nations to be roused to activity.

And intrinsically it placed no barrier against the wider and more comprehensive organization of nations, for "nation" is a spiritual and historical concept and therefore in the act of becoming, not a naturalistic and fixed concept like that of race. The very hegemony or primacy claimed for this or that people—by Fichte and others for the Germanic peoples, by Guizot and others for the French, by Mazzini and Gioberti for the Italians, and by still others for the Poles and the Slavs in general—was theorized as the right and the duty of that people to take its place at the head of all the nations in order to act as their leader in the movement towards civilization, towards human perfection, towards spiritual greatness. The German nationalists of that time said that the German people was the chosen people, but they added that this was because it was cosmopolitan and not purely national. And almost all of the other hegemonists said the same. Constitutions and representative governments must bring to efficacy and political activity men of greater ability and greater goodwill than those who had been active before, or rivals of these. A free press was an open forum for the exchange of ideas, for the clash and measurement of passions, for the elucidation of situations, for disputes and agreements; and, as someone has cleverly said, it attempted to take the place in the great states of Europe and of the world that the agora had held in the small cities of ancient times.

The favour in which men held the two great parties that made up the parliaments—conservative and progressive, moderate and radical, the left and the right—betrayed the intention to slow up the impetus of the social movement and avoid the havoc and bloodshed of revolutionary explosions, by making the struggle of interests mild and humane. In the face of the centralization and the administrative despotism of Revolution and Empire and that of the absolute monarchs who had been restored to their thrones, the anxious hopes and desires of local autonomies were troubled by the fear that centralization, by putting all on one level, would impoverish and sterilize the fulness of life in the very places where those autonomies were carrying on the best administrations and cultivating the best nurseries of political ability. Constitutional monarchies after the English model took a middle position between absolute monarchy (which was too historical) and the republic (which was too little historical), and were declared to be almost the only form of republic suited to the times. (After her Revolution, of course, statesmen of the old school considered England a republic, and not a monarchy.) Likewise, in general all the resumption of historical traditions was animated by the desire to collect and use whatever was still alive and adaptable to modern life, whether it was found in local institutions and customs, among the nobility or among the peasants, or in naïve religious beliefs. The breaking of the chains that had weighed down or still weighed down industry and commerce was in obedience to the necessity of giving an impulse to invention, to individual ability, and to competition, in order to increase the wealth that, no matter who produced it or who owned it, was always the wealth of society as a whole and contributed to its welfare and its moral elevation in one way or another, sooner or later. And the same was true of all the aspects and special purposes of these varied demands.

It might happen—and in the later course of history certainly would happen—that some or many of these liberal institutions would die, when the conditions that made them possible had disappeared. Others would become inefficient, powerless, or unadaptable, and these would have to be modified, or discarded and replaced. But that is the lot of all things pertaining to man; they live and die; they change and take on new life; or they become mechanical and have to be cast aside. And in every case the agent of that modification, readaptation, or destruction is always liberty, which by this method is taking on a new body, one endowed with fresh youth or grown to adult strength. So there is nothing to keep men from thinking, with the rigid and forward-looking logic that belongs essentially to the liberal concept, that when the contrasts which had given it life had grown antiquated, the two-party system would be changed into one of varied and mobile groups concerned with particular problems. Self-government would yield to the necessity for greater regularity and centralization, constitutional monarchies to republics; and national states would be combined into states of many nations, or united states, when a wider national consciousness (for example, European) had come into being. Economic freedom would be weakened and reduced to narrow confines by federations of industrialists and the nationalizing of various services. Certainly few of these liberals of the first generations believed in such possibilities; sometimes or even habitually they denied them. But nevertheless those possibilities were implicit in the principle they proclaimed, and they must be borne in mind now that we can perceive them after more than a century of manifold experiences and mental toil. This warning applies to all that we have been saying of this germinal period, in which we see, as we must see, in the germ the tree of which it was the germ and which alone could have made it capable of growth and not an aborted cell.

And it might also happen (and that is the reason that the new and Goethian figure of progress was drawn no longer as a straight line, but as a spiral) that in the crises of rejuvenation the liberal régimes would be subject to reactions and returns to authority, of different origins, of lesser or greater extent and longer or shorter duration. But liberty would continue to work within these and to eat them away until at last it would emerge once more, wiser and stronger. To be sure, even then the corporality that we have called spiritualized would be accompanied now and then by another that was not spiritualized, and was therefore unhealthy. The cult of nationalism gave signs, in some of its confused apostles, of being given over to vainglory and the insolence of material dominion, or of shutting itself off from the other nations in a sombre lust of race. And the cult of history and the past gave signs of perversion into inane idolatry; the reverence for religion, those of pseudo-religious fervour; the devotion to existing institutions, those of conservative timidity; the observance of constitutional forms, those of lack of courage to face the necessary modifications; economic freedom, those of the protection of the interests of this or that group; and so on. But these weaknesses, these errors, these omens of evils to come, were inseparable from the very value of the demands that were being made and the institutions for which they asked, and they did not lessen the substantial nobility of the liberal movement, its potent moral efficacy. This was irradiated by poetry, armed by logic and by science; it turned early to action and prepared for conquest and dominion.

Poets, theorists, orators, publicists, propagandists, apostles and martyrs bore witness to the profound seriousness of that ideal; and since they arose and multiplied around it, and not (or more rarely and less resolutely) around other ideals, they bore witness that its vigour would prevail, that the victory which awaited it was certain. And not only the facts but also the doctrine forbade any separation in the future—a separation that would be a grave sign of degradation and decadence—between theory and practice, science and life, public life and private life; as if it were possible to search for and find the truth without at the same time feeling it and living it in action or the desire for action, and possible to separate the man from the citizen, the individual from the society that forms him and which he forms. The mere scholar and philosopher, pacific and given to dreams, the intellectual and the rhetorician who treated of the images of the sublime but fled from the fatigue and danger of the duties those images evoked and imposed, and were prone to servility and the adulation of the courtier—these became objects of scorn. And all writing to order, getting oneself supported by courts and governments instead of looking only to the approval of the public for favour and the very means of livelihood, the compensation for one's work—this became an object

of reproach. There was a demand for sincerity of faith, for
integrity of character, for agreement between word and deed.
The concept of personal dignity was revived, and with it the
feeling for true aristocracy, with its code, its rigidity, and
its exclusiveness, an aristocracy that had now become liberal
and therefore wholly spiritual. The heroic figure that appealed to all hearts was the poet militant, the intellectual
man who can fight and die for his ideas—a figure that was
not confined to the ecstasies of the imagination and peda-
gogical illustrations, but appeared in flesh and blood on bat-
tle-fields and barricades in every part of Europe. The "missionaries" of liberty had as companions the "crusaders" of
liberty.

Now he who gathers together and considers all these characteristics of the liberal ideal does not hesitate to call it what
it was: a "religion." He calls it so, of course, because he
looks for what is essential and intrinsic in every religion,
which always lies in the concept of reality and an ethics that
conforms to this concept. It excludes the mythological element, which constitutes only a secondary differentiation between religion and philosophy. The concept of reality and the
conforming ethics of liberalism were generated, as has been
shown, by modern thought, dialectical and historical. Nothing
more was needed to give them a religious character, since
personifications, myths, legends, dogmas, rites, propitiations,
expiations, priestly classes, pontifical robes, and the like do
not belong to the intrinsic, and are taken out from particular
religions and set up as requirements for every religion with
ill effect. Such a process is the origin of the somewhat numerous artificial religions ("religions of the future") that
were devised in the eighteenth century; they all met ridicule,
which they deserved, since they were counterfeits and carica-
tures. But the religion of liberalism showed itself to be essentially religious in its forms and institutions, and since it was

born and not made, was no cold and deliberate device. Therefore at first its leaders even expected to be able to live in harmony with the old religions, and to bring them a companion, a complement, an aid. As a matter of fact, it set itself up against them, but at the same time summed them up in itself and went further. Beside philosophical motives it set the religious motives of the near and the remote past. Next to and above Socrates it set the human and divine Redeemer Jesus. And it felt that it had undergone all the experiences of paganism and Christianity, of Catholicism, Augustinianism, Calvinism, and all the rest. It felt that it represented the highest demands, that it was the purifying, deepening, and power-giving agent of the religious life of mankind. Therefore it did not point to the chronological dates of its beginnings, nor to new eras that cut it off sharply from the past, as the Christian Church and then Islam had done, and as the National Convention, in imitation of them, had done by its decree expressing the abstract concept of liberty and reason—a concept that lived for a brief moment a life as abstract as itself, and was first forgotten and then abolished.

On every side rang out the cry of a new birth, of a "century that is being born again," like a salutation full of promise to the "third age," the age of the Spirit, which Gioacchino da Fiore had prophesied in the thirteenth century, and which now opened out before the human society that had prepared for it and waited for it.

II. OPPOSING RELIGIOUS FAITHS

THIS religion of the new era found its contrast and its opponents in other rival and hostile religions, which although they were expressly or virtually criticized by it and surpassed by it, counted their own believers and attracted proselytes; they composed important historical realities, answering to certain ideal moments that are forever being repeated.

The first place among them was taken or deserved to be taken by the Catholicism of the Church of Rome, the most direct and logical negation of the liberal idea; that Catholicism felt itself and recognized itself to be such and wished to be so considered from the first appearance of that idea. It proclaimed and proclaims itself such with loud outcry in the syllabi, the encyclicals, the sermons, the instructions, of its pontiffs and its other priests, and always (except for certain passing episodes or illusive appearances) played that part in active life. And in this light it can be considered as the prototype or pure form of all the other oppositions and at the same time the one that, with its undying hatred, illuminates the religious character, the character of religious rivalry, of liberalism. To the liberal conception that the aim of life is in life itself, and duty lies in the increase and elevation of this life, and the method in free initiative and individual

inventiveness, Catholicism answers that, on the contrary, the
aim lies in a life beyond this world, for which the life of
this world is simply a preparation, which must be made with
heed to what a God who is in the heavens, by means of his
vicar on earth and of his Church, bids us believe and do. But
no matter how logical and coherent this authoritarian ultramontane conception of a world to come may be in the thread
of its deductions or compared with other similar conceptions
less solid in texture, none the less it lacks that logicality and
coherence which come from agreement with reality. The activity of the Catholic Church, considered in history, is either
directed to the ends of civilization, of knowledge, of custom,
of political and social policy, of the life of this world, of
human progress—as can be clearly seen in her great period,
when she preserved a large part of the heritage of the ancient
world and defended the rights of conscience and of liberty
and of the life of the spirit against barbaric peoples and
against the materialistic tyranny of emperors and kings—or
else, when she loses this function or at least the leadership
that she has held in it and is overcome by the civilization
which she has herself collaborated in creating, she shrinks to
being a guardian of decrepit and dead forms, of lack of culture, of ignorance, of superstition, of spiritual oppression,
and becomes in her turn more or less materialistic.

History, which is the history of liberty, proves to be
stronger than this doctrine or this programme; it defeats it
and forces it to contradict itself in the domain of facts. The
Renaissance, which was not an impossible return of pre-
Christian antiquity, and the Reformation, likewise not an impossible return of primitive Christianity (since each was an
approach to the modern conception of reality and ideality),
mark the internal decadence of Catholicism as a spiritual
power; and this decadence did not give place to a regeneration and was not arrested. Rather, it was rendered irremedi-

able by the reaction of the Counter-Reformation, when the
body and not the soul of the old Church was saved, its mun-
dane domination and not its rule over the mind, and a political but not a religious result was achieved. Science, which by
its support and co-operation demonstrates the superiority of
a determined moral and political ideal, deserted the Catholic
Church; and all the original and creative minds, philosophers,
naturalists, historians, men of letters, publicists, passed or
were forced to pass into the opposite camp, where they were
received and found disciples. For in her own field the Church
could only restore the edifice of mediaeval scholasticism and,
of necessity or through political shrewdness, introduce into
it some secondary variations, or add as a sort of ornament
whatever she could take—without attracting too much attention—from heterodox science and culture. The cessation of
the wars of religion, the new principle of tolerance, English
deism, the concept of the natural history of religions, rationalism and illuminism, antijurisdictionalism and anticurial-
ism, had been constantly at work destroying the conditions
favourable to the Church; so that the French Revolution
found her attenuated and also almost disarmed politically.

It is true that from that revolution itself, from the damage
and the suffering that it inflicted and from the rebellions and
the resistances that arose and took shape against her, the
Catholic Church derived an unexpected influx of forces, both
political, through the renewed support of the states and the
classes that had been defeated or that were threatened and
were struggling in their own defence, and sentimental,
through the longing that was making itself felt for the peaceful and suave images of the past as a refuge from the troubled
and harsh and arid present. But the first of these forces were
purely political and available only for political successes;
and the others were uncertain and quick to turn to the opposite side or to other causes, as is always the case with fancies

that rise and fall and desires that are mobile and to be distrusted—as in fact the Church very soon and one may say in general did distrust them. Thought and science continued to slip from her; as far as they were concerned her womb was stricken with sterility as if by divine punishment for having sinned against the spirit that is the spirit of sincerity. In the midst of these storms and fears, at most she beheld arising as her champion some pedantic polemist who was also, unfortunately, fanatical, abstractly logical, and pompous, a lover of the extreme and the paradoxical, one from whom she had reason to shrink rather than to hope for actual aid, as she scented a spirit foreign to her and a dangerous sense of independence. Above all, the historiography of Catholic sympathizers when compared with that of the liberal side revealed in manifest fashion the poverty to which Catholic thought had been reduced, and even its triviality and puerility. For whereas it reconstructed and understood and admired the history of Christianity and of the Church in the last centuries of the Empire and in the Middle Ages (and even, in some respects, in modern times, those of the missions overseas and the martyrs for the faith), it is well known that the Church considered the entire course of modern history as nothing but horrible perversion, and attributed the authorship and the guilt of so much evil to the Luthers and the Calvins, the Voltaires and the Rousseaus, and the other "corrupters," and to "sects," which, she said, by weaving secretly a web of intrigues, had gained a temporary and diabolical triumph. In short, instead of history, she busied herself with telling fairy stories of ogres to frighten children.

But more serious than all this was the penetration of the enemy into the very circle of the faithful, among those highest in intellectual elevation and purity of intentions. These men felt the attraction towards political liberty, the independence of peoples, the nationality and unity of states, freedom of religious conscience and of the Church herself, the spread of culture, technical and industrial improvements; they experienced currents of approval and sympathy for the creations of modern philosophers, writers, and poets, and took up the study and the independent scrutiny of history, and even of the history of the Church, which they loved especially in the times when she was different from what she had been since the sixteenth century and what she was at present. This effort towards accord and reconciliation, varying and often different in spirit in the several countries and variously tempered or fused, was called Liberal Catholicism. It is clear that in that name the substance is in the adjective, and that the victory has been won not by Catholicism but by liberalism, which Catholicism made up its mind to receive and which introduced a leaven into its old world. The Catholic Church watched it with suspicion and almost condemned it as she had Jansenism, whose successor it was in more ways than one and whose work it continued in the civil and political field; although, prudent and diplomatic as she is wont to be, she tried to refrain, as much as she could, from striking personally at some of the men belonging to it, and who were often writers of great fame and popularity and sincere and respected Catholics, whose condemnation would have caused much scandal and confusion of mind.

For all these reasons the Catholic conception and the doctrine that set it forth in a system and defended it with arguments, were not, in the ideal sphere, an opposition likely to trouble liberalism. The surest proof of this lay in the renunciation it made of, and even in the repugnance it felt towards, the continuance of the warfare that had been waged during the preceding centuries with arms and writing—particularly by Voltaire and the Encyclopaedists; the harvest of that had been reaped. But for that very reason it would have been as unbecoming as it was superfluous to persist in it; the rest could be left to the play of time. And more than unbecoming, it would have been vulgar and inhuman, because (Voltaire and his followers had overlooked this) the old faith was still a way, a mythological one if you will, to soothe and calm suffering and sorrows and to solve the painful problem of life and death, and it was not to be rooted out with violence or insulted with mockery. And it would not be very politic, either, because those beliefs and the consolation derived from them and their teachings were the basis, for many men, of the formula and the authority of social duties, and gave rise to foundations and institutions of social welfare and charity, and motives of order and discipline—all forces and capacities to be assimilated and transformed gradually, but not to be struck down without knowing what to set in their places or without replacing them at all.

The same attitude was taken towards Catholicism and the Church as towards everything past and surpassed, an attitude of impartiality, regard, respect, and even reverence. On the other hand, the liberal ideal, conscious, as we have said, of its own historical genesis, did not reject its bond with Christianity, which still survived in the Catholic Church, no matter how utilitarian and material she had become; and it considered all evangelical souls as its sisters, with whom it was able to establish mutual understanding outside the various veils of doctrine, and to work in the same spirit. Poets at that time liked to describe the figures of the good friar or the good bishop or the good priest, simple and upright and courageous and heroic, to whom they paid no less fervid homage than to their heroines of beauty and virtue and to their other heroes: although they took pleasure in contrasting them frequently with the rest of the clergy and with the Roman Church, and above all with figures of prelates and Jesuits. The necessity for severe vigilance and war was turned against Catholic policy, which had preserved a good part of its weight because of the support that it lent to conservative and reactionary régimes, and because of the lower classes, especially in rural districts, which it was able to arouse and which it had already excited, intoxicated, and guided in the storms of the Revolution and the Empire, such as the Vendeans, the masses of the Santa Fede and the Viva Maria—Christian and apostolic armies which, under different conditions, it was still able to excite and to unchain, and meanwhile was able to use, and did use, as a threat and a hindrance to the development of liberty and the progress of civilization. In order to describe the character of this struggle and to differentiate it from that against Christianity or against Catholicism in so far as it was Christian, a word was coined or at least enjoyed a new meaning and general use, the word "clericalism," and men said that they felt aversion not for Catholicism, but for "clericalism," for "black clericalism."

It is superfluous to stop to discuss the other churches and religious confessions that were either state churches and acted in unison with governments, or else had become rationalistic and illuministic, and at last idealistic and historicizing, and did not oppose but indeed rather favoured the liberal movement—so much so that the Catholic Church placed in a single heap Protestantism, freemasonry, and liberalism—and which did not therefore represent, or represented only at times in a less perfect form, the radical opposition, which was that of Catholicism to liberalism. Less radical than this, and indeed purely political in its technique and its tactics and therefore void of a religious background, seemed the other opposition that liberalism had to face and against which it undertook its first and principal and severe battle: that of the governments, that is, of the absolute monarchies, which are the only ones that need be considered here, for scarce and insignificant were the survivals of aristocratic and patrician régimes, which moreover led substantially to the others. But there is no ideal that does not depend, in the last resort, on a conception of reality and therefore is religious; and that of the absolute monarchy implied the idea of kings as the shepherds of the peoples, and of the peoples as sheep to be led to the pasture, to be mated and multiplied, to be protected against the weather and against wolves and other wild beasts. *"Mulets,"* they were in fact called by Richelieu, the minister of Louis XIII; and the philanthropic Marquis d'Argenson, the minister of Louis XV, treated them in the same way and wanted to form of them *"une ménagerie d'hommes heureux."* A similar idea of them was entertained by Metternich when he declared that it was the concern of princes alone to guide the history of nations; and by that Prussian minister of the restoration whose reply to the remonstrances of the city of Elbing was that the measures of the Government were "above the limited intelligence of the subjects."

This idea, in spite of the unbelief of many of its followers, invoked the divine institution of monarchy and the priestly character of the first kings; and even when, in the Middle Ages, Church and Empire entered into conflict, the theorists of the Empire did not abandon the point of that divine institution, as can be seen, among others, in Dante and his doctrine of the two Suns; nor did Lutheranism prove less obsequious towards the princes and the State, but, by holding that they were of divine order, contributed to their consecration with effects that still endure in German thought and customs. That is why even absolutism, particularly in the form that it took in France with Louis XIV, found its juridical completion in the theory of the divine right of kings; and the sovereigns of the Restoration, led by the most ideological and mystical of the conquerors of Napoleon, formed a Holy Alliance to govern *"comme délegués par la Providence"* (as is written expressly in the constituent act) the nations, who were *"les branches d'une même famille,"* applying in their gov-

ernment *"les préceptes de la sainte religion,"* precepts of
justice, charity, and peace. And Prince Metternich, in his
statement quoted above, added that for their deeds kings were
"responsible to God alone."

But the virtue of the absolute monarchies did not lie only
in this ideology, which political science had long ago dissipated and which English and French revolutionaries had
translated into rough prose by judging and sending to the
scaffold Charles Stuart and Louis Capet without their blood's
becoming baptism and chrism for new kings by divine right.
One of the great men but one of the least religious who have
ever appeared in history (if this deficiency is reconcilable, as
may well be doubted, with true greatness), without this ideology, or recurring to it only in some calculated phrase, had
recently remoulded a monarchy that in many things, and especially in its absolutism, was a model for the restored kingdoms. The Holy Alliance itself did not preserve the religious
halo with which its originator had meant to encircle it; and
kings and ministers moved its machinery without heeding,
or honouring with but an ironic smile, the profession of faith
that formed its theoretical preface. Here, just as in the Catholic Church, the true virtue lay in the services that the absolute monarchies had rendered and were rendering to civilization. For they had overthrown feudalism, tamed ecclesiastical
power, gathered the small states together into great ones and
even into national or preponderantly national states, simplified and improved administration, provided for the increase
of wealth, defended the honour of the peoples and gained
glory for them. In the period that preceded the French Revolution and the Empire they had generously opened the doors
to science and culture, turning themselves into enlightened
monarchies. During the Revolution and the Empire, spontaneously or by imitation, coerced or voluntarily, they had
carried to completion the work of abolishing feudal privi-

leges and traditions, and had reconstructed themselves into "administrative" monarchies, as they said.

The experience of the French Revolution and of the others that followed had created a disgust for republics, and the example of the Empire had given new life to the monarchical system. The monarchies were therefore still capable of history, and of satisfying the needs of the nations that asked for representation and participation in the government, of undertaking or of completing the independence and the unification of the state, capable of giving greatness to the nations and life to their aspirations. And the liberal ideal was prepared to breathe its spirit into them, thereby giving the best proof of that disposition which led it to combine the future with the past, the new with the old, and to maintain the continuity of history by preventing the dispersion of institutions and tendencies so painfully acquired. But instead of a Holy Alliance of independent and free nations, it appeared then to be what we have already implied, a conglomerate of absolute monarchies, in part formed by inheritance and including several nations, and in part fragments of nations. The promises and the hopes that were burning in the breasts of those who fought against the Napoleonic hegemony and despotism were not kept and not put into effect when the danger was past; and almost everywhere the restored monarchies had begun the defensive and the offensive against the old ally and the new enemy, national patriotism and the liberalism that animated and was animated by it. On the side of the monarchies stood retrograde and reactionary forces, the courtiers, the nobility, and the semi-feudal classes, the priesthood, the riff-raff of the city and the country, and, above all, that power which every established government has because of the simple fact that it is established. But there were also forces of a better quality, administrative and diplomatic traditions, armies strong and rich in glory, expert and devoted servants of the state, dynasties that had been associated with the growth of their nations for centuries and seemed inseparable from their fortunes and were still producing princes that were worthy because of their personal merits and because of the prestige that surrounded them: conservative forces that had their roots in the past, but were none the less precious for that, nor was it possible to allow them to be dissolved and to perish.

The problem was to persuade or to force the absolute monarchies to become constitutional, to take the step they objected to, to escape from the contradictory situation to which they clung, since, after what had happened in the meantime, they could neither go back to the enlightened monarchies of the eighteenth century nor further back, where the aristocrats would gladly have pushed them, to the semi-feudal and nobiliary monarchies; nor could they adopt in full the procedure of Napoleonic absolutism without its complement of military and imperial ardour, which had made it acceptable or imposed it by covering it with and enfolding it in glory. And so they were reduced to jumbling together as best they might the old and the new, and to binding them together by means of the police, the censorship, and severe repression. With the liberal constitutions, all that deserved to be kept would be kept, and at the same time renewed: the figure of the king, freed from the last traces of the priest and the shepherd of flocks, would have become not exactly, as had been said in the eighteenth century, that of the "first servant of the state," but rather that of the guardian of the rights of the nation and the poetic symbol of its living history. The "will of the nation," which once more made them kings, was not discordant with the "grace of God," which had first chosen and upheld them; just as the acceptance of the past does not deny the present or progress towards the future.

Notwithstanding the affinity of some elements of Catholicism and of the absolute monarchies with liberalism, and not-

withstanding the disposition of the latter to entertain them
and make them its own, the two systems remained hostile to
it and it hostile to them, and so it happened with a third
system and a third faith, which seemed to be confused with
liberalism or at least to unite with it in an indissoluble dyad:
the democratic ideal. The points of agreement with it were
not only negative in the common opposition to clericalism
and absolutism (which explains the frequent joining of their
forces) but also positive in the common goal of individual
liberty, civil and political equality, and popular sovereignty.
But this is precisely, amidst all these resemblances, where
the difference lay, because the democrats and the liberals
considered the individual, equality, sovereignty, and the nation in entirely different fashions. For the first, individuals
were centres of equal forces to which it was necessary to
attribute an equal field or an equality, as they said, in fact;
for the second, the individuals were persons, their equality
only that of their humanity, and therefore ideal or legal, a
liberty of movement or competition; and the people was not
a sum of equal forces, but a differentiated organism, varying
in its components and in their associations, complex in its
unity, with governors and governed, with ruling classes—
open, to be sure, and mobile, but ever necessary for this necessary function—and the sovereignty was that of the whole in
its synthesis and not of the parts in their analyses. The democrats in their political ideal postulated a religion of quan-
tity, of mechanics, of calculating reason or of nature, like
that of the eighteenth century; the liberals, a religion of quality, of activity, of spirituality, such as that which had risen
in the beginning of the nineteenth century: so that, even in
this case, the conflict was one of religious faiths. That the one
faith was the precursor and the parent of the other must be
granted, in the general sense in which Catholic theocracy and
absolute monarchy had been precursors of liberalism; and in

a more particular and closer sense, that modern thought passed progressively and dialectically from naturalism and rationalism to idealism, and Galileo and Descartes had prepared the way for Kant and Hegel; and in the other sense that in every individual life there is usually a youthful radical phase, one of negation and affirmation that are equally abstract. But once the transition was made, the two faiths, the living and the surviving, stood and still stand face to face, staring at one another with eyes now friendly and now hostile. The philosophy of idealism rejected the philosophy of natural law, the contractualism, the social atomism, of Rousseau; his "general will," which ill represented the will of Providence and historical reason; the opposition of the individual to the state and of the state to the individual—for these are terms of a single and indissoluble relation.

In the more distinctly political field, liberalism had completed its separation from democracy, which in its extreme form of Jacobinism not only had destroyed by its mad and blind pursuit of its abstractions the living and physiological tissues of the social body, but also by confusing the people with one part and one aspect—the least civilized—of the people, with the inorganic howling and impulsive mob, and by exercising tyranny in the name of the people, had gone to the other extreme and had opened the way for an equal servitude and dictatorship instead of one for equality and liberty. The horror of revolution that made itself felt at this time and which runs through the entire nineteenth century, which was yet to carry out so many revolutions, was in reality the horror of democratic and Jacobin revolution with its spasmodic and bloody convulsions, with its sterile attempts to achieve the inachievable, and with its consequent collapse under despotism, which debases the intellect and destroys the will. The terror of the Terror became one of the fundamental social convictions; and in vain did some undertake the defence of that method, arguing its necessity, and maintaining that it alone had guaranteed the benefits of the French Revolution and that it alone could ensure those of the new revolutions that were brewing—in vain because other, more critical minds were not slow in discovering and revealing the sophistry of this argument.

If somewhat later the image of the French Revolution cast a shadow over its worst aspects and set in relief the admirable side of its passions and actions, thanks to the effect of distance and still more to biased and flattering histories, it was then too near, there were still too many eye-witnesses of what had happened, for the democratic ideal to derive any strength and glamour from it: and indeed this ideal had issued from it in badly damaged shape and was rejected generally, and by the most different parties. Several of the surviving actors in the Revolution and authors of the Terror, the least inept for active works amongst the old Jacobins or those who had corrected and educated their natural capacity through experience, had entered the service of Napoleon and later that of the absolutist régimes of the restoration, and were counted among their most unprejudiced followers and their most inexorable instruments in the war against democracy and liberty: in agreement with what the most serene of poets observed, that every fanatic should be nailed to the cross at thirty, because he who has been under an illusion, when he comes to his senses turns into a knave. Others, candid souls, had preserved their illusions and survived in a mist, vaguely reliving with regret the errors and the betrayals and the accidents that had prevented their pure and beautiful ideal of equality and popular sovereignty from reaching the goal that had been almost in sight, prevented the happy instant from tarrying forever, beatifying the human race. And though the word "republic," as we have shown, struck an unpleasant note at that time, now strident and now dull, some, even of the younger generation, still cherished a regard for the republic because of its venerable classical memories or because of a rationalistic and simplifying longing. But neither republicans nor democrats at this time figured among the major forces at play; and liberalism, which had surpassed them in philosophy and politics, and had even operated many conversions among them, could on the one hand make use of surviving democrats and republicans in certain alliances that were offered spontaneously, and on the other hand watch vigilantly to prevent them, at decisive moments and on the days of upheavals, from compromising the fruit of their efforts by excesses, by acts of madness and disorder, and from unconsciously and unintentionally preparing for the offensive and victorious return of clericalism and absolutism.

Still less importance, amongst the forces at work towards the beginning of the century, must be attributed to another opposition, which was born just at this time and was soon to make itself felt and to grow ever prouder and more threatening; because of this threat it is advisable to examine into its physiognomy at once, to study its character and understand its origin: communism, which we call by its real classical name, and not by that of "socialism," with which it was tempered until it gradually became something else, developing into liberalism, into democratism, and even into Catholicism. We have said that it was born at this time, because it was then that this old idea, which has always accompanied the human race and has sprung up again many times in the course of centuries, assumed a modern form, and attached itself not to those Utopias and fantasies of the past, but to the conditions created by new ideas and activities.

Diversely from the communism of the past, and also from that of the eighteenth century, and even from that of Babeuf and his conspiracy of the *Égaux,* in which there still lingered

ascetic elements—tendencies to renunciation, to simple, elementary, and rude customs, an aversion for cities, a return
to the fields—as it made its appearance in the beginning of
the nineteenth century, like liberalism it proclaimed the im-
manental and terrestrial conception of life, called for the
enjoyment of goods and the ceaseless increase of wealth,
promoted science and technical inventions, machines, and all
the other instruments of economic progress. Herein lay its
affinity with liberalism, which included the same objects; and
liberalism did not substantially oppose it, as is and was believed by certain theorists, because communism aimed at the
socialization of this or that instrument of production or of
all of them (if to speak of all of them has any sense, which is
not the case) and liberalism, on the other hand, maintained
amongst its constituent principles the irremovable private
ownership of these or those instruments, and unlimited freedom of competition. It should by now be unnecessary to prove
that liberalism does not coincide with so-called economic
freedom, with which, to be sure, it has had many points of
resemblance—and perhaps still has some, but always in a
provisional and contingent fashion, without attributing to the
maxim of *laissez-faire* and *laissez-passer* any but an empiric
value, as being valid in certain circumstances and not valid
in others. Therefore it cannot on principle reject the socialization or nationalization of these or those instruments of production, nor has it indeed always in fact rejected it, for it has
carried out not a few reforms of this nature. And it only criti-
cizes it and combats it in given, particular cases, when, that is,
it must be considered to arrest or to reduce the production of
wealth and obtains the contrary effect—not that of an equal
economic improvement of the members of a society, but that of
an aggregate impoverishment, which often is not even equal;
not an increase of liberty in the world, but a diminution and
an oppression that is barbarization or decadence. Because the

only criterion for judging no matter what reform lies in its capacity or incapacity to promote liberty and life. "Property" itself has this double aspect and this double sense, which makes of it two different things in turn: that is, from one point of view it is a simple economic ordinance, subject to modification, and often modified in order to elevate man's moral personality, and from another it is a necessary instrument and form of this personality, which we cannot destroy or trample on without destroying and trampling on the moral and progressive life; as the saying goes, without going against the nature of man—it would be better to say against the duty and mission of mankind, which is not to live comfortably at ease, but to create higher forms of itself and, like the poet and the artist, to fashion the eternal poem of history.

Besides, communism itself had modified its programme. In the first period it had advocated, for its practical and integral accomplishment, government by scientists and technicians, or the foundation of little model states that would exercise an irresistible attraction by holding up patterns of enchanting happiness before the eyes of men. Then it had gone back to the methods of democracy and Jacobinism, conceiving or attempting violent seizures of power and *coups de main*. But it ended by recognizing that its accomplishment required as a *sine quâ non* that the course of history should lead to the alternative of either injuring and reducing the production of wealth, preserving the capitalist system, that is, private property, or else guaranteeing and increasing production, thus abolishing private property. It believed it could confirm and prove this by the economic crises and the destruction of wealth rendered from time to time necessary by the capitalist system in order to re-establish its equilibrium by means of upheavals and bankruptcies. And if that were so, liberalism would perforce approve and advocate this abolition of its own accord; and the whole point is merely this, whether things really do occur in this way or occur with the regularity and rapidity imagined by these theorists; that is, it is a question of experience and not one of ideals.

The conflict of ideals between communism and liberalism, the religious conflict, lies elsewhere: in the opposition between spiritualism and materialism, in the intrinsic materialistic character of communism, in its deification of the flesh and matter. Materialist it was at its birth in its first apostles of the nineteenth century, although it did not receive this philosophical name until later, and then not from its adversaries but from the strongest of its theorists. Its principle is the conception of economics as the foundation and matrix of all the other forms of life, which it considers as derivations or appearances or phenomena of this unique reality. Now if economic activity, in the living system of the spirit in which it rises from the other forms of activity and leads to them, is itself a spiritual activity, when it is torn away from that system, isolated, placed as a corner-stone, it becomes matter. And the sterility of matter will not bring forth and cause to blossom either morals or religion or poetry or philosophy, and not even economics itself, which requires the glow of life, keen intelligence, and eagerness.

In fact, the very first economists of the nineteenth century, the so-called utopists, gave proof of being foreign to the life of the spirit, all intent as they were on the miracles of machines, on the advantages of industrial organization, on the psychology of smug satisfaction with the works of economics and the safe and easy life that it would achieve. Not knowing or not understanding the lessons of history, they undertook to falsify it. And so they interpreted liberalism as the mask of capitalist interests, denied to modern civilization the character of a humane civilization, considered it as classicist and bourgeois, and reduced the political struggle to a struggle of economic classes; they treated religions as inventions for keeping the proletariat in slavery and somnolescence, and philosophies as structures of concepts raised with the same intention of defending the exploiters; and so forth with similar wild fancies. But a society conforming to this materialistic concept could never be any more than a mechanism; and since a mechanism, unlike the organic and spiritual life, does not work by itself and needs someone to set it in motion and regulate it, it had necessarily to be regulated by a perpetual dictatorship, which would oblige its components to revolve in certain designated circles, to profess certain tenets and keep away from certain others, and to bend or repress their intellects, their desires, and their wills. For if such a society is not a brotherhood mortifying itself for the kingdom of heaven, it will be an army for ends that are in the minds of those who hold it under dictatorship, or a crew of slaves well fed and well trained who will erect astounding pyramids; that is, it will in every case lack autonomy, through which alone a society is a society. And even if its labour, without the friction but also without the stimulus of competition, might perhaps increase the products of the earth and of the hand of man, it would forever impoverish the souls that would make use of this wealth, and in the end it would dry up the true fount of wealth, which is liberty of the human spirit, and men would become like those whom Leonardo defined as "passages for food": a religious ideal this too, but of true and actual and not metaphorical *abêtissement*.

To be sure, the Devil is never so black as he is painted and as we have had to paint him here to get to the bottom of his theory and his logic, and to deduce their ideal consequences; and communism, as long as it does not reach the fulness of its reconstruction, which is a demolition of human life, and does not become a continuous dictatorship and tyranny, shows that it too has virtues of its own. For with its criticisms and its demands, and also with its menaces, it com-

bats the egoisms of private economic interests and adds to
the common good; with its myths it animates with a political
ideal of some sort social classes aloof from politics, awakens
them and disciplines them, and in a certain way initiates their
education. It would therefore be foolish to reject it or to wish
that it were not in the world, as we may reject and theoretically annul its directing principle and its materialistic religion.

Such are the oppositions, either already formed or taking
form, which liberalism found on its path at its rise or during
its first steps. And as some of these declined and almost disappeared and others assumed greater vigour and consistency,
still other and newer ones arose, of which there will be word
further on, not only because they entered the field later, but
also because they did not have the original character of the
others, and may be considered as derivative, eclectic, and
variously combined.

The oppositions described above were fundamental, of a
different religion, and may be expressed in the formula *mors
tua, vita mea*. They must therefore not be confused, under
this aspect, with the varieties that liberalism held in its womb,
and with the conflicts and parties that were born of them.
For these things were consonant with its nature, were its very
nature, the rule, so to speak, of its game, which consisted of
the search for what was suitable and what was better, and
developed in discussions, associations and counter-associa-
tions, persuasions, and resolutions owing to the prevalence of
one majority or of the other, which determined what could
be asked for and obtained under given and yet modifiable
conditions. The opposing forces, on the other hand, hindered
and attempted to overthrow the whole liberal system, and
were not able to overcome it except by the same method to
which, in the last instance, one recurs in politics, by the *ex-
trema ratio* of force. This is a necessary moment of every po-

litical act and constitution: by the force of popular rebellions and wars, of armed vigilance and repression.

It is strange that the liberal method should so often be described as that of the unarmed prophet. Even without going back to its concept and the concept of every form of politics, the facts show that for no other idea have so many fierce battles been faced and won, for no other idea has blood been shed more freely, or a fight been led with greater stubbornness, or more readiness and eagerness been shown for self-sacrifice. But that accusation of softness and flabbiness was directed at something else, which was instead the *raison d'être* of liberalism and the cause of its pride; that is, at the law which it observed of still holding fast, indeed even by means of force, to what we have called the rule of its game, but of having as rule of the game this very liberty, which demands tolerance of the opinions of others, readiness to listen to and learn from opponents and in every case to know them well, and therefore to act in such a way that they need not hide their ideas and their intentions.

Thus with the establishment of the liberal order all ideals, the Catholic, the absolutist, the democratic, and the communist, would have freedom of speech and propaganda, with the sole limitation of not upsetting the liberal order. The contradictions in this way would become evident, and all the legitimate particular demands, all the motives of good, which those ideals from time to time took up in themselves and of which they proclaimed themselves champions, would bear fruit in the same way as do all other varieties of demands and proposals; and in every case the presence and the opposition of these adversaries would act as a stimulus to keep the faith alive and watchful, like the heresies and the sects of every living religion. This, as we have said, was reason for pride to liberalism, but it was also founded on a reason for modesty and humility; for ideals may well be theoretically divided into good and bad, into superior and inferior, but men—and the actual battle is one of men against men—cannot be thus divided and set off against one another, and each one of them contains within himself in varying degree the true and the false, the high and the low, spirit and matter. Each one, no matter how reactionary he may profess to be or may boast of being, can, in the concrete case, defend and further liberty, and no matter how liberal he may think himself, can go over to the other side. And all, in short, cooperate, in positive or in negative fashion, in the good that makes use of them, and transcends all of them in so far as they are individuals. As John Milton said in the *incunabula* of modern liberty, to suffocate, no matter where or in whom, a truth, or a germ or a possibility of truth, is far worse than to extinguish a physical life, because the loss of a truth is often paid for by the human race with tremendous calamities and the truth bought back by unspeakable suffering.

If the superiority of a philosophical system is measured by its capacity to dominate the other systems by receiving their truths into its own wider circle, putting them each in its proper place and making of them truths of its own, and at the same time by reconsidering their arbitrary and fanciful parts in order to convert them into logical problems and solutions, the superiority of a moral and political ideal lies in a similar receptivity, a turning into truth and adaptation and conversion of the virtues and the needs that are in the opposing ideals, whose condemnation is decreed, on the other hand, by their incapacity to carry out the same task because of their sterile and total rejection of their contraries. From this measure the liberal ideal did not wish to shrink, and submitted to it with full consciousness, convinced that it could withstand the test.

III. THE ROMANTIC MOVEMENT

CONTEMPORARY with the rise and growth of idealism and liberalism, and often in the same individuals, was the birth and expansion of romanticism; a simultaneity that is not a mere juxtaposition, but a relation or a multiplicity of relations, as it will be advisable to make clear and to keep in mind.

To this end it is necessary, first of all, to emphasize a distinction that has almost always been lost sight of by those (and they have been of late years and still are many) who talk of romanticism and write histories of it. Without this distinction it is inevitable that certain spiritual manifestations of a positive character fall, as it were, under a cloud of disapproval, and others of a negative character are illumined in a favourable light, so that the history one sets out to write comes forth contradictory and confused. The distinction is between romanticism in the theoretic and speculative sense and romanticism in the practical, sentimental, and moral field: these are two diverse and even opposite things to one who does not wish to limit himself to the surface and to appearances.

Theoretic and speculative romanticism is the revolt, the criticism, and the attack against literary academicism and philosophic intellectualism, which had dominated in the illuminist age. It awakened the feeling for genuine and great poetry, and set forth the doctrine thereof in the new science of the imagination called aesthetics. It realized the great importance of spontaneity, passion, individuality, and gave them their place in ethics. It knew and made known the right of what exists and operates in all its varieties according to time and place, and founded modern historiography, interpreting it no longer as mockery and derision of past ages, but as understanding of these as parts of the present and of the future. And it reintegrated and retouched all the aspects of history, civil and political history no less than religious, speculative, and artistic. It thrust back into their natural limits the natural and mathematical sciences and their correlative mental form, showing that, outside of their own field, they were impotent to resolve the antinomies with which the mind came into conflict no less than those which had to remain in abstractions and separations. It grasped life in its active and combative sense, and thus prepared the theoretical premises of liberalism. Even in its irrationalistic concepts, as in the primacy sometimes allotted to emotion and mystic ecstasy, there was a justified polemic against abstract intellectualism, and, in irrational and provisional form, a nucleus of rational truth. Even in its mistaken attempts, as in those of a philosophy of history over and above all histories and of a philosophy of nature over and above all the natural sciences, there was visible the activity of the profound necessities of a history that should be at the same time a philosophy and of a nature understood both as such and as development and historicity, and recognized again as such either beyond or at the bottom of the classifications and the conventions with which and on which the scientist properly so called is obliged to work. In short, this romanticism is not only in no wise in disagreement with modern philosophy, whether you choose to call that idealism or absolute spiritualism, but it is that philosophy itself, or certain particular doctrines of that philosophy, and therefore a duplicate appellative with its correlative double meanings and verbal paradoxes, as when the philosophy that goes from Kant to Hegel is called the "philosophy of romanticism" and then "classic idealism"—therefore at the same time "romantic" and "classic."

But the romanticism that is spoken of in the practical, sentimental, and moral field is something quite different, belongs to quite a diverse sphere. And if speculative romanticism is resplendent with truth, if the attempts to refute it have always been and always are vain, if it has indeed at various times been judged to be extreme and audacious and yet at the same time never been debased to infirmity, feebleness, and insanity, the other, on the contrary, at once assumed this unhealthy aspect and has always been the object of ethical reproval, more or less stressed, now indulgent and pitying, now severe and satirical, and the necessity has always been felt of treating it and bringing about its cure. The greatest liberators from the chains of intellectualism, the greatest fathers of idealism and romanticism in critical and speculative concepts, Goethe and Hegel, considered moral romanticism in this fashion, and shrank from it and blamed it, pronouncing it pathological and shameful. Most certainly the praises that later were spent on romanticism, defining it as "protestantism in philosophy" or "liberalism in literature," did not belong to it. The divergence between the two concepts, the one positive and the other negative, becomes apparent again in the distinction, which has become customary among historians, between the "first" and the "second" romantic generation, between romanticism's period of splendour and its period of unrest and decadence; but in truth the real distinction is not, or not exclusively, one of persons or chronology, but ideal and intrinsic. And still less clearly is the difference visible in the common contraposition of Latin healthiness and German morbidity; for if among the Germans there might be noted some of the first and more pronounced manifestations of that moral ailing, it was also among the Germans that arose the proclaimers of the thought and the ethics which alone were able to cure it; and so this thought and the ethics conjoined to it as well as the malady had their precursors and followers outside of Germany. For these phenomena corresponded to mental creations and psychic conditions that belonged to the modern age and were to be found or might have been found in any people. And in fact the malady received the name, which fitted the truth better, of *"mal du siècle."*

Romanticism was not, as it has so often been interpreted and represented, an effect of the departure from the hereditary and traditional faith, which had yielded certainty and tranquillity of feeling and will; because when an old faith is followed by a new one, the warmth and enthusiasm of the latter covers and makes almost imperceptible the pain and melancholy over the separation and severance from the former. In the eighteenth century society had become widely dechristianized in its intellectual and ruling classes, without any resultant formation of a divided or morbid state of mind, such as romanticism was, and the process even developed with a certain gaiety and cheerfulness. Even the violent rebels against the law, the customs, and the ideas of existing society, the *Stürmer und Dränger,* who for such aspects are considered as proto-romantics, in the achievement of their negations and their rage of destruction gave signs of disordered force rather than of confusion and weakness. But moral romanticism, romanticism as a malady, the *"mal du siècle,"* possessed neither the old nor the new faith, neither the authoritative one of the past nor the clear one of the present, and showed precisely that it was a lack of faith, travailing in eagerness to create one and impotent to do so, or to obtain satisfaction from those which in turn it proclaimed, or to stick to them as principles of thinking and living. For faith is born spontaneously and necessarily from the truth that obliges us to listen to it in the depths of our consciousness, and can never be found by going in search of it with the restless combinations of desire and imagination.

Rather than to the separation from the traditional faith, this malady was related to the difficulty of truly appropriating and living the new, which required, if it were to be lived and carried out, courage and manliness, and the renunciation of certain outworn motives now grown impossible, flattering and comfortable though they might be. To be understood and grasped by reason, and defended, it demanded experience and culture and a trained mind. This might be not impossible for robust intellects and characters, who followed its genetic process without allowing themselves to be entangled in it and, passing through their inner storms, reached the haven; and in another way it was possible for clear and simple minds and straightforward hearts who at once learned and adopted its conclusions and put them into practice, conquered and held by the light of their goodness and good. But it was beyond the powers of feminine souls, impressionable, sentimental, incoherent, and voluble, who stimulated and excited in themselves doubts and difficulties that they were not able to master, who loved and courted the dangers in which they perished. Unable to find their way back to the natural centre that they had questioned, they wandered here and there, clinging now to one point and now to another that could not possibly become a centre. They had severed the connections of the finite with the infinite, of the senses with the ideal, and now in despair they identified the infinite with this or that finite, the ideal with this or that phenomenon. They had lost the true God, and now they moulded idols, which they themselves soon unmade or which dissolved of themselves, because the part cannot stand for the whole, nor a phantom woven by wild fancy or caprice for the solid concept, which is light and strength.

And so these feminine souls, these "romantics," dreamed of returning to religious transcendence and the peace that it seemed to promise, to the cessation, in silence and in renunciation, of the doubts and anxieties of thought, to the norm accepted because of its very character as a norm that imposes itself and exonerates from all independent solution of the battles waged within the conscience. And as the highest expression of this sort of transcendence and of this imperative ruling was the Catholic faith; not only those who belonged to Catholic peoples and had been brought up from childhood in Catholicism, but also Protestants, Lutherans, or those of other confessions, or even men come from the most distant religions or from no religion at all, became Catholics again or for the first time and even were converted with the due rites, and yet none the less never became intimately or genuinely Catholics, and assumed an ambiguous aspect in the eyes of real Catholics. For this Catholicism of theirs was too rich in sensuousness and imagination, was too eager for colours, music, singing, ancient cathedrals, figures of Madonnas and saints, cradled itself too fondly in the pleasures of sin, in penitence and tears; in regard to dogma it did, in truth, give itself ultra-Catholic airs, but was not equally obedient and faithful to the Roman pontiff and to his decrees and his policy. They called themselves or believed themselves anti-Protestant, but in such a way that they could not refrain from frequent allusions to the necessity for a new form or for a reform that should be fundamentally Catholic, but should resolve within itself the dissonances of Protestantism and Catholicism. Others, or the same ones, would at times be seized by rage against Catholicism, or even against Christianity, and turn to championing a restored paganism, opposing to the figure of the Holy Virgin that of the goddess Venus, now the Hellenic one, now the Germanic-mediaeval. Others, attracted by the studies, initiated at this time, of Oriental languages and literature, borrowed from them ideas of ancient rites, or compounded eclectically new and bizarre ones, or recurred to the practice of magic. Others, last of all, flung themselves into a sort of pantheism, adoring Nature, losing themselves in the sensations that she seemed to provide them, and returning, as they liked to say, to the primitive religion of the Germanic peoples.

Those who were more metaphysically or sacerdotally disposed were followed, and often joined, by those who enjoyed a more erotic tone, who sought for redemption in love and for divinity in the beloved lady, not so much with a revival of motifs that had belonged to the *stil nuovo* of the thirteenth century and to the Platonism of the Renaissance, as with a refinement and sublimation of sensuality, which is the kernel of the romantic religion of love. The resulting figure was no longer that of the woman who is strong in her virtue and her chastity, who repels and chastens and educates the man who loves her and obliges him to purify his passion of every low and earthly desire and elevates him, thus purified, with herself to the Highest Beauty and the Highest Goodness, which is God; but a creature equally susceptible and loving, made to suffer and to die of love, a creature adored and sometimes deified, emanating a charm such as alone could lend warmth and meaning to human life. At times, this creature of love would rise with solemn gesture like a priestess of her God and celebrate acts of initiation and worship. There was pathos in the series of expectations, ecstasies, inebriations and disappointments and despair, from which, however, would always arise again the idea of this form of love and of this feminine figure, which would descend from time to time to crown with a heavenly nimbus the blond or dark head of this or that earthly woman, encountered on the earthly path.

In other spirits, or at other moments, the bent of the imagination was preponderantly ethical and political—"political fantasy" because "romantic politics," that is, a politics of the romantic malady, is a contradiction in terms—and in this case belief and happiness were sought for in social modes of living differing from the present ones and particularly in the restoration of past ages. And as the immediate past, that of the *ancien régime*, was still too clearly remembered, was too precise in its limits, and did not easily lend itself to idealization and sacred sublimation, their desire was transferred to the remoter past. Meanwhile learning had re-established the continuity of historical development, and investigated and better understood the Middle Ages, and so they turned to the mediaeval period, in which they saw or thought they saw shadows as solid figures, marvels of fidelity, loyalty, purity, generosity, discipline and lack of discipline at the same time, and what was constant alternating with what was unexpected, simplicity of life in a small and peaceful circle with the charm of adventures throughout the vast unknown world that was full of surprises. To this religion of the Middle Ages we owe the more or less academic restorations of old castles and old cathedrals, the false Gothic that raged everywhere in Europe, the false poetry that in dilettante fashion set itself to imitating the mediaeval forms of epic, lyric, and miracle plays, romances telling of knights and tourneys, chatelaines and enamoured pages, minstrels and clowns, romantic masquerades. And we owe to this the aspect given here and there to some of the ancient monarchies of the restoration, which sometimes beheld themselves grotesquely attired with emblems and costumes fished out of the antiquaries' shops, and the spirit that pervaded the Prince of Prussia, later Frederick William IV, and, with moderation, Louis I of Bavaria.

But if the religion of the Middle Ages was the main one and the most widely spread, it was not the only one; and next to it, and sharing the honours with it, there rose and towered the religion of the race and the nation, of thát nation which, because of scanty information and historic reflection, was considered the creative and dominant race of the Middle Ages, the Germanic, whose courage was now being sought for and discovered and celebrated in every part of Europe—where, historically speaking, should rather have been found, as a common foundation, the Romanic peoples, which for the first time gave it unity and consciousness. And it was exalted as an element of youth and purity, which had produced the histories of Spain and Italy no less than those of France and England, and even now, weakened or bastardized in those countries, still preserved itself youthful and strong, and ready to regenerate the world, in the Germanic race, in modern Germany.

Less fortunate were the other pure races or self-styled pure races that, instigated by this example, also raised their voices, the Latin, the Celtic, the Iberian, and the Slavic. Other religions of an ethical and political tendency also had their more or less numerous devotees, such as that idyllic return to nature and the country and the simple peasant's garb in which there breathed the inspiration of one of its principal precursors, Rousseau; and, opposed to it, the tendency to the stormy, the enraged, the titanic, in which persisted instead the impulse of *Sturm und Drang*. But above all worthy of notice, because of its capacity for proselytizing and the various off-shoots that it sent out, was the aestheticizing conception, of life to be lived as passion and imagination, beauty and poetry. This was in fact the contrary of life, for life demands the distinction and with it the harmony of all its forms, and does not admit the pathological superposition and supremacy of one single form over all the others, which are equally necessary, each for its own task. And it was also the opposite of poetry, which is the conquest of action in cosmic contemplation, a

pause imposed on practical activity, even if that is also the
preparation for new activity. Therefore romanticism, corrupting life, also corrupted to greater or less extent the poetic
form, reducing it to something practical, to an immediate and
violent expression of passionate reality, to a cry, a shriek, a
delirium.

All these, considered in their source, were perversions,
inasmuch as they substituted the particular for the universal,
the contingent for the eternal, the creature for the creator.
But into such diverse and complicated and intricate sentiments there crept also those which are more appropriately
called perversions, that is, not only exaggerations and usur-
pations but somersaults of values: lust and sensuality set in
the place of ideality, the cruel and the horrible savoured with
voluptuousness, the taste for incest, sadism, Satanism, and
other like delights, at the same time monstrous and stupid;
as can be seen or divined in poets and men of letters even of
the very highest class, such as Chateaubriand, Byron, Shelley,
in whom, fortunately, there is not only this, and even this
exists as a rule in incidental or evanescent fashion.

Here we do not mean to pause and portray in its varied
combinations and gradations, which run to infinity, the *"mal
du siècle,"* which moreover has often been portrayed, with
more or less skill, by others; for all that was needed was
merely to explain its genesis in relation to the philosophy and
the religion of liberty. This genesis, as we have seen, lay in its
impotence to appropriate to itself this philosophy and religion, although at the same time it took from it a few elements, which promptly corrupted it, and falsified historicity
by sentimentalizing over the past and by leanings towards
restoration, nationality by the fanaticism of race, liberty by
egoarchy and anarchy, and the value of poetry to life by
poetry-life and life-poetry. But we must not, on the other
hand, ignore all—and it was much—that the liberal faith was

able to influence in this romanticism, nor the way in which, according to the various cases, it transcended it or hemmed it in or subdued it to itself in varying degrees. This sentimental malady was a danger to every form of ideal and of pure sense of religion, and not only to liberalism but also to its very antitheses and oppositions, all of which it would have dissolved if it had prevailed, just as it would have weakened and spoiled all strength of thought and will in sensuality, in disordered desires, in untrammelled passions, in flabby fancies, in restless caprices. This danger was bound to grow all the greater, the smaller became the forces of resistance capable of defying it; a danger that, in its moral essence, belongs to all times, but which in modern society assumes a particular consistency and with this society's greatness and complexity dilates, and with the growth of its contrasts, or with the diminution of their nobility, puts on a more malign nature. Later, in fact, it spread in art, thought, feelings, customs, in national and international politics; and when it had grown more evident and more monstrous, it received, and often acknowledged with pride, the name of "decadence," which is after all nothing but the old moral romanticism, exasperated and grown uglier, whose fundamental motifs it repeats, applying them to less distinguished matter and behaving in a less distinguished manner.

But in the first decades of the nineteenth century, the religion of liberty was fresh with youthful enthusiasm, and the very oppositions against which it fought—the traditional religion, the traditional monarchy, the democratic school of natural law—wore an air of majesty and respectability that was lacking in the opposition which arose later. Moral romanticism operated in the midst of a growth of generous hopes, intentions, and works that confined it, tempered it, and often turned it towards the good. Superior spirits, taking part as they did in the drama of their time, did indeed suffer from this malady, but as from a growing-sickness, from which they recovered and from which they drew fruits of experience, powers of discipline, a capacity for a wider human understanding. And from their midst emerged the keenest judges and the severest critics of romanticism, such as Goethe, whom we have mentioned before, who defined romantic poetry as "hospital poetry" and manifested his aversion to the "sentimental people" who, when they are put to the test, always fail and show themselves to be little and bad, and Hegel, whom we also mentioned, who uttered the most caustic satire and the most varied analysis of romantic fatuity and vanity, up to which he held, so that they might gaze upon themselves as in a magic mirror, the good and savoury prose of real life with its unwearying activity, its physiological pains and physiological joys.

To be sure, not a few romantics, those who could never succeed either in overcoming and calming the uproar they had excited in their own breasts or in eliminating it by forgetting it and resuming their modest everyday lives, went to rack and ruin. Some of them ended in madness and physical suicide, others in moral suicide, in debauches or the insincere practice of a religion that was not serious and not felt. The greater part of them, in inactivity and groaning in solitude and ennui, were like Byron's Manfred, who spoke of himself as "averse from life" and who might have been (says someone who watches him) a noble creature and was instead

> an awful chaos—light and darkness—
> And mind and dust—and passions and pure thought
> Mix'd, and contending without end or order.

Yet there were some who, although unable either to triumph over the enemy or to forget him, did not wish thus to end their lives or drag them out ignominiously, and practically, in

action or in the moment of deciding upon action, clung to
that ideal of liberty which theoretically they could not defend
and assimilate consciously, but which alone, because of its
pure, radiant beauty, had power over their souls. And so some
of them, pessimists because they had not been able to disen-
tangle the tangle of their ideas, or desperate because of betrayed or hopeless love, or unable to support inactivity and
ennui, went out to fight and to die for the cause of oppressed
peoples; and others alternated romantic follies and depression with patriotic and civil ardour. In general, the romantic
features are very strongly marked in all the men of that age,
as can be seen in their letters and biographies, and even,
almost, by merely looking at their portraits, with the characteristic look, the hairdress, the pose, and the cut of the gar-
ments. And if in some countries where the feeling and the
activity for liberty did not stand in the forefront, the romantics (who politically were nothing, because they were simply
nerve-sick and fancy-sick) were able, by their words of consent or dissent, by the manifestations of their humour or ill-
humour, to pass as conservatives and reactionaries among the
peoples whose hearts beat with a quicker rhythm, in whom
the idea and the flower of the intellectuals were liberal, yet
their name soon became synonymous with "liberal," and
priests and police suspected and kept an eye on romantic
youth. The sorrow of the world, the mystery of the universe,
the impetus towards the sublimity of love and heroism, the
desolation and the despair over desired and unattainable
beatitude, the walks under the friendly moon, the Hamlet-like
visits to cemeteries, the romantic beards and curls, the romantic style, these and other like things furnished evidence
of unruly spirits, of whom it was to be expected and feared
that they might conspire in the factions and rise in arms as
soon as occasion presented itself.

The spiritual forces that we have seen rise and prepare to meet and fight toward the beginning of the nineteenth century are alone able to give us the thread that will guide us through European history in this century, the history of its religious and moral soul, which informs and governs and transforms the practical actions that are called political, military, administrative, diplomatic, agricultural, industrial, commercial, and, in short, are variously directed towards various utilities and therefore dependent on them. Certainly, these practical operations can also be taken up and considered each one by itself, in its utilitarian and economic function, putting each one at the centre of the tale and making it the principal character of it. In this case we will have, as in fact we have, histories for soldiers, diplomats, administrators, farmers, manufacturers, and so on; but not that history, or that historical perspective, which properly interests man over and above his particular profession, man as man, in his highest and most complete life.

And this, in any case, is history, and not that—although it is also so named—of events placed one after the other, which is at best but a chronicle; for events, as we trace them back in their series to their origin, reveal themselves to be nothing but either products of preceding actions (including acts of so-called nature) or concomitant and concurrent and conflicting actions, all of which things, from the point of view of the action of which we have undertaken to narrate the history, are either its material or the stimulus to its actual determination, and to its varying configuration and development, without which that action would not exist at all, just as a mill does not grind if it has nothing to grind. He who does not abide by this concept always ends by saying (as feeble minds say) that history is merely a juxtaposition and tangle of events, or that it offers on the one hand "regular evolutions," and on the other "interrupted evolutions," troubled, upset, or borne to unimagined ends, different from and opposed to those towards which it was originally directed. A conclusion that is just as illogical as it is depressing; nor is there any surer proof of historical nullity than the depressing effect that issues from these deceptive narrations of events; for true history always strikes a warlike note for the battles of life.

On the other hand, that is, for the clear consciousness, which it is no longer possible to do without, concerning the impropriety of all historical determinism, we do not wish, at the beginning of the history that we are discussing, to place, as is commonly done, one event or another, the so-called industrial revolution, or the admirable discoveries of applied science, or the changed relations between the lands of American Europe and those of old Europe, or the formation of the modern colonial empires, or the rapid increase of population, and such matters, which are facts and not factors of this history. But we must also avoid placing in the lists a series of spiritual factors, the one independent of the other and limiting the other or even in so-called reciprocal action amongst one another: that would be, under an idealistic semblance, another sort of naturalistic determinism. The forces that we have described above, if understood in the light of our interpretation and exposition, are not placed as factors, are not a multiplicity, but compose a unity: a single process, in which what we have called the religion of liberty is confirmed in conflict with its own inevitable oppositions, is growing and assuming new attitudes with the elements that it assimilates from the oppositions or with the forms that it creates in this struggle for the purposes of victory; just as the oppositions, on their part, strengthen themselves with new elements or arrange the old ones differently, and in their turn display a certain spirit of invention in new defences and offences, in new modes of resistance and new obstacles; and in this spiritual travail, this religion suffers and continually transcends the corresponding malady, which is romanticism—it too changing its semblance.

And does this process exhaust itself in the course of the nineteenth century? And is it today, in the twentieth century, exhausted, so that we can speak of this century not only as a chronological division, but as a moral entity, as the beginning of a new process, with a new soul? Which is the same thing as asking whether, in the latter part of the nineteenth century or in the early part of this one, there was born a new religion that is religion, and broader and more powerful than the other, so much so that it transcends it and takes its place. To answer this question is the highest task of a narrative of European history during the period indicated; and in effect, whether we wish it or not, consciously or not, around such a problem, more or less obscurely stated, revolve all the narratives that have been given of it and which can be read in all the history books and manuals. We do not intend to reshape these narratives from the beginning and in detail; that would be but a vain labour, when all we need do is to recall them by broad hints, or even to take them for granted, so well known are the facts and the series of facts out of which they are woven. But we wish to obtain greater clarity and relief for that problem by continuing and setting forth in detail the exposition begun above, and by noting the achievements and the ulterior struggles and the successive forms of the fundamental motive already described, the achievements and the fortunes of the liberal idea—that is, the history of a war of the spirit, which is truly the "great war."

IV. RESISTANCE AND OPPOSITION TO ABSOLUTISM
AND THE VICTORY OVER IT
(1815-1830)

THE decade and a half that stretches from the fall of Napoleon to the revolution of July, 1830, forms, in common opinion, a historical period with a dominating theme of its own that it develops to a relative conclusion. This theme is made to consist of the reconstructive work of restoration and the corresponding action of the Holy Alliance, which opposed and thrust back and attempted to dissolve the liberal movement; but if we look at the bottom of the process which then took place, and at its positive moment and the event in which it was fulfilled, we can say with greater accuracy that in those fifteen years the liberal ideal resisted the absolutist ideal, fought it without giving truce, and in the end won over it a victory that was permanent because it was substantial.

In a certain sense, the Holy Alliance never existed anywhere else than in the imagination of Czar Alexander I, as a dream or a Utopia founded on conservative, pacific, even liberal motives—but pertaining to a liberalism paternally tolerated and watched over—and religious motives as well, or at least motives given religious unction. In this same circle, which is ideological, too much significance is introduced when one attempts to read there the presentiment of a necessary future in which the European nations are to give to their cultural unity a corresponding federal or unionistic form.

This idea was better adumbrated in this same period by Saint-Simon, but in order to become a political concept it required the extension of the liberal system, the independence and unity of the several nations, and after that a slow and laborious elaboration passing through illusions and disappointments and divagations and painful tests. So incoherent and feeble was the idea of the Holy Alliance that it did not awaken any intellectual movement, did not propagate itself roundabout through large circles, and had no original publicists or literature of its own.

The only real elements covered by this name, or that allowed this name to be given to them, were the intentions of the restored sovereigns to preserve their system of government and to prevent the revolution or transformation heralded by the desires and demands for constitutions, and by the factions, conspiracies, and revolts aimed at obtaining them. These intentions united with and supported each other reciprocally in order to extinguish the revolutionary sparks wherever they threatened to break out or did break out, in order that the fire might not spread from the neighbour's house to their own. Whether on September 26, 1815, the two monarchs of Austria and Prussia did or did not, to please the monarch of Russia, sign the Declaration of Paris that formed the Holy Alliance, nothing substantial was given to or taken from the presence and the strength of those interests and the activity based on them. England, which did not, because of constitutional obstacles, not to mention the sceptical and realistic foresight of her statesmen, join this pact, and the Pope, who remained outside because he was unable, in the name of religion, to sit beside orthodox and Protestant sovereigns, co-operated none the less in this international defence against revolution, England for a few years and somewhat passively, the Pope, because of intrinsic affinity, in a more continuous fashion. Austria, without recurring to any Holy Alliance, had already provided for the muzzling of the Italian states, either by means of princes belonging to her imperial house, or by engagements that she had exacted from other princes, such as the King of the Two Sicilies, never to grant constitutions to their peoples. Nor, as a consequence of having formed this pact, did Russia, Austria, and Prussia sacrifice their particular and divergent interests to the common end, as could be seen not so much in the personal liberalizing attitude of Alexander I, so soon relinquished, as in the three powers' disagreement with, and diverse policies towards, the Greeks when they rebelled against Turkish rule, and towards the colonies of Spanish and Portuguese America who had declared or proceeded in turn to declare their independence, and, more openly this time, towards the revolutions in France and Belgium. England, before all the others, because of the greater importance and complexity of her political and commercial interests, the public opinion of her people, her profound political sentiment that did not fear liberty with the conflicts and dangers in its train, announced through the mouth of Canning in 1823: "Every nation for itself, and God for us all. The time for Areopagus, and the like of that, is gone by": and abandoned for her part the function of guardian of the restorations. On the other hand, the plan, proposed by Metternich at the Congress of Verona, of a police of polices, that is, a league of the police forces of the various Italian states under a single director—a plan that was also inculcated by a reactionary animated more than Metternich by firm conviction and good faith, the Neapolitan minister, the Prince of Canosa—even if it did not take shape in that particular fashion, still did take some shape; those police forces did have an understanding, and worked in accord. Military action under international mandate, deliberated in common even if not always unanimous, had been carried out and continued to be carried out against the constitutionalists of Naples, Piedmont, and Spain; and restrictive provisions were imposed on the separate states of Germany by the will of Austria, who dragged Prussia after her and ended by dragging in the Czar, notwithstanding his inclination to put into execution the various parts of the programme of the Holy Alliance; and this task of vigilance and pressure extended as far as Switzerland.

But the liberals had to struggle neither against the phantom of the Holy Alliance nor against the far from imaginary understandings between the absolute monarchies, against which it was not given to them to set unions of liberal states as once Protestantism had set leagues of princes against leagues of princes, and as of late the French Revolution had set republics founded around its own republic against kings. They worked, first of all, with all the means at their disposal or that they were able to procure, against the absolutism of the states of which they were subjects and not citizens. They let the conflict between this common interest of the conservative monarchies and their differing particular interests create a rift in the reactionary unity of the so-called Holy Alliance and provide propitious opportunities for and aids to liberal action —and grave enough for the former, and extremely favourable for the latter, was the lukewarmness of, and then the desertion of the allies by, England, the greatest maritime power. They concluded, in their own way, an alliance among themselves, not of states but of spirits, the "alliance of the peoples," as it was then called or invoked. And this union of theirs was cemented by intellectual and moral force, which was lacking in the Holy Alliance, or even gave place to its opposite; it manifested itself with the spontaneity of life, finding and gathering together its components in all countries, translating itself into action by means of intellect and knowledge, discussion, oratory and poetry, by sympathy between those who suffered and fought the same things, by generous

reciprocal aid, by setting up against the international mercenaries, the Swiss—still in the pay of several absolute monarchies—the international volunteers of independence and
liberty.

Secret societies of a national and international character, which prepared minds for action, could certainly not be
lacking, as they had not been lacking during the eighteenth
century nor during the Napoleonic empire, and some, under
the names of Sanfedists, Calderai, Apostolics, were also on
the side of clericalism and absolutism. Especially important
among the liberal ones at this time was the Carboneria, which
from Southern Italy spread through the peninsula, flourished
in France, and had imitators even in Russia; and similar societies were formed in the oppressed countries, such as Poland.
But the efficacy of the secret societies was far less than was imagined and believed by those who were frightened by them,
and indeed almost negligible beside the great coalition and
spiritual and effectual conspiracy that was neither hidden nor
capable of being hidden, to which they did some service but
also some harm. One of Metternich's advisers, informing him
in 1820 concerning the state of mind in Lombardy, remarked
apropos of the belief that the opposition consisted of the
Carboneria, that it would have been a good thing if it had
been the affair of a faction, but that unfortunately it was the
question of a whole political party, made up for the greater
part from the middle class, and all of the best elements of the
nobility as regards intelligence, knowledge, and social forms.

Absolutism, which needed an inspired and original con-
structor, did not possess even such a reconstructive reactionary
force as might have overcome the liberal order where it
already existed, and have removed the changes that had been
operated in economics, custom, and culture (which created
needs where they did not already exist), and might, in short,
have brought European society back to the inertia of remote

times—although there never had been such inertia as appeared to its imagination. It found it best, therefore, to accept
all or almost all of the economic and juridical reforms introduced among those nations over which the power of victorious
France and Napoleon had made itself felt directly or indirectly—reforms that pursued the task of levelling the old
monarchies and were inherent in their principle, but which
for that very reason pressed and urged those monarchies
towards the future. Anecdotes were told, which in turn
aroused smiles and laughter and anger, such as these: The
King of Sardinia thought he could re-enact the royal constitutions of 1770 and (except for the gaps created by death)
the court calendar of 1798, as though nothing had happened
in the country or in the world; the Duke of Modena wanted
to wipe out all or almost all of the laws passed since 1791;
the Elector of Hesse-Cassel, hateful because of his caprices
and his ignominious conduct, abolished all the reforms of the
French period, declared null and void the sales of state lands,
annulled the public debt, restored the court calendar of 1806,
reintroduced the queue, but preserved the increased taxes;
and the Pope in like manner abolished codes and courts established by the French and desired to return to the old order,
again shut the Jews up in the ghettos and obliged them to
follow the rites of a religion that was not theirs, and even
forbade vaccination against smallpox, which mixed the lymph
of beasts with that of men.

All these were vain efforts that in time had more or less to
give way to the needs of the age. At the Congress of Vienna
the diplomats had urged moderation in undoing and had
recommended administrative reforms and the representation
of interests to Pope Pius VII for the Legations, which were
restored to him; and Austria, by the treaty of Casalanza,
guaranteed to the kingdom of Naples, against the King who
was returning from his Sicilian refuge, all that had been

accomplished by Joseph Bonaparte and Joachim Murat. The boy had grown, and it was seen, or found on trial, that he was no longer able to wear his old clothes. Only the more stolid and the more wilful of the returning *émigrés* abandoned themselves to the belief that he might be reduced to his former proportions by a sort of magic operation and with the touch of a wand of force. But such of them as in their foreign sojourn had observed and compared and meditated, and had obtained political and moral education, such as the minister the Duke of Richelieu, knew that this was neither possible nor desirable. So that absolutism assumed a form that was not precisely reactionary, but conservative, and reactionary only for the ends of this conservatism. Forced to compromise against its ideal, not only had it been obliged to tolerate the existence of old political régimes opposed to its own and ever affording perilous examples, but even to consent to the formation of new ones, which might actually serve as a stimulus and as encouragement to innovators and rebels. Notwithstanding the rôle she had played against the Revolution and the Empire, and her collaboration with the old monarchies, England did not lessen by a line her ancient constitution; not one of the most rigid Tories would ever seriously have returned to the path of absolutism, and the Stuarts had died out not only in their physical but also in their spiritual descendants. And although France had twice been beaten and prostrated by the absolutist coalition, it was impossible to refuse her that constitutional charter which had been granted at the first restoration, replaced by Napoleon with the other charter called by him the additional act, which was finally confirmed after Waterloo, at the second restoration. How was it possible to lead France back to the conditions that preceded 1789? And other constitutional régimes established themselves in the kingdom of Holland united with Belgium, in a few minor states of Germany, and, by wish of Czar Alexander, who for a brief time looked with favour on German constitutionalism, in Poland. The demoniacal power, liberalism, was still in the world, waylaying it; but what was worse, it possessed recognized spheres of dominion, in open contradiction to the principles proclaimed as alone containing salvation.

And if the German and the Polish constitutional régimes were fictitious and more or less impotent and counted for little, and if the far from liberal Dutch-Belgian régime at once saw itself occupied with the preliminary and exclusive struggle of Belgium with Holland, in England and France, on the other hand, liberalism resumed or started its ascending movement. England in the first years after the peace had found herself upon various occasions obliged to recur to exceptional laws, suspending the habeas corpus and muzzling the press; she had committed acts of repression, sometimes with bloodshed, to put down disorders and insurrections excited by unemployment and by other economic difficulties, and in which at that time the workmen vented their grievances against machines; with Castlereagh she had joined the powers of continental absolutism; she even sought, like these, for support among the clergy, spending great sums for the construction of churches and for curbing unbelief and irreligion, which were considered revolutionary. But even in the short time of the conservative reaction, Parliament with its debates, the law-courts with their sentences, and the other guaranteeing institutions stood fast, and limited and sometimes annulled the extraordinary measures that were resorted to. Meanwhile public feeling agitated and worked for a policy that might solve social problems by a different or an opposite method.

Literature and poetry were full of antireactionary attacks and took sides with the nations that were rising against foreign domination and against domestic despots; to aid them, committees were formed, volunteers set out, legions were raised, expert officers were sent. Lord Byron, who followed up his rhymed poetry with real poetry by going to the aid of the Greeks, and ended and sealed it with his death at Missolonghi, became a symbol of this generous outburst, which was not philhellenic alone, and not British alone. In another order, the ideas of Bentham, and the Radical party, which had risen in opposition to both the Tories and the Whigs, proposed reforms in every branch of English life, which had grown topheavy from too many residues of the past, the remote past and the Middle Ages as well as the age of religious wars: political privileges of landed estates, Draconic penal laws, unequal distribution of parliamentary representation, exclusion of certain classes of citizens from the exercise of political rights. Economic development, which set industry and trade in the forefront, was hampered by the existing tariff system of protection for agriculture; and to 1820 belongs the petition of merchants, which was the forerunner of the later and vehement agitations of the free-traders.

Public opinion had prevented England from participating with arms in the suffocation of the constitutional movements and of those for national independence. The reactionary crisis was thus soon passed. In 1824 a member of the House of Commons was able to exclaim with astonishment that a few years before everything had been "restriction," and that now everything was "liberty." The transition was achieved under the ministry of Canning, from 1822 to 1827, when at home the penal laws were reformed, many duties were abrogated, and the tendency towards free trade was furthered, the freedom of trade-unions was allowed (followed by a great number of strikes and therefore restricted but still preserved in 1825), and laws were made against hunting-rights and such privileges. And abroad, the Government refused to take part in the campaign against the Spanish revolution, viewed with favour the constitutionalist party in Portugal, recognized the new states born from the separation of the Spanish colonies in America, gave diplomatic and military support to the Greek rebellion, and abolished Negro slavery. That in this activity England was protecting and furthering her power and her economy, extending her transoceanic trade, and maintaining the exclusion of Russia from Constantinople and the Mediterranean, is not at all, as short-sighted materialists and idealists without ideals interpret it, a proof of the selfish character of this policy, but only a proof of the possibilities and aids which a moral idea finds here and there in the course of events and in the combination of interests, and which therefore presuppose the existence of this directing idea; just as it would be a sophism to say of a man who performs a good deed permitted him by his actual conditions, and in which he finds himself not only not damaged but furthered, that he has cultivated his own selfishness. In 1829, under the Conservative ministry of Wellington himself, took place the emancipation of the Catholics, who owed this long-delayed act of justice to liberal feelings; meanwhile work was intensified and the discussion became many-sided and general for the fundamental reform, that of the franchise. Here might be witnessed another typical case of liberal mediation, in the face of the abstractions of Bentham and the Radicals, who, in breaking with the superstitious intangibility of the ancient English constitution, went to the other extreme and based the new laws on calculations of utilitarian mathematics. Whereas liberal minds, averse to superstition but not for that reason averse to the past itself, caused more moderate tendencies to prevail, which were to lead to the reform of 1832. The French Revolution reacted, with its rationalistic logic, on its greatest enemy, who also needed this logic for certain cases and in a certain measure, but who also possessed traditions and acquired tendencies that neutralized its sterile and dangerous consistency, and an education of the moral conscience that Methodism, so widely spread in English society, had contributed to keep alive and to retemper.

France had found herself in a very different situation, forced from the outset to defend her constitutional charter against a confident party which had accepted it reluctantly and insincerely, without inner consent, and which, although it did not dream—except for a few of its exalted adherents—of formally abolishing it, aimed at hampering it or trammelling its consequences and performances, of letting it exist as law without any corresponding custom, and of actually governing, over its head or through it, with the king, the clergy, the nobility, and even, if necessary, with the populace. It was but a juridical and formal difference that the charter had been simply granted and not negotiated; but it became a political and substantial difference in this struggle, in which the predominance of one or the other party gave it its true character; so that the problem on the liberal side consisted of knowing how to win what had been only granted and in changing, if not formally, at least actually, the granted charter into a popular constitution. The events in France during these fifteen years all have this one meaning. The offensive was represented, first of all, by the often renewed restrictions imposed on the press and by the re-establishment of the censorship, by the various attempts to modify the electorate in order to place power in the hands of the great landed estates and through them in those of the nobility and the court. Nor was this in disagreement with the means, directly opposed to it, to which the extremists of the nobility would gladly have recurred, universal suffrage, calculated to submerge the bourgeoisie and the educated classes and to exalt the clergy and the nobility. The monetary compensation to the *émigrés* for their confiscated and sold estates, the reintroduction of the entail and the impediments to the division of property, served the same end. Secondary aids were obtained by entrusting education to the clergy, by favouring the congregations, by welcoming the Jesuits; and the form of government that the reactionaries intended to restore also received a new or a strengthened lustre from revived monarchical ceremonies, such as that which was staged for the coronation and anointment of Charles X in the Cathedral of Rheims, and still more from the revived *guerres de magnificence,* such as that of 1823 to restore as absolute monarch a king of the Bourbon family, and that for Greek Christians fighting against Islam, and the last against Barbary and the Dey of Algiers.

The defensive too had its extreme wing in the republican group of Lafayette and the French Carbonari, not to mention the conspiracies and armed rebellions which, especially through the activity of former Jacobins and Napoleonic soldiers, were here and there devised and attempted, particularly in the first years of the restoration. But its true strength lay in the members of the parliamentary centre, who did not cease to oppose the electoral modifications in a reactionary sense; censorship and the persecution of the press; clericalism and its control of the schools; the indemnities, allotments, and favours demanded by the nobility and the returned *émigrés;* the small and great transgressions of the statutory charter; and who, with intent entirely different from that of the absolutists, defended as their own the cause of Greek independence and celebrated as a real triumph the destruction of the Turkish fleet at Navarino. The movement of French politics in those years was a varying sequence, and almost a seesaw, of greater or lesser observance of the constitution and greater or lesser violation and disregard of it; of the franchise regulated with one intention and then with another; of aristocratic chambers and liberal chambers, full of nobles or full of bourgeois; of censorship and press trials and suppression of newspapers; of clerical control of education and lay reaction; of the discharge of teachers and their recall to their chairs. There was a period during which a certain equilibrium was preserved, even if it was somewhat unstable, during the reign of Louis XVIII and the ministries of Richelieu and Decazes, and another during the reign of Charles X and the ministry of Villèle, in which the instability increased, and, after the moderate intermezzo of Martignac, overflowed with that of Polignac. In this long struggle the aristocrats of the old régime were emptied of their not very copious contents. These *ultras* troubled and annoyed even Louis XVIII and his ministers; they called them "true disturbers of the peace" and "white Jacobins," inclined, as they indeed were, to ally themselves with the red Jacobins against the liberals and the moderates. The clerical party, the *parti prêtre*, made itself heartily disliked. The Bourbon dynasty of the elder branch lost all its prestige. The methods and expedients of the reactionaries and conservatives were discredited, whereas, on the contrary, the men of the middle class issued from the struggle with renewed vigour, for they had conducted it throughout not only with talent, eloquence, and constancy (things that not even the other side, in its affection for the past, was quite without) but also with that consciousness of expressing a need of the times which fortifies the soul and gives it confidence, perseverance, and courage. *Help Yourself, and Heaven Will Help You* was the motto of one of the societies of young liberals operating at this time under the direction of Guizot.

In the countries in which the restoration had held to its system of government or extinguished the constitutional régime established by revolution, the process, which was the natural course of things, pursued its inevitable way, even if it was not apparent to the eye or if men believed it to be interrupted and arrested. In Italy, placed under her direct vigilance, Austria had with her army destroyed the constitutional liberty that Naples had created for herself, aided in

suppressing the similar revolution in Piedmont, foiled and
severely punished the Carbonari conspiracies in Lombardy
and Venetia, urged and supported the Pope and the other
minor princes in a similar activity, and established everywhere a sort of terror, which could never be peace, since it is
impossible to found on fear a quiet and trustful tenor of life,
but which did not, except at times, generate despair and discouragement. That is always the case, moreover, with such
feelings, which do not last in man, if they do last in animals
subject to the tamer's whip and glance. The pursuit and attempted reconstitution of the factions, the conspiracies, the
outbursts of rebellion, isolated and feeble as they were, and
quickly suppressed, bore witness to the flame that was smouldering under the ashes. But more intense was the intellectual
activity, which turned to the general and the substantial.
From every region of Italy men of courage and spirit went
into exile, and gathered again in England, in France, in Belgium, or wherever they could. They were men of culture and
ability, rich in faith; they formed an Italy outside of Italy,
and sent combatants for liberty to Spain, Greece, America,
Poland. Of these, side by side with Byron, memory has preserved, as representative of all the other Italians, Santorre di
Santarosa, who fell fighting in Sphacteria. And these exiles,
who were the lesser number, and the greater number of their
companions of faith who had stayed in Italy, vexed by the
Government and the police, made ready for events, and going
over the past vicissitudes and strengthening themselves with
those bitter experiences, pondered better ideas and prepared
for more suitable forms of action.

The constitutional upheaval in Naples in 1820-21, and
that of Piedmont as well, although the torch of liberty had
been raised in both, had not been upheavals from the depths,
that is, for a renewal of the entire soul; they had been willed,
the first especially, by officers of the Napoleonic wars, mor-

tified and discontented and troubled about their lot, and by property-owners equally uncertain as to the preservation of their recently acquired property. They were carried out by a factional network that was ill fitted to take the place of the moral consent of and agreement between the best men, interpreters of the needs of their people; they were unaccompanied by political sagacity in their ideological disregard of the international situation and of actual political forces. So that there was a great piece of work to be accomplished for the education of Italian youth, a difficult task, because it had to be performed amid suspicion and hindrances and prohibitions from above, and therefore with many precautions; and yet in spite of all this the task was carried out. And now the truth appeared in utter clearness as it never had before or as it had not been generally recognized, the truth that the only possibility for free life and civilized progress in all parts of Italy was to shake off this Austrian rule, which was not only foreign, but illiberal as well. So that political education had to be at the same time Italian and national education, in order that through it might be gained a knowledge of all Italian history and of the line of its development. And new paths were entered on and followed which had never been even imagined before; and then was sown the seed of Italian liberal Catholicism, directed towards the independence and liberty of the nation, and invoking the memories of the mediaeval pontiffs who defended Latinity against the Lombards and formed a league with the communes against the German emperors: memories and comparisons of great importance in a Catholic country like Italy, for they won over to liberalism large sections of society previously hostile to it, they stripped it of the suspicion of being antireligious and antichristian, that is, Voltairian and materialistic, they permitted it to insinuate itself and grow in places where, without this reconciliation with Catholicism, it could not easily have penetrated.

On the other hand, even the absolutist régimes could not acquiesce in subjugation by Austria, rivals as they were in territorial questions and jealous, in every case, of their own independence; nor could they accept the reaction, to which they had at first clung, because they had, after all, to govern, and that in the long run was not possible without the collaboration of men of ability, who were certainly not to be found among the reactionaries. And so they waited for the right moment to loosen the reins, to grant amnesties, to recall the exiles, to accomplish the desired reforms and works of civilization, and to give signs of good intentions and goodwill. If this was not within the capacities or within the decisions of men like Charles Felix of Sardinia and Francis of the Two Sicilies, it was hoped that it might occur with their heirs and successors. In one part of Italy, Tuscany, there was respite, because the House of Lorraine governed reasonably and mildly; and here not only was refuge to be found for exiles from the other Italian states who here learned to know and understand one another, but for many years a periodical was published, the *Antologia*, which continued the Lombard *Conciliatore*, and in which many noble minds took part, as in a *conversazione*. Austria caused it to be suppressed, but only after it had exercised its beneficent effect and produced its fruits.

Spain had for the first time founded her constitutional régime in the midst of the national war for her kings and against the French, with the constitution voted at Cadiz in March, 1812. This established a single chamber, partly because of the persistent tradition of the old Cortes, and partly because of the French example of 1791, adopted later by the Carbonari of Naples, who were very vague about its origin and nature. On parallel lines, Sicily, still at war against the French, had in the same year, 1812, established a constitution in part going back to the tradition of her ancient parliament, and in part after the English model and with the help and almost with the protection of England. The first, the Spanish one, was formally annulled by the Bourbon King when he returned to the throne that he had deserted and which his people had defended, and the second, the Sicilian, was annulled in fact by the other Bourbon King, as soon as he was able to return to his Neapolitan capital. Both the one and the other had come into the world too suddenly. In Spain, where national sentiment had been alive for centuries and had recently demonstrated this vitality in admirable fashion, modern ideas and culture, however, were lacking (for the ancient Spanish culture and science had ended in the eighteenth century with the expulsion of the Jesuits), and the modern form of nationality was lacking; so that it may be said that nationality there was instinctive and the liberal constitution abstract, and that the main body of the country did not understand it or know what to do with it. None the less, just as in Sicily, who always remembered her constitution and made efforts to recover it, so in Spain the constitution of 1812, improvised though it was, marked a beginning, the beginning of the formation of a new Spanish people.

The proclamation of Cadiz had been followed by the abolition of the Holy Office of the Inquisition, the suppression of the monastic orders, the distribution of state lands, the reduction of the estates of the Crown, the subjection of all orders of citizens to taxation, and other such favourable measures. And the king, Ferdinand VII, when he annulled it, could not cause what had happened not to have happened, at least not in the minds of his subjects; he did not destroy the needs that had been expressed in it, nor was he able, in other ways, to satisfy these, even in a temporary and provisory fashion. In vain did he decree, in 1816, that the two conflicting parties were to be regarded as wiped out and that even the use of the words *liberal* and *servil* must vanish. Such things cannot be car-

ried out by decrees. His government, among the worst and
clumsiest of the restoration, run by a notorious camarilla of
priests and buffoons and low menials, restored the Holy Office,
recalled the Jesuits, reintroduced the monastic orders, once
more exempted the clergy from taxation, imprisoned persons who had served under the French king and even some
who had taken part in the Cortes of Cadiz, and offended public confidence by despoiling those who had bought estates of
ecclesiastical origin. All this was more than was needed to
prepare the way for a revolution, and in fact in Catholic
Spain, as in France under the pressure of the *parti prêtre*,
the books of Voltaire and the Encyclopaedists and other
French publicists and polemicists were once more sought after
and eagerly read. With scarcely controlled impatience the
men of action and the soldiers looked on; in the struggle for
the honour and independence of old Spain they had fortified
their hopes for better times, and now beheld this epic followed by such ugly prose; and those who were living in un-
accustomed economic difficulties provided at that time, in
Spain and elsewhere, the inflammable material, the element
ready to take part in revolt. In Spain the revolt broke out in
1820, in a military movement that proclaimed the constitution of 1812; this was re-established and was sworn to a few
months later by the King. The Cortes were convoked, and for
over three years and a half Spain found no rest between the
hostility of the clergy and the absolutists and their king and
the European powers and the Pope on the one side, and the
lack of discipline of the army, the demagogic excesses, the
immaturity of the men of the constitutional régime, on the
other, until French intervention put an end to this disorderly
agitation.

But the fearful reaction that followed, which went against
nature, that is, against history, not only aroused affection
for what had been enjoyed for such a brief period, but ended

by seriously embarrassing even the King who had started it. For he found himself at the beck and call of a faction, over-powered and ruled by the ultra-royalists, by the Apostolics, the Carlists (as they called themselves, from the name of his brother, the standard-bearer of obscurantism), and fiercely op-posed even in the law of succession which he had proclaimed in favour of the daughter born to him from his last marriage. And feeling the lack of those forces of opposition through which it is possible to restore the lost equilibrium and to gov-ern, he was obliged to take thought in order to defend him-self against the supporters of absolutism, and to ponder meas-ures of justice, and, in the last resort, even to consider the constitutional attitude not altogether absurd and to suspect that it had its advantages. This conviction of his own interests became explicit in the young Queen, soon to be the Regent, Maria Christina. Neighbouring Portugal passed through sim-ilar vicissitudes, from pronunciamentos by officials and lib-erals, in order to obtain the Cortes, to the overthrow of the constitutional régime by the action of the King's brother, Dom Miguel, who was acclaimed by the populace, and to the liberal reaction by means of the opposition of Dom Pedro. All this was mixed up with a question of succession through the female or the male line. In the course of these events, Brazil became independent, somewhat after the fashion of the Spanish colo-nies; and absolutism, because of lack of strength, and liberal-ism, for reasons of logical coherence, were unable to combat this independence effectively and had reluctantly to accept it.

Discontinuous and feeble was, without a doubt, the liberal formation of Germany, not to speak of Austria, which was all court, army, bureaucracy, and the quiet life. The reason is to be sought for in what has already been suggested concerning the Reformation and Lutheranism, which with liberty of thought and private judgment had prepared the way for free research, criticism, and philosophy, but at the same time had

established the cult of the prince and the state, leaving the
two diverse forms of activity, the speculative and the political,
in a sort of dualism, each respectful of the other but without
close relations of lively interchange. Liberalism, with its rest-
lessness and its revolutions, said Hegel—and we may agree
with his remark without agreeing with the disapproving judgment or the offensive epithet—is an affliction of the nations
who have not, like Germany, enjoyed the Lutheran revolution; and he believed that after the restoration of the well-
ordered Prussian state there was nothing else to be done in
politics, and that one should return to the inner life, to the
kingdom of God, to philosophizing. What in Germany was
known as inner liberty was very great, and as it did not collide with any political obstacles, it was not induced to convert
itself, for its own protection, into political activity. Political
action was accepted ready-made from the hands of the prince
and his functionaries, and good citizens had nothing to do but
to obey it and co-operate with it. Thought proceeded boldly
along its own paths, without realizing that if it did not collide
with any political obstacles this was because it did not wish to
or did not know how to do so, because it had accepted the
limitations obsequiously. German philosophy had no martyrs,
as, for instance, had the Italian, which derives from this its
quarterings of nobility. Nor did men even notice that from
this acquiescence in separation and abstention German science
derived an academic and scholastic, a pedantic and heavy air,
an absence of concreteness and practical qualities, all that it
was reproached with by other peoples, both in its content and
in its form; this placed obstacles in the way of its European
diffusion, only partly overcome because the depth and importance of some of its concepts were grasped, and through
the goodwill and efforts of those who busied themselves in
translating them, in explaining them, in developing and illus-
trating them. A few foreigners heard with amazement from

the lips of learned Germans arguments against liberty of thought based not on political motives but on the risks that, with the journalism which it would bring in its train, it would create for austere science, whose maiden chastity it would compromise. The pedantic Wagner truly relived in these savants, in the hearts of these savants, and that is where the poet had found him, listening to their utterances, watching their behaviour, and had enjoyed him and caused him to be enjoyed by others with smiles and with laughter.

Nor, on its side, did the state realize the loss of agility and strength that was caused to it by citizens so submissive and devout, who kept thus aloof from political mêlées; and it attended to its own defence and to good administration, to bureaucracy and the army, so that when a German historian, who was one of the latest and most fervent representatives of this conception of the state, wanted to say what humanity and civilization owe to Prussia, he exalted the law of September 3, 1814, concerning obligatory military service as "one of the legislative acts that mark an epoch and help understand what history really consists of" (almost as though this very law might have arisen without the precedent of the French Revolution and its conscription, that is, without its democratic ideas). But if between internal and external liberty, between theory and practice, there was no adequate communication and interplay, still a particular manifestation of liberty which at this time was making headway proceeded, as it were, by itself and detached from all else: the national impetus, the conviction of German individuality and the will to provide it with increased power in the world. This impetus at times disturbed the tranquillity of German science and literature, contaminating the one with extraneous passion and the other with prejudice; at other times it embarrassed and frightened separate states and governments. But it was not fused, or at best very rarely and sporadically, with the ideal of political liberty, as should have lain in the nature of things and as often happened among other peoples, who had not risen, on a footing with the Germans, to the loftiest heights of speculation, and who could not, like them, boast of solid military institutions, but who in the place of these possessed simpler and more limpid and coherent concepts of reality and life. Therefore it was observed that whereas patriotism widened the hearts of other peoples, in the case of the Germans it narrowed them and made them meaner, and closed them to understanding and sympathy. In truth, even in their interest for other peoples they mirrored their own tendencies and imaginations; so that German philhellenism, diversely from that of England, France, or Italy, did not turn so much to the Greeks of the present moment as to Hellas and the Ionians and the Dorians set up by classical philology; and in Italy they did not see the men of the Risorgimento but amused themselves with rediscovering in the remnants of monuments, and in the customs of the lower classes, vestiges of the ancient Romans and pagans, contemplating them with the satisfaction of the archaeologist, and even admiring them as signs of the persistence of the race they were considering.

The restoration and Prince Metternich, who protected it and directed it in Austria and in all Germany and in Prussia itself, came together here, not precisely in the vanguard with the liberals, but with those fiery patriots and nationalists who had coined the word *Deutschheit*, who delighted in roughness and rudeness, and of whom foreigners, observing them, noted with amazement with what rage and madness they seemed to be seized, which was baptized "Germanomania." A young Italian liberal, Alessandro Poerio, a poet and a follower of Goethe, who went to Germany in 1825 with open mind and open generous heart, full of affection for German thought and German poetry, shrank back at the contact with the fanatical German students, repelled, half in anger, half in disgust. The governments of the restoration suppressed this movement, punished its manifestations, suspended or prohibited its newspapers, persecuted and imprisoned its leaders, did not spare any even of those who had been the orators and the heroes of the war of liberation; either because even in this uncouth and erratic form they felt the breath, hostile to them, of a new age, or because the actual problem at the bottom of this fervour, the problem of German unity, threatened the entire structure so laboriously put together in the Congress of Vienna and could not be solved except by a war between the German states, which none of them at this time could face. In this problem, and in the inevitable war entailed by it, the agitators, who did not connect it with the problem of political liberty, were unable to point out a straight path; they meandered and grew entangled in vague and confused ideas, and many of them concocted something not unlike the Holy Roman Empire, and—since semi-Slav and recent Prussia was badly fitted to form the centre or the summit of this edifice—looked towards hoary Austria, which had for centuries been the seat of that empire. Others looked towards the states of South Germany, which were deemed the most purely German, "Alemannic," as opposed to the Nordics and Prussians. The most concrete achievement on these lines during this period was not their work, but particularly that of Prussia: the Germanic Zollverein, undoubtedly a premise and a promise of state unity, and a notable step in this direction.

Notwithstanding all this, even that indolent political organism began to be pervaded by flashes of liberty. There was not much, but there was something. The parliaments reformed or instituted after 1815 were docile, imbued with bureaucracy; those of Bavaria and Württemberg and Baden —the King of Prussia did not grant the desired constitution that had been promised—were dissolved at the first signs of resistance. The others were puny and often ridiculous. All of them were continually opposed by the federal diet and by Austria, who presided over it and who would only too gladly, if she might, have wiped them off German soil. Political journalism was inexpert, practised as it was by professors and savants, and constantly suspected and watched and often punished or actually suppressed, as happened, among other cases, after the deliberations at Carlsbad in 1819. In spite of this, and little as it was, there still emerged the obvious impossibility of altogether excluding similar institutions and suppressing the needs manifested in them, which they would gradually strengthen and amplify. In the associations of young nationalists, in the outbursts of Teutonism there was mingled the hatred of tyranny and the tempestuous passion for every kind of liberty; this was, to tell the truth, a somewhat old-fashioned state of mind, *à la Sturm und Drang,* or (as we Italians would say) Alfierian, libertarian rather than liberal, and yet it was an emotional life from which a political life might arise.

On the other hand, in the doctrinal and publicistic spheres there began to make itself felt a tendency to illustrate and inculcate a more practical and more political concept of liberty. Some dreamed of institutions resembling the English, half-way between the modern and the mediaeval, with local autonomies and feudal privileges and representation of states and classes—that is, they wished to oblige Germany in the nineteenth century to go through the development of English institutions at the very time when in England this development was reaching a crisis of rationalization. Others, instead, preferred French examples, but even here not without a retardatory process, recalling the constitution of 1791 and not seeing or not accompanying with full sympathy the fruitful constitutional struggle in France in their own times. The Rhenish populations and those of South Germany, who had experienced the reforms and known the administration of the French, did not conceal their love of France and her manner of life, and often dared to invoke the "conquest of neo-Latin rights," to the scandal and horror of the Teutonists, and professed themselves quite as "liberal" as the Prussians were "feudal," and (such was the consequence of having split the national movement from the liberal one) shrank from German unity out of aversion to Austria or Prussia, who were differently but equally illiberal.

Poland, meanwhile, experimented on her own body as to the impossibility of reconciling a constitutional régime with national dependence, with the diet that the Emperor of Russia had conceded (but the sessions of which he suspended for a number of years, prohibiting, moreover, public debates), and with her other liberties, which were, according to the moment, now enjoyed and now suspended, restricted, or abolished. But Poland had received a deep imprint of Italian and then of French culture; she belonged to Europe, notwithstanding her singular and backward social composition, and could not resign herself or submit to this fate, but always tended to independence and a settled mode of living. And the peoples of Europe felt for her, and took part in her misfortunes and her hopes and compared them, not indeed without illusion, to their own. Whereas it was impossible to say that Russia already belonged to Europe, in spite of all that Czarism had done to imitate European absolutism in its administrative and military institutions, and in spite of the varying European dilettantism of her aristocracy, and certain imitations of European factions among her officers, and the generous but headstrong attempt of 1825, called "of the Decembrists," in which the regiments of the guard, set in motion by aristocratic and idealistic officer-conspirators, acclaimed the "constitution," believing, as was known later, that this was the wife of Grand Duke Constantine. Even the "Pan-Slavism" of the reactionaries, of which the ideal and sentimental basis was laid at this time, was born of European romanticism, and in particular of the German "philosophies of history," of which it was an imitation and almost a parody. A supporter of absolutism who had passed in review the nations of Europe in the years that immediately preceded 1830, and those nations which seemed to offer the best response to his ideals, when the constitutional revolutions had been repressed, and Austria, and, for her, Prince Metternich, dominated in Germany and Italy, and Spain was ruled by Ferdinand VII, and Portugal by Dom Miguel, Sardinia by Charles Felix, the Two Sicilies by Francis I, Russia by Nicholas I, and France was governed by the Prince de Polignac— he would with difficulty have drawn from all this motives for satisfaction and rejoicing, or reasons for tranquillity. The inner voice would have whispered to him that not all had been done, and that therefore nothing had been done: the restoration had held its ground, but the spirit of Europe was not changed. Metternich confessed about this time that public opinion was against him and against the party that he represented; and that their victories were regarded as crimes, their ideas as errors, and their plans as follies. Chateaubriand visited Italy in 1829, found her girded and guarded by every sort of heavy or light chains, and judged her "ripe for revolution." And then what was this strange enthusiasm for foreign and distant peoples, and the idealization, in which all men of goodwill took part, of Greek brigands and pirates no less barbarous and cruel—as they cannot have helped noticing at times—than the Turks? And what was the other marvellous idealizing transformation, the admiration, the fanaticism, the regret, the tenderness, that was to be observed in all countries for Napoleon, for this despot who had trampled on all liberties, and who had now become, not only among the young but among those too who had seen him at work, almost a hero of liberty or one who had given to the nations, together with so many other great and useful things, liberty as well? And beside this the aversion to the paternal figures of the legitimate sovereigns, and the coldness towards the valiant leaders who had conquered the Corsican adventurer, the Wellingtons and the Blüchers? Why was the vanquished usurper set up on altars and the conquerors set aside, if it were not because of the memory that this man had with his arms renewed the youth of Europe, and shaken and thrown to the ground customs and institutions that it had been better never even to have dreamed of restoring and which, after him, it was advisable to suppress in order to progress towards new forms, foreshadowed by him and not by the restored monarchies—with a shadow that the imagination changed into a promise or even a beginning?

The life of the intellect, on the other hand, was aflame in liberal men and liberal circles, because, as we have remarked, the greater and more direct and systematic opposition, Catholicism, gave out, besides its philosophy and theology and apologetics for seminarists, nothing but invective, deprecation, and confutation flung at the "errors of the century." A few thinkers, not without talent, who came from the lay world, served the Church at first for certain occasional ends, but did not enter into and become part of her tradition, and did not modify or add to the body of her doctrines. Such, for instance, were Joseph de Maistre and Haller, who have been given an undue importance, the first for the doctrine of the Pope as most absolute sovereign over all the absolute sovereigns of the world, and the second, for his anachronistic resurrection of the proprietary conception of the state; but they are both more noteworthy for their criticism of certain aspects of natural law and of eighteenth-century contractualism, and because they restored their proper importance to facts and history and to the force that generates states, and to the Providence that educates the peoples, arousing to this

end revolutions and all such horrors. On these points of doctrine they were in agreement with the analogous proofs and
theories of the liberals, and sometimes anticipated them, so
that they found perhaps more readers and students among
them than among the clergy, readers better able to interpret
and to understand with objectivity and thoroughness their
tendentious and unilateral doctrines.

At this time the writings of Madame de Staël, of various
French *émigrés*, and of other intermediaries won a reputa-
tion in every part of Europe for the philosophy and the historiography and the aesthetics of Germany, and for the literature and the poetry of the same people, equally preg-
nant with philosophical problems and philosophical ideas.
Kant and Fichte and Schelling and Hegel, and Johann
Müller and Niebuhr and Savigny, were translated and variously interpreted, condensed, and commentated; the tragedies
of Schiller were read and became popular, and attempts were
made to master the difficulties of *Faust;* and at the same time
the cult of Shakespeare was first introduced into the neo-Latin
countries, and that knowledge of the poets of all peoples and
of all times heralded as *Weltliteratur* was transplanted to
France and elsewhere. This was truly the great European age
of Germanism, far better and far greater than that other of
the barbaric invasions, when, no matter what idle fancies may
have been repeated later, the Germans were unable to offer
any valuable contributions and had to let themselves be in-
structed and civilized in the school of Byzantium and Rome.
This German thought gathered up the heredity of the Reformation and humanism and went back through Rome to Hellas
and then from Hellas to the Indo-Europeans and the oldest
East of all, whence it came down, with widened gaze, to the
knowledge of the modern world. It provided, as has been
observed, the solid speculative and historical basis of liberty,
even if several of its national authors and devotees set up on

this basis old and poorly restored political or governmental idols, and, above all, that of conservatism; the greater part set up nothing at all, considering it complete in itself, the end of their efforts, inert doctrine and contemplation.

But that intrinsically this thought was progressive, and even revolutionary, was unconsciously confessed by the parallelism in which Fichte, Hegel, and others with them placed the two revolutions, that of the French, which was political, and, contemporary with it, that of the Germans, which was intellectual. But this parallelism could not continue long and logically led to this consequence, which they had not foreseen or which they had cast aside or ignored: that, just as abstract rationalism had given birth to the Jacobin revolution, the new and concrete rationalism or idealism must beget another, different in spirit and in rhythm, which was perhaps already in act. In France, in fact, who had already opened her arms to German thought, and in Italy, who through French writers, and then directly, made use of it to further her spiritual growth, the conclusion was drawn; and those philosophers and historians who in Germany were conservatives, and even reactionaries, in the other countries assumed, let us not say the Phrygian cap, but at least the insignia of liberty, and were revered, because of what they had thought, as masters of precisely that which they had not wanted and which they had practically rejected. This fusion of speculative thought and practical politics confers historical efficacy upon men like Cousin, although it must be admitted that the fusion did not take place in him because of critical depth and by way of speculation, for he was but a feeble philosopher, but through the very conditions of the different milieu. It may even be said that there was some misunderstanding. Words like these which Cousin pronounced in his lectures, carrying his audience of young Frenchmen away, and which are more or less the same as Hegel's: "History, in its beginning as in its end, is the spectacle of liberty, the protest of the human race against anyone who would lay shackles on it, the affranchisement of the spirit, the reign of the soul, and the day when liberty ceased in the world, would be that in which history would stop"—such words sounded and had their effect quite differently in France from the way they did in Germany. So that Heine jested about the "providential ignorance" of Cousin, so useful to the French, who (he explained), if they had truly known and understood German philosophy, would never have staged their July Revolution: only a jest, moreover, because it did not go to the root of that objective logic which, beyond the imagination of the individual, leads whither it must lead.

In this way we can also understand how there came from Germany at the same time currents and trends of thought that both absolutism and Catholicism greeted as allied forces, and other thoughts or the same which they deprecated in turn as the pernicious corrupting action of German thought in Catholic countries. The new direction taken by historical studies was mainly due to German ideas and to their immediate or variously mediated efficacy, and their rapid spread on all sides was owing to the leaven of liberty. These studies had remained completely barren in the era of Napoleonic despotism, because only one who hopes and works for the future looks backwards, cautious in all that he plans and desires, conscious of his own responsibility, and only the country for which we work and for which we feel with passionate desire is the country that we love; and, since its personality is its historic life, we look into its history. In France, during that decade and a half, Augustin Thierry published his letters on the history of France, and his history of the Norman conquest of England, and his brother Amédée his history of the Gauls before the Roman domination, and Thiers and Mignet their histories of the French Revolution, and Guizot

those of the origins of representative government and of civilization in France and in Europe—taking care to join the past
to the present—and his other history of the English revolution, that is, of the first great liberal revolution. Quinet translated Herder's work on mankind; Michelet translated Vico's
Scienza nuova and wrote his essays on the philosophy of history and on the modern era; Cousin and Villemain and
Sainte-Beuve wrote their first works of philosophical and
literary history. Likewise in Italy, where the *Républiques
italiennes* of Sismondi had already been much read and the
admonitions that ended the narrative had been received with
attention, Manzoni and Troya investigated Lombard history
and the origins of the Italian people, and innumerable others
accompanied them and followed them with alacrity on this
path, and Vico and his speculations and interpretations returned into favour.

In England could be seen in Hallam as it were the transition from eighteenth-century historiography to that of the
nineteenth century; savants began to take up the elaborate
methods of German philologists; Grote undertook his reconstruction of Greek history; and Macaulay wrote his first essays in the *Edinburgh Review*. This was the science of the
new century, as was soon perceived and proclaimed, just as
that of the preceding one had been physics; this does not
mean that physics and the other natural sciences were neglected and did not progress, and did not moreover benefit by
historical ideas, as was seen in the teachings of Lamarck,
nor, above all, that the Baconian function for the potentiation
of human activity was belittled. Indeed, in those years industrial applications, and particularly the new means of
transportation and communication, were tokens of fervid interest and winged hopes, almost on a footing with political
problems and ideals as ways for the broadening of human

life; so much so that Byron, in *Don Juan,* remarked that at this time

> Mankind just now seemed wrapt in meditation
> On constitutions and steam-boats of vapour.

The first Italian liberals and Carbonari discussed not only arguments of literature, history, philosophy, in the *Conciliatore,* but also, like Confalonieri, dealt with machines, and river steam-navigation, and kept in view the progress that England was achieving in these fields.

Similar outbursts of liberty pervaded all literature, by which we mean, as here we ought to, not only works of poetic inspiration (and indeed these only in certain aspects, because, owing to this very character of theirs as things of beauty, they are ill adapted to manifest, and still less to document, historical tendencies) but also the complex of poetic and non-poetic works, works of effusion, confession, imagination, exhortation, and entertainment. The lord of men's fancies at this time was Byron, fiery declaimer and playful conversationalist, polemicist and satirist and wit, with rare sparks of poetry properly so called, but always aggressive and biting against every race of tyrants. He hated English conservatives and priests, and soldiers and wars, for he could admit no wars beyond those for liberty and no warriors other than Leonidas and Washington. The mad passion for liberty is also apparent in his pictures of corsairs and adventurers and outcasts and men guilty of wrongs and crimes, as it was in all the others of like kind that for a century furnished heroes for dramas, novels, and poems: great-hearted brigands, homicides from virtue, women who proclaim the rights of passion and burst their marital ties, courtesans purified by love and able to die for love, clowns with profound feelings who suddenly discover their inner tragedy, dissolute geniuses, and so forth. These figures have been harshly censured as incoherent, absurd, and morally monstrous, almost as though they were persons of flesh and blood, whereas, since they are creatures of sentiment, we should only search for the sentiments that generated them, among which we cannot deny that there was also, together with others less worthy or even unhealthy and generally dominating them, the passion of which we have spoken, so violent as to deform the objects towards which it was directed, so rebellious against unjust laws as to rebel against the good and just ones as well, so blinded by its raging desire as not to perceive that it sometimes linked together and enfolded in the same desire things that were essentially contradictory. Even the candid Silvio Pellico at this time outlined the adulterer-patriot, raising to this dignity the Dantesque lover of his sister-in-law, who was held up for admiration because of this double rebellion against the subjugation of Italy by foreigners and against the iniquitous bonds that had tied the gentle Francesca to the ugly and uncouth Gianciotto—because of this double and equally generous passion. The same mystic marriage was celebrated between the romanticism of sadness and desolation (of which Byron was one of the most eminent representatives) and noble political sentiment; and this occurred particularly among the romantics of Latin countries, who in literature as in life differed from those of Germany. The latter, during these years, after passing through the most troublous follies were now being mentally dissolved and were fast losing their charm, surrounded as they were not only by critics but by mockers and parodists.

Chateaubriand, who in certain morbid feelings resembled the Germans, and was in addition a royalist and legitimist, when he found himself face to face with censorship and other forms of oppression of thought resolutely sided with the freedom of the press. Constant, who had the same inclinations and who was never able to give peace and harmony to his

emotional life, was among the first and most subtle and elo-
quent champions and theorists of the liberal system. Ugo
Foscolo, oppressed by the spectre of death and the dissolution of all things in the darkness of nothingness, saved as sole
reality what he called illusions, beauty and heroism, and not
only was his poetry virile, but his life was nobly inspired,
and he ended it in rebellion against the Austrian restoration
and in voluntary exile. Giacomo Leopardi, who scorned
civilization and progress, and considered free thought to be
that alone which, free of these phantoms, recognizes the desperate nothingness of all things, was in spite of this regarded
as an unconscious liberal by his youthful contemporaries;
and this was perhaps not so much illusion as sympathetic
clairvoyance, and in any case was the conclusion that the
young men personally drew from his sorrowful songs. The
romantics who did not redeem their inner disorder and remained in their troubled dreams were few at that time and
found no followers, not even when they had the genius of a
Stendhal, who was not understood by his contemporaries and
whose often exquisite art was not appreciated. There were,
to be sure, hints of conservative or reactionary or royalist-
legitimist politics in novelists and poets who unearthed and
adorned the Middle Ages, such as Walter Scott, and, in the
first years of the French restoration among several French
writers as well, and later also in Victor Hugo and Lamartine,
who at this time were very young; but in these last they were
soon replaced by quite different ideals, and Scott's intentions
were not incorporated in his novels, and certainly did not
pass over into his readers—who at that time may be said to
have comprised all who were able to read—of whom the
greater or the better part derived nothing but an increased
interest and a sort of affectionate *pietas* for the customs and
the events of the past, and admiration for brave men and
charming women, and a liking for wise, kindly, and witty

people. The poetry of patriotism and liberty was voiced in eager, manly purity, half heroic, half melancholy, by lyric souls like the Italian Giovanni Berchet. Manzoni's Catholicism set out with the same sentiments; and with the others of his school he belongs, to tell the truth, to the liberal circle and not to the Catholic or clerical, which did not produce thinkers or at best heterodox or scantly orthodox ones, and hence in Italy had no poets or writers of any account.

The Catholic Church was thus shorn of her life-giving element, and incapable of generating new forms or even new religious orders—as she had still been able to do in the sixteenth century—to such a degree that the best she could do was to restore the Jesuits whom she herself had abolished. And so she was unable to follow her opponents into the lofty spheres in which they moved, and was gradually reduced to becoming a predominantly political power. Under this aspect she was not, indeed, trifling or negligible, for she had on the contrary acquired possibilities in which before she had been lacking, and means of offence and defence, and capacities for giving assistance or inflicting damage, and, in short, manifold resources for negotiating and extorting concessions and favours and gaining what was to be gained. The Revolution and the Empire had put an end to Gallicanism and the national churches, abolished ecclesiastical feudalism and the privileges of the clergy and with them the ties that linked them to the other classes of the nation and to the temporal sovereigns, mediatized the territories of the prince-bishops, and accomplished many like functions. But Catholicism had with all this been in no wise abolished, and all this had simply fostered what was known as ultramontanism and turned the clergy of the various peoples and states towards Rome and placed a new and worldly power in the hands of the Pope. With this power the Catholic Church, in the first place and during the first period, as we have said before, supported and received the support of the absolute monarchies against revolutionary and liberal onslaughts. Those monarchies she had considered as enemies when they represented the modern state in formation, but now that they had grown conservative and so were depressing the spirit of intellect and morals, they were acceptable to her, seeing that after passing several centuries in conditions of intellectual inferiority, she now felt the same necessity and exercised the same depressing influence. And so she concluded a series of concordats, to her own advantage and reconquering positions that she had lost in the eighteenth century, even one with Naples, which had known the influence of the Giannones, the Tanuccis and the Caracciolos, and a few particularly scandalous ones, such as that with Bavaria. And so the Jesuits and the crypto-Jesuits, and the congregation that they instituted in France, and their intrigues with the *ultras,* and the so-called missions of propaganda, repentance, and expiation, and the Frères de la Doctrine Chrétienne, obtained all sorts of successes for the Church and for a time subjected public education to her authority.

Things were even worse in other countries, like Italy, where the priest again made his appearance beside the prince and his ministers, and the episcopal censorship was added to that of the Government, and everywhere might be perceived a mingled odour of sacristy and police station; not to mention Spain, where the conduct of the Catholic Church was so foolish in her obstinate clinging to the past as to cause to burst from the rebellious bowels of the land a ferocious movement of anticlericalism, quite unheard-of before in such a people with such traditions. But the agreements with the states, political as they were, concealed, like all transactions of a like nature, discord and hostility; and already some in Germany had attempted to set up a national German church against the Roman curia, and Prussia had had severe struggles with the

Pope and had resorted to the imprisonment or the expulsion
of bishops and archbishops; and in Austria, where the books
of unorthodox writers and even the Bible were prohibited,
Josephinism, under Metternich's government, persisted. In
England one of the objections against the emancipation of
Catholics was their dependence upon a foreign political
power; and among the French legitimists a protest was voiced
in 1826 by the legitimist and feudal Comte de Montlosier
against the alliance of the throne with the altar, and against
the intrigues of the Jesuits. A contrary but analogous protest
came from a Catholic and a priest, Lamennais, who, expressing grave disapproval of the alliance between Catholicism
and the absolute monarchies and their particular interests,
and invoking first of all freedom for the Church, was to end
by assigning a new task to the latter, an alliance with liberalism and democracy, certain as he was, in the strength of
his belief, that such an alliance, with its consequent total
separation of Church and State, would procure new triumphs
for Catholicism by the path of liberty and confer new life
upon it. "Liberalism," he wrote in 1829, "is right: liberty
will save the world; not, to be sure, its own, but that which
it is unconsciously preparing." Lamennais's opinions at once
obtained wide approval in France and elsewhere; but the
Church, after a first period of assent, was to draw back, as
might have been foreseen, for she realized the dangers of
that proposal and in the last resort was to utter a decided
condemnation of her too zealous and too audacious defender.

But meanwhile the reciprocal interests operated in various
fields and created a first gap in the friendly agreement of the
Church with the political order of the restoration, and forced
her into understandings and unions with patriots, liberals,
revolutionaries. This happened not so much in the frequent
alliances of Catholics with radicals and democrats in England for the reforms that included their emancipation, and in

the protests against the intolerable conditions in Ireland, as, above all and not without the influence of Lamennais's doctrines, in Belgium, in the common resistance and the common preparation of Catholics and liberals for the revolt against Holland, with whom Belgium had been linked in a single state. Other similar alliances would appear later on; but they were all of a political character, rendered advisable or inevitable by events, and as such they confirmed once more the obviously non-political nature of the Church. This found its formula in the doctrine of indifference towards the forms of government, a formula that is already to be found on the lips of Leo XII; it is after all the same utilitarian maxim adopted by the states against one another in their international relations, and which, no matter what attempts may be made to justify it with the evangelical dictum concerning the obedience to be rendered unto Caesar, is a renunciation of the true moral character of a religious creed, to which nothing can ever be indifferent.

Far less ambiguous than these alliances and, since they were more loyal, also more fruitful, were those which liberalism formed with democracy. The latter by this means was gradually transformed, not, to be sure, in its conception, but in its actuality, in its men and its tactics, and became almost an extreme wing of liberalism itself, which with its radicalism helped to fight against survivals and abuses, and to repulse the attacks on liberal institutions, and with its determination in showing fight was even necessary in desperate cases. This was shown in France by Lafayette's group, and by politicians and orators like General Foy, and again in the July days, when the Cavaignacs and the Raspails and the other young republicans shoved aside the hesitating moderates and revealed their ability to set students and working-men in motion and to take up arms and to construct barricades. But it was also seen on various occasions in Italy, in Spain, and in the course of the English agitations and reforms. Communism had not yet risen to the strength of a social movement and a corresponding party; but already in the agitations of English working-men various voices called for the return of the land to common property and expressed other similar radical proposals, and, what is more important, the first theorists and framers of communist programmes, Saint-Simon, Fourier, and Owen, were already maturing their opinions and beginning to attract attention. The stimulus was offered by the actual conditions of modern society and in particular of modern economy: so that at this very time a liberal writer, Sismondi, found himself facing those conditions and felt their gravity and was almost bewildered by the evils and the dangers that he perceived and foresaw; whereas among the non-liberals, the aristocrats and the feudalists took them up as material for observation, comparison, disparagement, and sarcasm. Saint-Simon, developing the ideas of the *Lettres d'un habitant de Genève* written in 1802, published in 1821-22 his *Système industriel;* and he gathered around him listeners and disciples, men of science and technicians and young historians and philosophers, such as Augustin Thierry and Comte, and shortly after his death his school started a vivid propaganda, with Enfantin at its head. Fourier, who as early as 1808 had published the *Théorie des quatre mouvements*, published in 1822 the *Traité de l'association agricole domestique* and in 1829 *Le nouveau monde industriel et sociétaire*, and he too had a school, a more restricted one but full of enthusiasm. Owen, who for a number of years in his cotton-works at New Lanark had offered an example of thoughtful care for the workmen's needs, had come forward as a social reformer in 1812 with his book *A New View of Society*, followed in 1820 by his *Book of the New Moral World*, had exercised an assiduous and varied activity as apostle, and founded, in 1825, the colony of New Harmony, Indiana. All this formed the object now of simple curiosity, and now of more serious interest, now of expectation and benevolence; but it was still outside the circle of real political activity.

As this opposition was still in the embryonic stages, it was not against it but rather against the three others that liberalism, during these years, directed its principles, its particular concepts, its institutions. This, together with the disintegration of monarchical absolutism, was the most important factor of these active and creative fifteen years, out of which liberalism issued not only victorious but strengthened in a complex of doctrines and corresponding modes and practices on which it thrived for a long time and on which it may be said to be still living today. It is self-evident that a similar theoretical development could not take place in Germany and in Italy; but it did not take place even in England, who already had this system at work, opposed by nobody, and therefore had little need to spend much intellectual activity over it or to provide doctrinal justifications, contenting herself with deducing the last consequences. For the other questions in which she was particularly involved, industrial growth, taxation, tariffs, England preferred to cultivate the science most useful to her, political economy, which at this time produced its Malthus and its Ricardo. English philosophy, represented by Bentham and thinkers of the same turn of mind, worked, however, with the concepts of the interest of the individual and the interest of the whole and of their harmony, and held liberalism, in theory, back to much of the abstract utilitarianism that derived from seventeenth-century rationalism, and so did not allow it to observe the dialectical and historical currents demanded by the new century. The religiosity of the various sects was utterly practical and moral, and the discussions concerning the Catholics and the Anglican

Church, even in the so-called Oxford movement, notable for a certain romantico-mediaeval trend, had no speculative importance. Not that England had lessened or lost her zeal for ideals in an entire devotion to action and business, as was said then and later; but her attention was turned from general questions to particular ones.

The country in which this doctrinal development was truly effectuated was France, highly conscious of the necessity for defending liberty against absolutists, feudalists, clericals, and republicans, and prepared for this task by the influence of German speculative and historical thought, to which she had added the requisite political elements. The work was enthusiastically begun by Madame de Staël and carried on by Constant, who in this was almost a pupil of hers, and carried further by the group known as the Doctrinaires, which was formed, indeed, in the drawing-room of the Duchesse de Broglie, Madame de Staël's daughter. The principal men of this group were imbued with political passion and lived in the midst of parliamentary and newspaper struggles. Several of them, like Madame de Staël and Constant, had lived in Germany or Switzerland, and others by other ways had grown familiar with German literature and science or had felt their influence indirectly. If you read the books of science and history and the political speeches of Royer-Collard, Guizot, De Broglie, Jordan, Barante, De Serre, you find there, magnificently expressed, a full consciousness of what liberalism was and meant, and of its differences from what the other systems were and meant. The tradition of 1791 had been dispersed in France amid the vicissitudes of the Convention, the Directory, and the Empire; and the generation born towards the beginning of the century—as Quinet narrates in his autobiography—no longer grasped the meaning of "constitution," "Girondins" and "Jacobins," "statutes" and "guarantees," almost as though they were words of a dead language,

and they did not hear spoken, on the lips of the people, of
the soldiers, of everyone, anything but the language of despotism, which is so easily understood because it is simple and
of few words. Nor was it feasible to attempt to resume those
tendencies of a quarter of a century ago, seeing how many
changes had occurred in the order of facts and in that of
ideas. What was needed was to begin all over again, and that
is what these writers did. After the Jacobins, they gave a non-
Jacobin idea of liberty and of the revolutionary process itself; after Napoleon, a non-usurping and non-despotic idea
of monarchy; after so much violence and brutality, an idea
of political activity that was neither violent nor brutal; after
all that orgy of warfare, a civilized idea of the function of
the peoples, and last of all, after so much arid irreligion and
hollow ecclesiastical orthodoxy lowered to an *instrumentum
regni,* a humano-religious idea, heedful of spontaneous de-
velopments and intent on preserving the ethical elements of
the old religions too.

Such was the work accomplished by the Doctrinaires. This
unattractive name was given to them by their opponents, and
also by the superficiality of many minds in their country,
minds unable to brook what was solid and what to them
seemed heavy. Perhaps, later, they did deserve it in a certain
measure, because they stopped, wrapped themselves in their
first concepts, and fell into decadence. But history looks at
their moment of creative activity, and is obliged to pronounce
this name with different feelings and with gratitude. "To
maintain the restoration, without yielding ground to reaction": that is the formula Guizot used in his memoirs to sum
up the way in which the problem and the duty appeared to
them in 1815. It was a problem of history to be taken up
again and carried on, a problem of conservation and progress
that answered to the necessities of the new situation. In relation to this duty and this problem, they studied and erected

into a system English political experience and political science, and gave particular development to the institution of the constitutional monarchy as they conceived it, strong in its past and alive in its present, and to the institution of the electorate, which they wished restricted to the maturer social forces, capable of understanding what is meant by government and what the national interests are. At this time these were to be found in the so-called bourgeoisie, and in the world of culture, which, although its sphere of growth lay within the same social circle, yet passed beyond it, precisely because of its cultural qualities. And so they objected both to any attempt to obtain indirect or two-class suffrage and to all proposals of a franchise so broadened as to become an instrument of reaction in the hands of the *ultras* and the clergy. And for the same reason they endeavoured to preserve the conservative and historical forces, and even the hereditary peerage. At the same time they defended first of all the primary and fundamental institution of liberalism, the freedom of the press, and together with it liberty of conscience, without at the same time favouring the cruder forms of anti-Catholic illuminism. These, and the other institutions formed or adumbrated at this time and which later assumed clearer outlines and grew more supple and more adapted to new conditions and needs, and the practice of the constitutional and parliamentary life, and the debates in the French chambers, were the school of liberalism for the other countries of Europe still lacking a constitutional régime. For all of these France was working at this time, taking advantage of the charter that had been granted to her and which she would no longer allow to be stolen or torn from her. The constitutions of 1848, and, to give an example, those of Italy and among them that of Charles Albert which became the constitution of the kingdom of Italy, gathered the fruits of this labour, for they were modelled after its resultant, the statute of 1830.

Since, then, as is shown by this rapid résumé of the facts
and events of these fifteen years, the liberal ideal at this time
had an actual and not merely a theoretical preponderance
over the others, and if the better and more combative forces
were on its side and bent and dominated the opposing forces
not from the outside but from the inside, what was the July
Revolution? Was it, as several historians have judged, the
consequence of an error that might have been avoided if
Charles X had not let himself be guided by his Polignacs,
who in their turn hoped for counsel from fervid prayers to
the Virgin Mary, or if, when he had come to his unalterable
decision once more, to dissolve the chamber, with its liberal
majority, and proclaim the Ordinances, he had also taken,
as he failed to do, the requisite military precautions? Or, as
others believe, was it an accident, which might just as well
not have happened, and would liberalism have won in any
case, in other ways? These cogitations concerning abstract
possibilities, which, thus qualified, are implicitly refuted,
ought not to distract us from the reality, which is only what
happened. And considered in the light of their reality, the
days of July were nothing but what everyone sees and knows:
the moment when the struggle that in varying shape and with
varying rhythm had lasted for years, between liberalism and
absolutism, turned into an armed conflict, in which the two
hostile parties respectively affirmed the same character that
had appeared in the preceding events, and in that very fact,
and by means of the conflict, the one increased the energy
that it possessed, and the other diminished and lost its own,
and was defeated.

With it, all European absolutism was morally defeated
and, on the contrary, European liberalism, which was struggling and bridling in repression, became an example of how
to face the enemy in extreme cases; a proof that in this way
victory is certain; an aid in the fact itself that a great power

had reached the plenitude of liberty; and ground for confidence in revolutions soon to come. After fifteen years, after all the efforts of the governments, the wiles of the police, the labours of the gendarmes and the militias, absolutism, which in the intellectual field had shown its feebleness and lack of logic, allowed itself to be beaten even in the field that was all its own, and in which it felt itself more at ease, in that of the force which it is customary to call material. And, in these fifteen years, liberalism had made such great progress as to render democracy dependent on it and to attract the better elements even of the aristocracy and Catholicism. These combats in the streets of Paris attained to the significance of a world-battle; it seemed to the anxious watchers that the thick black clouds which were lowering on the horizon of European political life had suddenly been scattered by the sun, by the "July sun."

V. PROGRESS OF THE LIBERAL MOVEMENT:

FIRST CONFLICTS WITH SOCIAL DEMOCRACY

(1830-1847)

A HIGHER spiritual temperature in Europe was what is generally called the "effect" or the "effects" of the July Revolution—in other words, a glow of action and reaction after that important event, which had been the relative resolution of a state of tension, the winning of a great battle, but not the end of a war—for in the moral life no wars are truly ended. The liberals resumed their activity with eager confidence, and the absolutists hastened to the breaches with the wiles and devices rendered advisable by events, and sent into the fray such of their forces as were still intact. The reciprocal proportions were no longer the same as before, either between the two parties or in their relations with the others. The effort undertaken in 1815 by absolutism to establish itself in the European world and remould it nearer to its own desires had in the beginning been not so much a self-confident offensive as a defensive, and now lowered its aim even further, so that it was legitimate to speak of the "failure of the Holy Alliance." On the other hand, liberalism obtained not a few advantages and acquired more and more the characteristics of an offensive. Meanwhile in the various liberal organisms that had taken shape, problems and conflicts of varying nature were making themselves felt.

The first of the "effects" that are generally attributed to

the July Revolution was the restored national independence of Belgium. The new kingdom that arose provided itself with a constitution much more liberal not only than the somewhat antiquated one enjoyed by Belgium in her union with Holland but even than that of France of 1830, especially in what concerned the organization of the municipalities and the provinces. The disagreement between the two peoples had been constant since the very beginnings of the union, in spite of the not slight commercial advantages that the Belgian provinces obtained from it. It concerned the inadequate representation of the Belgians in the Dutch assembly, the distribution of financial burdens, the Dutch employés in Belgium, the centralization of the higher courts in The Hague, but above all the treatment of religion and of language, and the press regulations, things that offended and revolted the sympathies of both Catholics and liberals. A few years before 1830 there took place the agreement between these two parties for common national ends and for those that coincided externally, even if internally they were different, and were pursued by both. The July days had no immediate consequences there, and did not lead to the radical solution of separation from Holland, an idea that had not yet reached maturity. The Belgian insurrection of August 25 gave rise at first to negotiations towards an agreement; and it was only after the street fights in Brussels of September 23-26 and the repulse of the Dutch troops that the provisional government and the national council that had been convoked proclaimed, on November 19, Belgium's independence and, on November 24, the fall of the House of Orange. Through a series of various military and diplomatic events, under the wing of France and England and with the intervention of the French army, which drove the Dutch from Antwerp, the kingdom of Belgium was founded, under the Coburg dynasty and, at the wish of the five powers, neutralized; a kingdom that soon

flourished in traffic and industry and was among the first to
establish a close network of railways.

The acceleration of a process already begun was also seen
in the great English electoral reform, demanded with growing
insistence by manufacturers and working-men after the events
in Paris, by means of agitations and demonstrations, mass
meetings and processions, which at times assumed a threatening aspect and were in vain opposed by the Wellington ministry. This ministry was overthrown in November, 1830, and
the negative vote of the House of Commons and another of
the House of Lords were unable to defeat the measure permanently; it became law in 1832, increasing the number of
voters by more than three hundred thousand and modifying
their quality, so that the ensuing elections gave a wide representation to new classes and returned a majority of liberals,
and in addition a certain number of radicals. Even in smaller
countries, such as Switzerland, the patrician régime, which
had been reaffirmed in 1815 and which criticism and polemics
had undermined, was overwhelmed by the liberal movement;
and in November, 1830, a demonstration in Zurich was the
signal for a change to a constitution and for the introduction
of similar institutions in twelve cantons, although in a few
others the old order was preserved and in still others, according to the older and the newer ideas, the city was separated
from the country. This happened between 1830 and 1833;
and about this time Portugal beheld the end of the struggle
between the constitutionalists of the young Queen Maria, supported by her father Dom Pedro, and the absolutists of Dom
Miguel. The latter, whom Wellington had viewed with no un-
friendly eye and whom Charles X and Ferdinand VII had
recognized, received the *coup de grâce* from the combined
forces of France under Louis Philippe, England with her liberal ministry, and Spain. Spain, in her turn—after Ferdinand
VII, hostile to the House of Orléans, had met an invasion pre-

pared in France by the Spanish exiles and repelled it, and
had then proceeded to tighten the curb—had witnessed, at
the King's death, a fight for the succession between the Queen-
Mother Christina, as regent for her daughter Isabella, and
her brother-in-law Don Carlos, and was gradually drawing
aloof from absolutism. The Regent looked for support to the
liberals and in 1834 promulgated an *estatuto real*, or a first
constitutional charter, and with the assistance of the liberals
drove out not only the Portuguese pretender but even the
Spanish one from Portugal, where he had established himself. And so Spain entered upon her series of vicissitudes
which—no matter how troublesome and entangled they might
be, and which, because of the frequent military pronunciamentos (an inheritance of the immediate post-Napoleonic
period) and because of the frequent and more or less dis-
guised dictatorships were anything but liberal in their development—never bore her back, at least not formally, to
the absolutist régime.

Elsewhere, attempts were made and failed, as in Italy in
1831, with the insurrections of Modena and Parma, Bologna,
the Romagna, the Marches, and part of Umbria, in which
the tricolour was unfurled and provisional governments were
set up that legislated in a liberal sense; they were soon overthrown by Austrian intervention. The modest and elementary
reforms that the powers, after the repression, recommended
to the sacerdotal government in their memorandum remained
without any effect. In Germany, a few small states, such as
Brunswick and Hesse-Cassel, drove out their stolid prince-
lings and obtained constitutional charters from their successors; the King of Hanover was constrained to make the same
concession; in 1831 Saxony reformed its assembly of estates;
the parliaments, where they already existed, and especially
those of Bavaria and Baden, took on a new life, the oppositions waxed bolder; in the chamber of Karlsruhe the doc-

trinaire oratory of men like Rotteck and Welcker won the admiration of all Germany, and Grand Duke Leopold was complimented on having left the management of the finances and the other branches of the administration to this assembly and on having amplified the freedom of the press. In Rhenish Bavaria, Wirth and Siebenpfeifer published audacious and almost republican newspapers. There had for several years been symptoms of new growth in the associations of young students, which were partly political in tendency.

But Prussia remained immobile, and her King, following as a rule the leadership of Metternich and in union with the two Emperors, co-operated towards the severest repression and compression. The looked-for opportunity for this soon appeared with the gathering at Hambach in May, 1832, for the anniversary of the Bavarian constitution. Thirty-two thousand persons, for the most part from Rhenish Bavaria, took part in this and proclaimed the principle of popular sovereignty, the unity of Germany, the German republic, and the confederation of the free states of Europe. Besides the lawsuits and the convictions that the Bavarian Government was obliged, because of these excesses, to impose, in June the federal diet prohibited popular societies and festivals and gatherings and the displaying of the national colours, renewed the measures of Carlsbad concerning the universities, and what was more, enjoined the princes to reject every attempt to diminish their sovereignty, every request for a constitution, and prohibited all legislation whatsoever differing from the maxims that guided the diet. They decreed, furthermore, that a permanent committee should be set up and entrusted with the legislative proposals of the separate states. In consequence of all this, Baden was obliged to suspend her law on the press. The *coup de main* at Frankfort in August, 1833, on the part of a handful of conspirators, attempting to remove the diet and to set up in its place a provisional government, led to the dissolution of the chamber of Hesse-Cassel, the country from which the greater part of these conspirators had come, and to an increased vigilance over all the states. In the Treaty of Berlin of the same year, the three absolutist powers reiterated their right to give aid in foreign or internal affairs to every sovereign who asked for it, without the other powers' having any right to complain. Far more grave and terrible was the defeat of Poland, who rose in November, 1830, and held out, in a stubborn and heroic struggle, until September in the following year, against the overwhelming Russian army; because after that immense effort for liberation had proved vain, a pitiless revenge was inflicted on the Polish people, who lost all the institutions conceded or almost conceded by Emperor Alexander and what little independence still remained to them, and were for many decades unable even to attempt to shake off the yoke imposed on them and now rendered more and more burdensome.

This rally and these victories of the absolutist powers, this arrest of the extension of the revolutionary movement towards independence and liberty: Austria flinging herself on Italy, without the interference of anyone, in order to suffocate every breath of life; Russia subjecting Poland to her utter autocracy and sending patriots to the scaffold or to places of punishment; the spectacle of the Polish fugitives, who gathered particularly in France, joining and fraternizing with the Italian exiles of the recent and the earlier revolutions; the disdain for the downtrodden and oppressed nationalities, the sadness over the sorrows witnessed, the pity for the victims, the admiration for courage in affliction—all this made a feeling of bitter disappointment follow the delight of the first moments, and made people think and believe and say that the July Revolution had failed in its purpose. And it was only natural that this should be the case among the contemporary spectators, and still more so among those who were struggling and suffering. But this feeling cannot be shared by the historian, who does not measure facts by hopes, in respect to which (for they are measureless) the former always appear small or inferior; instead he looks only at the facts that preceded them, and observes in what sense the conditions have been modified and what has arisen that is new and positive.

And this was the new element, that absolutism had collapsed in all Western Europe, and the liberal régimes had been strengthened and had grown better able to answer to the economic and social conditions. In fact, the Quadruple Alliance of 1834 against Don Carlos and Dom Miguel might appear for a certain time as an answer to the Triple Alliance formed in the previous year by the central and eastern powers. Here legitimism sank from a practical ideal to an imaginative one and to a romantic aspiration; from a political party to little gatherings of high society, composed of stately old ladies and accomplished gentlemen, who segregated themselves from the present, withdrawing into the salons of the Faubourg Saint-Germain and other similar élite corners of the world. Sometimes this imagination attempted to come down to reality, as in the enterprise of the Duchesse de Berry in the Vendée, of which it was said that the blame was Sir Walter Scott's, and which by the irony of events was robbed of its glamour by a particular physiological condition that the heroine of the golden lilies had incurred, unable, poor weak woman, to endure for a long time the chill loneliness of widowhood. In this adventure there were some who succeeded in shedding their blood for their former kings; others laboured to lend assistance in arms and money to the pretenders of Spain and Portugal; others (and among these Bourmont and several with him) offered their swords to these monarchs of legitimism, as they did later to Austria, who represented the good old times, or—why not?—to the brigands who in the name of the dethroned princes were spreading rapine and murder. These were the last remnants or late and rather artificial imitations of the legions of the *émigrés* and the Vendéans in the days of the great revolution. Even in Spain, which some twenty years before had risen in every region against the French importers of rationalized civilization, now only the Basque provinces, attached to their *fueros* and mediaeval customs, sympathized in direct fashion with Don Carlos and offered him a point of support.

The polemics of absolutism were poisoned by these collapses, which cast shadows of others to come before long; as may be observed in Italy in the books of the Prince of Canosa and in those little dialogues of Count Monaldo Leopardi that covered the face of his son with blushes and extracted cries of amazement and horror from Lamennais. The three absolutist powers had been obliged to accept, with rage and vexation (and indeed some of them, and in particular Russia, had seriously thought of recurring to arms), the partial destruction of the work wrought by the treaties of 1815. They viewed with dismay the substitution in France of the House of Orléans for the Bourbons *majorum gentium;* in Belgium, the independence of Holland; in Spain and Portugal, the expulsion of the pretenders, the champions of their sacred ideas and recognized by them or on the point of receiving their recognition; and in all these countries, the formation or the progress of liberal constitutions. They, who were still in particular fashion bound to one another by what to the new conscience of the peoples seemed a *pactum sceleris,* the dismemberment and division of Poland, were still powerful through their weighty armies and their diplomacies; and a few years later the Austrian eagle even went so far as to lay her talons on the free city of Crakow and to befoul herself with the blood of Polish nobles, against whom, in Galicia, she urged the Ruthenian peasants on to slaughter. But these were triumphs that could be accounted as defeats, and the opinion of the civilized world was being set more and more strongly against them, against their sovereigns, against their ministers, against their very armies, whose qualities and feats of valour were not an object of admiration but one of commiseration and regret, and did not stir hearts, those hearts that were profoundly moved over the pages of a little book by an Italian, which narrated at this time, without emphasis and without discussion, *Le mie prigioni*, the imprisonment he had suffered for the cause of liberty under the Austrian oppression.

And yet there was not only, in those years, the bitterness of the disappointment of which we have spoken, but another emotion, a spiritual revolt because of broken faith, almost an accusation of treason, of which France was the object: France, to whom the Italian insurrectionists had looked in 1831, certain that in word and in deed she would veto Austria's intervention in favour of the papal government; France, the hope of the Polish rebels, who expected from her as well as from England battalions to aid them, and had sent their representatives around to ask for them; France, the hope of the German liberals on the Rhine, who at the festival of Hambach toasted Lafayette. The hopes were based not only on the sympathies of individuals and private persons and on the opinions of writers, but also on words of encouragement and instigation pronounced by the French committees for Italian emancipation and for the reconstruction of Poland, and by some of the most responsible men of her political world, and also by a few ministers in office, and in the beginning even by Louis Philippe, who allowed an expedition of Italian exiles to be prepared, which was to gather at Marseilles—and then was countermanded. And in a more general way they were based on what France boasted of having been throughout her long history, and above all in her glorious Revolution, the liberator of peoples, the enemy of oppression; and on what she boasted of having become once more in her last revolution, which was to continue the work of the other and to carry it on in a spirit different from that of Napoleon, and to burst the chains of the peoples, and, with them all, to create a new Europe. Quite recently her historians, men like Guizot and Michelet, had, in this respect, conferred the primacy on her, as the country that was "the centre and the cradle of European civilization," so the first said; or that, said the other, was to effectuate, after the Christian revolution, another, no less grandiose, a purely human and social one; or that, added Buchez, "alone was able to understand and carry out a disinterested task." And now she had fallen short of this primacy, these promises, this trust, and after egging the peoples on to rise, she had abandoned them to their butchers, had come to terms with the kings, and through the mouth of her ministers had declared "that the blood of the French belongs to France alone" and coldly announced that "order reigns in Warsaw."

There was, in this French attitude, a reality and an illusion, or rather the reality of a certain kind that is turned into illusion when it is transferred to another kind. The reality was the actual disposition of the French mind, already indicated by the language, so supple and conversational, so adapted to the diffusion of reason and to rendering it practically fruitful, that reason which is at once humanity and equality and liberty and justice. And there was a generous impulse, even though sometimes confused with self-satisfaction in the eagerness for *la gloire*, an impulse of which traces might be found even in the Middle Ages of chivalry and in the Crusades and which burst forth with the outbreak of the Revolution and founded a tradition and a school. But the French people who fostered this mode of thinking, and in part practised it, was not able to coincide with the French people in so far as it made up the French state, which, like every state, obeyed the laws of politics and therefore the laws of its own safety and preservation. And although modes of thought do not remain inactive even in politics, they operate in it only in so far as politics is able to absorb them and to make them its own, that is, mediately and not immediately—as is so strangely expected when they are invoked to dictate the conduct of politics or to take its place. The difference had already been experienced and suffered in practice by the Italian patriots and Jacobins when the French descended on Italy with Bonaparte and their other generals, who were desired and hailed and awaited as conquerors, but who instead milked the Italian population for the benefit of France, left them at times to their fate, and even treated them as objects for bargain, as with Venice at Campoformio. Lafayette and his other friends and co-religionists unified too much these two diverse aspects of things, and promised and gave reason to hope what was granted neither to them nor to others to realize. The French state, issuing from the July Revolution with its new king, had internal and external dangers that it had to face or to avoid, difficulties and interests for which it had to make provision.

Russia, who hesitated to recognize Louis Philippe, would have started war, and would perhaps have dragged Austria in with her, if the Polish insurrection had not kept her busy at the right moment, and if Austria had not been occupied with the affairs of Italy; and Austria, meanwhile, having Napoleon's son in her hands, threatened to raise the Bonapartists against the Orleanists. In France the republicans were raising their crests and inciting to revolution. The principle of non-intervention, which the new régime had affirmed against that of the Holy Alliance and which had caused the wings of so many hopes to sprout, was, and could only be, a political formula, with the requisite double meanings and with the oratorical effects of political formulas, and meant (as was explained when the time came) that France would

reject any foreign intervention in her internal affairs and
would keep it remote from the countries that lay within the
circle of her own nearest interests; that in these cases she
would intervene when her own politics permitted or demanded, as she did in Belgium and in Portugal; and that she
would on the other hand allow Russia to intervene in Poland
and Austria in Italy, when she was unable to prevent it without becoming entangled in a disastrous or extremely risky
war. At best she would act as she did in Italy: she would
occupy Ancona in order to show Austria that she did not mean
to permit her to extend her dominion in Italy and to induce
her, after she had carried out her military and police operations, to evacuate the occupied territories. This did not mean
that the French policy was lacking in civilized and liberal and
humanitarian features; just as England was not lacking in
them, although she interpreted intervention and non-intervention in the same way. Certainly no one—no matter how often
she has been cursed as "perfidious Albion"—would want to
deny all that she has done for the independence, the liberty,
and the civilization of the nations. Every other form of participation in the causes of enslaved and oppressed peoples was
and had to remain, in England as well as in France, a thing
reserved for private individuals. In this Lafayette and his
friends did good work, and those Italians and Poles whom the
French state was unable to succour in their country found
among the liberals in France, and also in England, Belgium,
and Switzerland, friendship and encouragement, were often
protected against certain hardships exercised by the governments of France and the other countries, and founded there
the battalion of soldiers of nationalism and liberty, the symbol of the brotherhood of the nations above all the struggles
for existence of the separate states.

But looking more closely at this idea of the French primacy entertained by the peoples who had believed in it and

who had been confirmed in this belief by the July barricades, and who had waited for the fulfilment of this obligation of nobility, we find that there are two sides to the case. On the one hand we must allow for the desperate conditions in which the peoples found themselves, divided and scattered and disarmed under the pressure of powerful military states that held them within a network of fortresses and garrisons and through their police forces watched over every gesture and every word. Their anxious expectation, as Manzoni said of the Italians, for the appearance on the Alps of a friendly banner was the need for an event able to break the iron band at some point and to open a loop-hole for their insurrection and battle. On the other hand they were guilty of distrust of their own strength, and from a justifiable prudence sank into an unjustified depression and cowardice, forgetting that the line of what is possible can be considerably altered by means of the inventive audacity and the creative force of the will that really wills. The wisdom of no longer hugging fond illusions or expecting from the policy of states what it does not furnish, at least not by its own activity, of no longer counting on the French primacy and the French duty of "initiative," should have been combined with an awakening of that confidence in themselves, in their own "initiative," the education of the will by action, and with trying and retrying and never giving up, rebelling, accepting eventual or even certain defeat and rebelling once more, with the generosity of sacrifice in the certain consciousness of final victory, which was to be sought for on this its own highway, and not in the combinations of particular interests and in dreams of possible fortunate accidents.

It is in the perception of this truth, and in the inflexible resoluteness to act in a manner agreeing with it, that the true greatness of Giuseppe Mazzini lies. In 1831 the Piedmontese Government allowed him to go into exile, without realizing that this exile was to give Italy, and all the peoples striving for liberty, their greatest teacher of life. But less slow to become aware of him and to know him were the Austrian police and Metternich, who qualified him as "one of the most dangerous men" of the youthful and restless faction. Mazzini saw that there is something more fundamental than the politics manipulated by statesmen, something that must be done when the other cannot be done, and before the other is done; that is, to awaken in man the sentiment of the universal, the ideal, and with it the consciousness of the mission that is assigned to each one, and of the duty that is derived from it, and of that dedication of one's entire self to this duty which potentiates forces and renders possible what to men of little faith seems impossible. So that in opposition to the antiquated Carboneria, which still survived here and there in Italy and to which he himself had belonged, in opposition to those who had grown old in these ideas and in these attitudes, in 1832 he founded the Giovine Italia, Young Italy, which went back to the religious sources of virile and combative character. In opposition to the waiting for the French "initiative," and in the delusion awakened in him too by the July Revolution of all the hopes fixed on foreign governments, he inculcated in the Italians and in the other peoples the "initiative" of each. And he outlined, in contrast with the French hegemony, a Young Europe. "The tree of liberty does not fructify," he liked to repeat, "unless it is planted by the hands of citizens and rendered fertile by the blood of citizens and guarded by the swords of citizens."

This greatness of his (as, moreover, is generally felt and recognized) is moral greatness, the greatness of an apostle who lives what he believes and operates equally with the illuminating and inflaming word and with his example, and advises and urges to similar conduct those whom he addresses and whom he gathers about himself. All the rest, in the com-

plex of his ideas, is either not his own or else is secondary
or vague or erroneous. The idea of the republican unity of
Italy already belonged to the tradition, from which he may
have derived it, of the Italian Jacobins, who, like himself,
from disappointment and disgust with the activity in Italy
of the France of the Directory were led to outline the Italian
republic as one and indivisible. At that time, in the days of
the Batavian and Swiss republics, such an idea was certainly
less remote from reality than it had become in the nineteenth
century. But they did not bring to it, as he did, religious feeling and the fervour of the apostle, and their idea did not take
root and had, as the phrase goes, no dynamic efficacy. The
concept of the nations, and of the missions incumbent on each,
came from the German philosophers and historians, and belonged to the common intellectual heritage, even if it was
validly promoted by him and implanted in the consciousness
of Europe and popularized. The substitution, which he proposed to make, of the Italian primacy for that of France has
no value beyond that of a myth useful to encourage the pride
of a people that needs to rise from the ground and fight. He
had been preceded in it, moreover, not only by the myth of
the French but also by that of the German primacy, asserted
under analogous conditions by Fichte; it was accompanied
and followed by the different "primacy of Italy" of Gioberti
and the Polish primacy of Cieszkowski, and, if you will, by
the Swiss, Melchior Hirzel, who prophesied Switzerland as
the generating centre of the European republic, free of Christianity and governed by modern philosophy.

Mazzini's doctrinal combinations must be judged more crit-
ically. In these he was animated by a vigorous feeling for
liberty, and viewed the forces of liberalism as the source of
the movements for national independence; but a lack of speculative depth and historical sense prevented him from theoretically formulating and deducing the concept of liberty.

And indeed theoretically he compromised it, and almost disowned it. For from Saint-Simonism he accepted the principle of association as opposed to that of competition, and the new humanitarian religion with dogmas, cult, and discipline, and, if not actually with a Pope, at least with a religious council placed at the head of the peoples, and poetry and art subjected to social ends, and such things. From democratic ideology he accepted the vague idea of the People, oscillating between the whole and the part, and, in short, a general representation the main elements of which were supplied by the Spanish peasants of the insurrection against the French and by the volunteers and soldiers of the wars of the republic in 1793, which made him dream his dream of a guerilla insurrection to be kindled from one end of Italy to the other, as well as in all the other countries that needed to be liberated.

Despite all this, despite the fact that he was neither a coherent thinker nor a statesman, Mazzini rose to intellectual, moral, and also political power in the life of Europe. Patriots and revolutionaries of all countries found their point of contact in him; and against him the absolutist and conservative governments waged a daily warfare with all the resources of espionage and intrigue. And if, in those years after 1830, there arose or rather increased (because it was never lacking and even now is not lacking altogether) a common European consciousness, a common base of ideas, a common judgment, a common opinion, a common sensibility, and almost a tribunal whose sentences cannot be disregarded with impunity, this was certainly not the work of one man, and indeed sprang from the essence of the liberal movement, inasmuch as it was the continuation of the illuminist movement. But at the same time Mazzini contributed to it both in the general and in the particular, with the afflatus of his religious spirit and the love that made him feel for and understand and embrace all the different peoples, not only the Italian but the

German people as well, and those Southern Slavs whom he was the first to discover and to whom he revealed their future. The voices of discouragement (natural incidents in all wars and enterprises, and, because of their logical emptiness and practical sterility, destined to be gradually submerged by the need for action and progress) were also silenced by opposing voices, such as that of Lamennais, who in 1835 wrote to Mazzini himself: *"Prenez courage, monsieur; les meres enfantent pour vous."* And the mothers accomplished this function so successfully that in Italy in 1846 the poet Giusti, warning a reactionary personage that the *galantuomo* Time was wending his way towards liberty, added:

> Believe 't or not, but the cathedral-bell
> Is there to speak for who has ears to hear:
> Each time it tolls, a liberal is born,
> Or a *bandito* lies upon his bier.

In Italy, the youthful sovereigns of the two principal states, the kingdom of the Two Sicilies and that of Sardinia, were both antiliberal, bound by oath and treaty not to grant constitutional liberties, and hostile to these because of their clerical and almost bigoted minds. One of them, however, Charles Albert, a soldier by temperament and by education, nourished ambitions of aggrandizement and therefore viewed Austria as his natural enemy; the other, Ferdinand II, had no such ambitions, and did not oppose Austria, although he was keen on governing without the interference of Austria or of any other power. Less fanatic and more wary, he conceded amnesties to political prisoners, recalled exiles, employed the men of the Napoleonic decade of the revolution of 1820, was indulgent towards those who were conspiring and plotting insurrections and planning to take his life, refused to listen to any talk of international absolutist intrigues; whereas Charles Albert gave support to Carlism and Miguelism, and, out of hatred of the July monarchy, supported the Duchesse de Berry and punished with merciless cruelty the first conspirators of Young Italy, his subjects. But both of them undertook administrative reforms, restored the finances of their states and the economic life of their countries, negotiated treaties of commerce, constructed railways, with more extensive and more intensive results, with regard to the geographical situation and the historical precedents, in Piedmont than in Southern Italy. Thus the one and the other, indirectly and unconsciously, assisted and prepared the progress of liberty, just as the gentlemen and the educated bourgeoisie in Piedmont, Tuscany, and elsewhere in their turn busied themselves with agricultural experiments, schools, and asylums for children, with mutual instruction and public welfare in general. The congresses of the Italian scientists, which followed regularly upon that at Pisa in 1839, and which the princes neither prohibited nor favoured, led to the same results.

In the states of the Church, where the movement of 1831 had been followed by a lurid government of cardinal-legates who made use of bands of malefactors, everything was immobile to such a degree that after about fifteen years the liberals were able, by means of Farini, to adopt as their own demands, in the *Memorandum of Rimini* of 1845, the memorandum presented to Cardinal Bernetti by the powers in 1831; and as regards economic progress, the saying of Pope Gregory XVI has remained famous, that railways and steam-traction were works of Satan; which was, moreover, a saying not void, in its way, of insight and logical coherence. The Young Italy association spread with rapidity, especially in Northern and Central Italy, and its adepts were counted by the tens of thousands. The writings of Mazzini circulated, escaping the eyes of the police, and although they did not convert people to their social and religious concepts, and did not even gain much headway for the republican idea, they opened a path for the revolution and prepared men for audacity and sacrifice. But the longed-for popular and general revolution did not burst out, and after the unhappy attempt in 1834 to organize an expedition to Savoy, even the frustrated attempts became rare, such as that of Romagna in 1843 and that of Cosenza in 1844, and last of all the landing of the Bandieras in Calabria. However, in London, where, driven away from Switzerland, he had taken up his residence, Mazzini did not cease to ponder and to invent new plans with his emissaries and correspondents, among whom was Fabrizi in Malta.

In contrast with Mazzini and his political concepts and his method, and outside of all factions and conspiracies, there was formed and grew up in Italy the other party that became powerful at this time, that of the moderate liberals. These, unlike Mazzini and his followers, in their religious convictions were all or almost all Catholics, and, by way of reminiscence of mediaeval history, received the name of neo-Guelphs. These were those Catholic-liberals mentioned by us in delineating the dialectics of the political creeds toward the beginning of the nineteenth century, and they must be carefully distinguished from the others of the same name who at the same time sprang up and attracted attention in France, Belgium, and elsewhere. In order to distinguish their genuine nature and real character these latter deserve rather to be called clerical-liberals or liberalizing clericals. It is all the more necessary to detach them from those others because not only have they often been confusedly bunched up with them but also, owing to this confusion, they were unfavourably judged by men like Quinet, who accused the Balbos, the Troyas, the Rosminis, the Giobertis, of working to destroy the last refuge of the Italian spirit—thought—thus giving the *coup de grâce* to their people, and of being followers of men like De Maistre, De Bonald, Görre, Günther, and the like.

It is sufficient to recall, as far as their religious ideas are concerned, that their Catholicism was either a simple revival of the ethical and spiritual motives of Christianity, or a continuation and reflection of Jansenism, which had reacted so powerfully on the royalists and reformers and revolutionaries towards the end of the previous century, and the influence of which had reached even Mazzini. And let us remember that some among them would gladly have deprived the Pope of all temporal power, restoring him to a purely spiritual function, and that all, from the greatest to the least, had in mind a more or less radical "reform of the Church."

Their moderation was political sense, which regarded as a fool's paradise the idea of an Italian republic and even that of the political unity of the whole nation, and considered as utterly fantastic the appeal to the imaginary people that would rise in the fields and the factories to drive out with their improvised arms the foreigner and the domestic tyrants. They attributed little importance to conspiracies and viewed as dangerous the method of "everything or nothing." So that they thought it would be necessary to go back to the educated classes, and not to despair altogether of the kings and the other princes; to prefer open-air conspiracies to those in secret; to ask gradually for what they might hope to obtain, administrative reforms, representation of interests, councils, and, later on, political constitutions; and to consider the international situation and take advantage of the opportunities that it offered or might offer to drive the Austrians out of Italy and to compose a federation of Italian states. In these two aims, Italian independence and political liberty, they were in agreement with the Mazzinians and the democrats and the anticlericals, although they differed from them in the way they pictured the future and in the means to be adopted in the present, and in the general tone of their polemics and propaganda. De Sanctis observed that the two parties or "schools" manifested all their diversity in their prose: in the moderates or liberals, an analytical style, a language very near to the spoken language, simplicity, easy speech, reasoning persuasion, the use of irony; in the Mazzinians and the democrats, a synthetic style, a solemn language, pompous and often rhetorical modes, invective, sarcasm. The first had a real people before them whom they were trying to educate, the others an imaginary people whom they were trying to excite. But in reality the one party did not throw down or uproot the other, but rather each made up for the shortcomings of the other.

This became apparent later in the course of events, and might be seen meanwhile in the passage of several of their men from the one to the other, in the need that some experienced at times for greater audacity and others for greater moderation (Balbo being the more conservative, Gioberti inclined to democracy, and D'Azeglio ready to do away with delay and to demand independence and liberty at the same time). This was true in the co-operation that they resolved to accept, not to mention the fact that Mazzini himself, even if at brief moments, did not shrink from yielding precedence to Charles Albert, and perhaps even to Pius IX, and to the monarchy capable of satisfying the national aspirations. All of them were practically drawn, whatever their illusions may have been, to what was practical and feasible. As to what was not feasible, the Mazzinian idea of the Italian republic was in conflict with actual conditions, which are changing, but that of Gioberti, of a nationalistic and liberal Pope, was in contradiction with logic, which does not change. None the less, even this Giobertian idea, although it contained ambiguous elements, deriving as it did from a somewhat ambiguous author (a hater of Jesuits but not far from their tortuous methods and pretences, and in any case confused or vague in his concepts and susceptible of many metamor-

phoses), produced beneficent effects. If the clear-sighted saw
the fallacy of it, for many Catholics, for many young priests
and even for several high personages of the clergy, this papal
myth opened the way to their intense desire for a national
Risorgimento, for civil progress and a renewed religious life.

At this time the moderate school of liberal Catholicism produced almost all the books of philosophy, the histories, the
novels, the poetry, that cultivated these desires among Italians. The list is long, and goes from the treatises of Rosmini
and Gioberti, the histories of Troya and Balbo, Capponi and
Tosti, to the novel and the tragedies of Manzoni, who was the
precursor, to the *Ettore Fieramosca* and the *Niccolò dei Lapi*
of D'Azeglio and the satires of Giusti. But because of the
unity of fundamental intentions in the two opposing schools,
just as many readers became acquainted with the less substantial books of the so-called Ghibellines, such as the antipapal
and antiforeign tragedies of Niccolini, or the less educative
books, such as the convulsive novels of the Byronic Guerrazzi.
And all that there was of good or of true in them was assimilated. To the moderate school is also due the more realistic
development given to political discussions, in Balbo's *Delle
speranze d'Italia*, in D'Azeglio's *Degli ultimi casi di Romagna*,
and in the books of Durando, Galeotti, and others. It was also
in its midst that might be noted the first signs that Italian
politics were being centred in Piedmont. Outside the pale of
the Catholic-liberal school, in the field of pure modern philosophical and critical thought (which in the ideas of that school
is found mixed and reconciled in a more or less extrinsic
fashion with traditional religion), a few among the younger
minds showed signs of life; and equally outside of it, in liberal and lay thought, another young mind was taking shape,
that of Camillo di Cavour, who received a strong impetus
from the July Revolution, and did not follow the ideals of
Mazzini but accepted the temperate, middle path in politics.

About this time Cavour wrote: "There is no great man who is not a liberal; the degree of love of liberty is proportionate in every man to the moral education attained by him"; and again he wrote, in his diary: *"Nous autres qui n'avons pas de foi religieuse, il faut que notre tendresse s'épuise au profit de l'humanité."* And it was to be his lot to carry out in concrete form and to actuate a great part of what the moderate school had desired and willed and prepared, including the relations with religion, and the proclamation of Rome, now held by the Pope, as the capital of the kingdom of Italy.

The other people that, like the Italian, was to solve at the same time the problem of liberty and that not of independence but of national unity, the German people, not only did not enjoy this good fortune of having its various parties, under diverse appearances and with varying stress, moving towards the same end, but persisted in its dualism, so that it was unable to unify the two problems. The unifying force of the liberal character was always, in this nation, somewhat rare and intermittent. The Germans, as Balzac remarked at this time, giving playful expression to a common European conviction, *"s'ils ne savent pas jouer des grands instruments de la Liberté, savent jouer naturellement de tous les instruments de musique"* (*Une fille d'Ève*, 1839). The society Young Germany, of which there were premonitory signs in certain aspects of Börne and Heine, and which began to attract attention towards the first years after 1830, was similar only in name to the Mazzinian association, and consisted of mediocre men of letters, writers of novels and various things, who cried out against the separation of literature and politics and professed a literature of "tendency," but were void of concepts and true political passion, and whenever they were put to the test of life and action cut a very sorry figure. The German men of letters who in transitory effusion embraced the ideas of liberty and progress turned easily in the other direction,

like Menzel, who in his period of effusion was among the first
to make out the case against Goethe for his apoliticalism (and
it is curious that of all people a great poet and a genius of
contemplation should have to bear the burden of blame for
what was, at best, the fault of German culture in general),
and then changed into an ultra-German and anti-French nationalist, a monarchist and an absolutist, an opponent of the
liberals. In a country of savants, worthy of admiration for
the multitude and quality of its instructors and pedagogues,
there were no writers to direct this people in the great problems of the national life, as there were, after all, in Italy.
Moreover, even the weighty wings of speculative thought were
then being folded, and the original and creative minds were
followed by their imitators. Historical criticism flourished
almost alone, in every branch of history and especially of
Christianity, which was bringing to fruit various concepts of
classical philosophy.

And if the French had been able to derive so much vital
nourishment from German philosophy and historiography
and poetry, the Germans learnt nothing or but little that was
substantial from their neighbours, a people far ahead of them
in what constituted the moral needs and the political experience of the modern age. The French had considerably
rectified, by means of historical studies, the abstractness of
their eighteenth-century ideals of liberty, equality, and fraternity; but the Germans, who fled from this abstractness instead of correcting it, plunged into a sort of mysticism of the
past, into an adoration of the irrational that always emanates
from the past when it is disjoined from the living present,
into one of the various forms that we have seen of unhealthy
romanticism, which had more power over them than clear
ideas, soon overwhelmed them and swept them away, and
prevented their gaining strength in general opinion. Among
the liberals there were, however, several scholars and profes-

sors, seven of whom, Dahlmann, the two Grimms, Gervinus, Weber, Albrecht, and Ewald, let themselves be dismissed for having protested, in 1837, against the King of Hanover, who annulled the constitution granted by his predecessor. And among these Gervinus, with his historical books, became the principal doctrinal representative of the party.

The parliaments of the lesser constitutional states, as soon as the storm of repression had passed over, endeavoured to regain a minimum of efficiency; and the parliament of Baden continued to distinguish itself, sensitive as it was to the influence of neighbouring France and Switzerland. In some of the Prussian provinces, that is, outside the Rhenish regions (where from 1842-43 was published the biting and critical *Rheinische Zeitung,* so soon suppressed), in East Prussia and in Silesia, requests were voiced from time to time for a participation of the people in the government, since the eight assemblies, one for each province, that had been established in 1823 had only consultative powers and so were not able to answer the purpose. The need for institutions in conformity with the times, although it did not find the way to expression and accomplishment, certainly was latent in Germany as well as elsewhere, because it was born from things themselves. But Frederick William IV, whose accession to the throne was hopefully greeted as the beginning of a new era, was, as we have remarked and as his contemporaries noted with amazement, the personification of mediaevalizing political romanticism. An administrative monarchy of the type of Frederick the Great's did not appeal to his imagination, because he felt too keenly in it the frigid intellectualism and rationalism of the eighteenth century; but neither did he sympathize with the modern parliaments, which another sceptred romantic, and a poetaster to boot, Louis I of Bavaria, had turned up his nose at as being highly prosaic. He had in mind, indeed, a parliament, but one of a mediaeval character, formed of

the representatives of the states, and with corresponding ceremony and corresponding activity. He toyed with this favour-
ite fancy of his without getting up the courage or without
devising the way to actuate it, and hesitated in his behaviour
towards the liberals, at first granting them amnesties and
mitigating the censorship of the press, and then placing on
trial or forcing into exile those who supported proposals contrary to his sentiments.

Under these conditions, the other problem, that of German
unity, since it could not be solved by means of a country rendered politically homogeneous and with its national will expressed in its assemblies, had no other road than that of conquest and assimilation on the part of one of the states. Now
of the two stronger states, Austria represented the opposite of
the principle of nationality, so all that remained was to look
to Prussia, and to the revival that she had encouraged, in
this regard, of the tradition of her Frederick II. But this tradition was antiromantic no less than that of the bureaucratic
state, and the King shrank back from it with a shudder of
horror, because he revered in Austria the symbol of the Holy
Roman Empire and beheld her once more at the head of a
Christian-German state, in which the King of Prussia would
assume the place and figure of the great and foremost vassal,
famous for his fidelity and his valour. In this state of mind,
although he was a Protestant, he was filled with an undiminished tenderness and reverence for the Catholic Church, a
shadow, no less than Austria, of the vanished European unity
of the Middle Ages, and here he encountered fancies like
those which had flourished in South Germany among the
"Alemannen." Just as these political ideas concerning the
national unity were uncertain and inert, so the feeling of independence, that is, of hatred of France, was ready to burst
forth. At one time France had trampled on Germany, she still
possessed ancient lands of the Empire, and now she seemed to

be longing for the left bank of the Rhine. This hatred exploded in a formidable fashion in 1840, because of the suspicion aroused by Thiers's policy, and was voiced in songs that were Germany's only truly political songs, the "Marseillaise" of a people that never had the other, the true one, against tyrants and for the oppressed. And since there was no foreign domination in Germany, this feeling of independence, only in part justified as a defence against possible menaces, would have remained void if it had not contained not a properly patriotic, but a nationalistic and imperialistic motive. This was made manifest not only by the idealized image of the Holy Roman Empire, but also by the fact that those German patriots did not dream of the rights of independence of the other nations, and in their plans included, together with Austria, the continuation of her dominion over the lands of Italy and over those of the other nationalities comprised within her state. These intentions were seen as early as 1848, and in the Frankfort Parliament. In fact, the Ottos (lofty memory!) had attempted to descend as far as Southern Italy, and the Swabians had held this as well as Sicily.

Liberal in inspiration, although not entirely free of imperialist germs, were the movements for independence that began to stir among other peoples, and all of them, in Hungary, in Bohemia, in Croatia, in Serbia, had their initial symptom in the effort to restore national languages to honourable place, to elaborate them artistically, to restore them to common use; and in general in the cult of customs and national history. In this regard, since we have recalled Mazzini, who readily took up the nascent aspirations of those peoples and became their herald, let us also remember that around 1840 an Italian of Dalmatia, with similar sentiments, Tommaseo, collected and translated the folk-songs of Illyria. Outside the pale of the Austrian Empire, among the populations subject to Turkish rule, Serbia was achieving a sort of autonomy, thanks to the skilful manoeuvres of the Obrenoviches; little Montenegro enjoyed a *de facto* independence with a prince of her own, and Moldavia and Walachia, protected by Russia and modernized by Western (especially by French) culture, were also gradually becoming independent. Poland was crushed by the three absolutist powers and was represented almost exclusively by her numerous refugees. Russia was unable to escape the force of the national idea, which, shorn of its liberal content, had modelled itself on the pan-Germanism of the mediaevalizing German romantics and other similar reactionary political writers and utopists, turning into Pan-Slavism and imperialism.

Western Europe, too, was looking on at a painful effort for independence in the heart of its freest state, Great Britain, in that Ireland which religious divisions, uprisings, and conquest had reduced to a pathological condition that was not easy to cure, in spite of the inflamed speeches of her O'Connell and the initial reforms proposed by Peel but rejected by the House of Lords. In 1845 she was devastated by famine, lost a fourth of her population, and could find no other remedy than in the depopulation of the country by the emigration of her sons to American lands. England was unable to live either with her, in a tranquil and prosperous union, or without her, because of the danger that would be created by separation from this island placed at her side by nature.

Wherever the movement was purely national, it was not slow to be followed and inspired by the movement for liberal constitutions. In Bohemia, the diet of 1840 began to insist that the vote on taxation should be recognized, and in Hungary, in 1832, Kossuth demanded not only economic reforms, but also political reforms of the old constitution, in order to shake off the preponderance of the magnates and to make room for the lesser nobility. In 1843 Greece, after an insurrection in Athens, received from her King Otto a constitution providing an upper and a lower house. In Austria, where the reform movement had been arrested towards the end of the preceding century by the Josephs and the Leopolds, the examples offered by South Germany, and such books and newspapers from the Occidental countries as were able to penetrate there in spite of the prohibitions, awakened a certain spirit of criticism and a wish for innovation. It is superfluous to pause over these and similar signs, which showed the more or less spontaneous and rapid spread of liberal thought. So too, for other reasons, we shall have to take for granted all the activity exerted at this time, with ever growing intensity, by Europe, and especially by liberal Europe, in the way of colonization and the conquest of countries noted for their historical passivity. Therefore we must pass over the labour of England in India, where she gradually took the place of the East India Company, got rid of barbarous customs, and abolished slavery; and the new empire, guided by new principles, that England too was forming in the place of that which she had lost in the eighteenth century; and the beginning, with the conquest and organization of Algeria, of the French colonial empire; and all that happened in Egypt under Mehemet Ali; and so forth.

All this ferment in the world, of ideas, efforts, attempts, and expectations, in 1846 generated, amidst universal emotion, a creature that was the paradoxical expression of the inevitable necessity and the virtue of the liberal idea, which is capable of attracting and bending to its own ends men and institutions that it should only have wished to cast down: it generated a liberal Pope, Pius IX. An impossible thing, in logic and in reality; one of which with reason Prince Metternich said that it was the only thing of which he, with his foresight and his calculations, had never dreamed. In fact it was real only in so far as the impetus of that ideal movement lent him its soul and made him accomplish gestures and acts like a man in a dream, fascinated, unwilling, but which, substantially, was a projection of the heart, a fantasy carried out in a theatrical performance for which Rome, Italy, and the world furnished the stage, and the nations the choral masses. Even as early as this there were some who caught a glimpse of what was happening, and it was at this time that a *stornello* was composed, which said:

> Pio Nono is not a man, it is not he
> Who saws the air sitting on his faldstool:
> Pio Nono is the child of our mind,
> An idol of the heart, a dream of gold:
> Pio Nono is a banner, a refrain,
> A name fit to be sung in chorus. . . .

And Gioberti boasted of having, with his "ideal picture of the Christian pontificate," set in motion the autosuggestion of that Bishop Mastai who became Pius IX (who, in his moments of distress, protested that he was nothing but a "poor vicar") and the still stronger collective suggestion. Beyond a doubt, *Del primato morale e civile degli Italiani* was the book of Galeotto, but it would not have exerted its fascination if it had not been led up to by all the busy labours of Catholic Liberals, and especially by the liberal-national-papal epic that they spun about the Lombard League and the Battle of Legnano.

Meanwhile, the revolutionary force that issued from this poetic symbolism was extremely great, in Italy and throughout the world. Liberals, of no matter which religious persuasion or outside of any religious persuasion, by embracing it saw all their demands taken up without any objections, and all the obstacles to their task fall. A great part of the clergy opened their arms to those whom hitherto they had been obliged to view as their enemies and the enemies of religion. The absolutist régimes lost the aid that they had been receiv-

ing from the Church. Amnesties, abolition or palliation of the
censorship of the press, demands for and promises of consultative bodies, requests for and creation of civic guards
and national militias, followed upon one another in rapid
interplay from 1846 to 1847, in Rome, in Tuscany, in Piedmont. Already the phase had started of demands for constitutional charters and parliaments. And in Naples, where
Settembrini was issuing his *Protesta,* the liberals were raising their heads and the Government was obliged to have recourse to imprisonment; meanwhile in Reggio and in Mes-
sina uprisings were taking place. And in Lombardy-Venetia
the congregations were laying aside their customary docility,
the population was singing hymns to Pius IX and wearing
his ribbons; as a protest against Austria smoking was discon-
tinued; and the Austrian soldiers had recourse to their usual
brutality.

The congress of savants held in Genoa in September,
1846, had sung the praises of Charles Albert and of liberty,
those of the independence and the Risorgimento of Italy.
The year after, efforts were made to establish a commercial
league between the Roman States, Tuscany, and Piedmont;
every incident, the funeral of Confalonieri or an Italian archbishop's succeeding to the Austrian prelate in Milan, provided
an opportunity for showing what were the feelings that were
raging in the public mind. The occupation by Austria, who
had grown nervous, of Ferrara in August, 1847, excited an
immediate reaction, and gave occasion for Charles Albert's
offer to defend the rights of the Pope. Garibaldi, a Mazzinian
exile of 1833, of whose feats in South America rumours had
arrived, was planning to become the champion of the liberal
Pope, and was preparing to return to Italy. And other officers
were returning who had fled after the previous revolutions
and conspiracies, and had fought for other peoples, since they
had not been able to fight for their own. Cobden, with the

laurels of the victory he had gained for free trade, was progressing through Italy, and was made much of. Palmerston, who had turned into a defender of liberty against absolutism, sent his agents to the various capitals of Italy to advise and encourage the princes to grant reforms and constitutions.

The agitation spread into other countries, either through the Italian example or for the same motives that had generated that. In Switzerland a crisis was reached by the disagreement and conflict with the seven cantons faithful to absolutism, to the clergy and to the Jesuits, which had seceded from the Confederation in 1845, creating the Sonderbund. Towards the latter half of 1847 their resistance was broken with arms, the unity of the confederation was re-established, and the Jesuits were driven out of Switzerland. In Germany, Metternich, scenting the wind, realized that this was no time to commit acts of imprudence, and in agreement with Prussia he calmed the ardour of the new Elector of Hesse-Cassel, who was preparing to change the constitution granted by his father. In Baden a liberal cabinet took over the reins of office and for the first time an opposition was formed of democrats and radicals. The King of Prussia, meanwhile, decided to convoke, in February, 1847, the congress of the united diets, which, according to the constituent law of 1823, was to reach a decision concerning loans to be contracted by the state. In his opening speech, he reiterated that he would never consent to insert between his subjects and God (that is, the sovereign chosen by God) a charter that with its formalities would take over the government and occupy the place of the ancient loyalties. All the same, these united diets, which legally had only a right of petition in internal affairs and a deliberative vote on bills that the King might be pleased to submit to them, started an opposition, conducted principally by the representatives of the Rhenish provinces and those of East Prussia, directed at obtaining the fulfilment of the constitution promised in 1815 and regular sessions of the assembly. Contemporaneously, the question of the succession of Schleswig-Holstein, which was threatening the German fatherland with the loss of a Germanic territory, caused the national feelings to boil over and rendered the problem of unity more acute than ever.

Thus, after the first great revolution of modern history, which was the defeat of mediaeval theocracy in the struggle between the Empire and the Church and the formation of the great states and the Renaissance, there was being completed the second revolution, equally great, which had begun in the middle of the seventeenth century in England and had become European with the French Revolution—the substitution of liberal régimes for absolute monarchies. In this process the first oversimple ideal of these régimes, which was abstractly democratic and Jacobin, had been left behind. Of the men of the old ideals, the theocrats of the supremacy of the Church or of the agreement between State and Church, the supporters of royal or patrician absolutism, the former Jacobins and terrorists, some drew to one side because of intransigence of creed, or from a feeling of dignity, or from disdain and annoyance, repeating to themselves that the victorious cause had pleased the gods but the defeated cause had pleased Cato. Some resigned themselves to what had happened, that is, took part in the liberal régimes in order to pick up the lesser evils that might fall to their share, hoping in their hearts for and secretly looking forward to the better and the best, which was sure to return; meanwhile they animated the extreme wings of the liberal party. Some, practising the lesser evils and pondering them, gradually acquired a new spirit and a new mind, and were educated and turned into pure liberals. This triple movement (which naturally did not exclude the passage of single individuals from one to the other of the three situations described) was shared by the clericals, one part of

whom did not withdraw to pray and curse, but pretended to
accept the new political conditions, considering them as provisional and to be destroyed by the very arm of liberty; and
another part ended by accepting them loyally and sincerely,
as good and healthy. This last development did not occur
without a sort of secret and almost unconscious reform in a
rationalistic and idealistic sense. Dogmas were relegated to a
corner of the soul, with respect for their own past but rendered constantly more inactive, and in truth were replaced by
a different system of thought, which was what really operated
and acted. The Reformation, in the countries in which it had
not taken place in the sixteenth century, was carried out in
this fashion, skipping or abbreviating the stages that elsewhere had been gone through more or less slowly. Even in
Italy this process was visible, more or less audacious, more
or less stressed, in Manzoni, Rosmini, Gioberti, Lambru-
schini, Ricasoli, and others.

But there was always the Church of Rome, firm in these
dogmas, ready to intervene and remind everyone that the
enemy of Catholicism had once been catharism and evangel-
ism and now was liberalism. This occurred with the 1832
encyclical *Mirari vos* against Lamennais, which expressly
condemned liberty of conscience, of worship, of the press;
the separation of Church and State, and all kindred *delira-
menta*. It caused serious embarrassment to the Catholics of
liberal countries, the French, the Irish, and above all the Belgians, who alone, thanks to their union with the liberals, had
succeeded in shaking off their dependence on Protestant Holland and on that condition had accepted the liberal constitution, and were making use of it and supporting it. This union
bore the character of national necessity. On the other hand,
it was evident what advantages Lamennais's Catholic friends,
who did not follow him in his separation from the Church—
men like Montalembert and Lacordaire—derived or would

derive from negotiating their support of liberal ministries: the salvation of various ecclesiastical and especially of educational institutions and the use of the freedom of the press for the protection of ecclesiastical interests, according to the example given by Lamennais in *L'avenir,* which was imitated by Montalembert and, with violence and virulence, by Veuillot.

And both the Catholics who were obedient to the Church and the Church unremitting against liberalism, the former as political as the latter, satisfied the demands of conscience and those of authority by the customary expedient of casuistry and compromise, distinguishing between "dogmatic intolerance," to be rigidly preserved, and "civil tolerance," to be permitted, and between the "principle of liberty," which the Church and every good Catholic must condemn and abhor, and the "practical and limited liberties" established by the constitutions, which might be approved. These were sophistries in logic and offences against the moral conscience in ethics, and a sincere mind, reading certain speeches made at this time by Monsignor Dupanloup or the *Cas de conscience* of Bishop Parisis, cannot repress a movement of repugnance. None the less, they were good politics. At the same time might be noted the first signs of the approach (judged to be inevitable by Cavour) of ultramontanism toward socialism, among the social-democratic Catholics, such as Ozanam, and in Buchez, who had passed from Saint-Simonism to Catholicism. This occurred at the very time when Kingsley of the Anglican Church was coining the phrase "Christian socialism." As in liberalizing clericalism, here too substantially conflicting conceptions were reconciled, which at first covered their heterogeneous nature with mediaeval trappings of revived guilds and corporations, and later passed frankly to less anachronistic projects. The "popular party" that was formed in Italy in our day, and the others with the same or a different name but with a similar character in other countries, take their remote origin from the effect exerted on these clericals by the July Revolution, the defeat of absolutism, and the rise of new social conflicts. For in these years indeed were laid the capital bases of the political struggle that is still going on. Communism, which then for the first time seized minds and imaginations and shook them and overturned them, was foreseen as triumphant in the near future, greeted with a blaze of joy, repelled with horror. It also formed at this time its system and its methods, and conceived its full thought, so that nothing essential was added or changed later. Its material was furnished by the revolution, fulfilled or in process of execution, in industry and commerce, thanks to the use of machines and means of rapid transportation. This revolution, which greatly accelerated productive processes, upset the stability of the economic classes, crowded great masses of workmen into the cities, lowered wages because of the unemployed, made use of the work of women and children at low wages and for long hours, enriched rapidly and to an exaggerated degree contractors and capitalists and, correspondingly, landowners, gave rise to the predominance of financiers and bankers (represented by the world-famous Rothschild) and, with all this, let loose a competitive battle with ensuing crises and bankruptcies and misery; not to mention the tumults and the working-men's riots that occurred not infrequently, and the dangers to the social order from them. These facts and these conditions did not of themselves produce, as some like to mythologize, communism or any other political system by determinism, or in the form, as it were, of an immediate result of the workmen's sufferings, but they set before thinkers (and these and not the working-men were the authors of communism, as of every other political system) economic and moral problems, the need for a better organization of production, for justice and humanity and civilization, and for the exhortation and education of new social classes towards political feelings and desires.

These problems are doubtless substantially the same as those which have always woven the web of life of human societies and through which the thread of their history runs, but because of the conditions to which they were referred they now appeared with a new perspective and a new physiognomy. To solve them was the political task of the present, but to solve them in relation to the present, to the intellectual and ethical forces now at play, to the ways that were open or that might be opened, and, therefore, with the consciousness that, with the ulterior change in things and as an effect of these very solutions themselves, the problems would from time to time appear again in other ways and with other possibilities of action. For to have wished to solve them all radically and forever would have been the same as to have wished to set up a goal for human life and an end to history. However, if this aim did not exist, if it did not always rise anew in men's minds, we should not have what is called a Utopia, which is precisely the idea of such an integral and definitive solution, and the dilation of particular and circumstantial problems, which alone are actual and solvable, to a total non-existent problem, one called, for instance, the social question, a question *"qui n'existe pas,"* as a French politician once exclaimed. And he was right, and it would be more obvious how right he was if the formula "social question" were translated into the other synonymous one "historical question," or "question of human history"—which is clearly a question that does not exist.

And there were other utopists; for instance, some were struck by the increase in production and prosperity which, under given conditions, had derived from the abolition of shackles on industry and commerce, and in particular, and lately, from the effects of the great and victorious battle fought in England against the tariff on grain; and so they were inclined to believe that the social question or the "question of history" would be solved simply by elevating free-trade economic expedients into absolute principles, into a law of human association, which promised the pacification of all conflicts, the smoothing out of all difficulties, the happiness of humanity. This could only be conceived, in the last analysis, by placing the law of history outside of history, as may indeed be observed in the most popular of these champions and utopists of free trade, Bastiat, who at bottom had a religion somewhere between faith in nature according to the philosophy of the eighteenth century and a faith in a providential God.

Different and opposing utopists, inasmuch as they planned in their turn a definitive organization of society and human life and a superhistorical government, were the communists, who changed into an absolute the relative and particular and circumstantiated negation that can be posited of free competition, and into an absolute the equally relative affirmation of the value of authoritative intervention in the regulation of production, and thought of replacing competition either with an arrangement that obtains harmonious ends not by means of struggle and competition but by spontaneity and enjoyment, or with the learning of savants regulating everything scientifically. Noble as were the sentiments and the intentions that inspired men like Saint-Simon, Fourier, Owen, their conceptions lacked the consciousness of human life in its spiritual and moral entirety. In fact, Owen was confined to materialist preconceptions, and Fourier abhorred "morality" and "duty" and would hear of nothing but "passion" and "attraction," without labour, without struggles, without dialectics. And all of them, but especially Saint-Simon and his school, were hostile to liberty, which, so Saint-Simon said, "is a vague and metaphorical idea" that impedes "the action of the masses on the individual"; that designates "a system of sentiments" and not a true "class of interests," and is of use, at the very best, as an instrument to combat the old theological system, but hurtful to the true society, which is entirely scientific and rational, in which the individual must be "bound and dependent on the complex," and in which we cannot conceive either political liberty or liberty of conscience for him, in the same way that there can be no liberty in chemistry, physics, and astronomy. Liberty, Louis Blanc repeated, is a "word," a "bait for the ingenuous," since there can be no other true liberty beyond that which is obtained in the·state by the "organization of labour." The Saint-Simonians were therefore admirers of Catholicism, for they too placed at the head of their imaginary society a sort of papacy, although of a scientific character. And Enfantin was full of reverence for Austria, "who alone had resisted the imperfect dogmas of liberty and equality, and who alone represented order, and filled a sacerdotal function." So that, not unlike a certain type of clericals when the July Revolution had brought with it the triumph of liberalism, the Saint-Simonians proposed to demand and encourage all liberties—of association, of the press, of education, of religion—not from love of liberty, but in order to reach its opposite through the means it provided. And they did not even grant liberty to science and art, which they wished to be the slaves or the employés of their government, to be composed of new priests, scientists, and industrials. It is no wonder that, with such a concept of the human soul, they tended to award predominance to enjoyment, and preached the dogma of the "regeneration of the body," which is the part of Saint-Simonism that most pleased Heinrich Heine and the writers of Young Germany. Nor is it a cause for wonder that the best that Saint-Simonism conceived and foretold and produced was economic institutions and activities—such as stock companies, banks, railway networks—

and that after its adepts had performed a bizarre religious comedy (in which beside the "Father" there was also
the "Mother," that is, woman) and had fallen into ridicule
and been dissolved as a school, the remaining Saint-Simonians and their chief, Enfantin—who had, like many of them,
received a polytechnic education—devoted themselves to business and speculation, to engineering works such as the projected cutting of the Isthmus of Suez, and, in utter indifference
to politics, got on fairly well with the Bonaparte of the Second
Empire, while their philosopher, Auguste Comte, justified
the *Coup d'état* and what ensued, meditating over his "positive politics."

How different from Giuseppe Mazzini, who had taken over
from Saint-Simonism all the worst elements that he introduced
into his system—the aversion to competition, association, the
religion of the future, and such things—yet laboured inde-
fatigably for liberty, endured all kinds of burdens and hardships, defied all kinds of dangers, and was persecuted by the
Bonapartist police and by all the others of Europe without
a truce, surrounded like a hunted beast! And Mazzini, who
always deemed communism "materialism," after the fashion
of Lessing saw in history the education of the human race,
and after that of Herder, the epic of the nations. Whereas
Saint-Simon inaugurated its economic or materialistic
(whichever you choose) interpretation, and saw in the French
Revolution nothing but the ascent of the bourgeoisie to power
and contributed to enlarge the concept of "bourgeoisie" in the
economic sense to that of the spiritual form of the modern
era, which was a falsification or a gross confusion of disparate
concepts. From the communists and the socialists and, by way
of imitation, even outside their fold, this abuse of the concept was kept up (in obedience to which it would have been
logical to say that the inventors of communism were "bourgeois," or even that this idea, which is purely economic, is

the "quintessence of bourgeoisism"). And as a consequence of the same impulse contemporary French historiography laid stress on class warfare, and accustomed itself to hunt, under the veils of ideologies, for the kernel of economic interests, in which it was assisted by the reminiscence of the explanation, frequent in the eighteenth century, of religions as inventions of priests for their purposes of rule. The philosophy of history with a predetermined plan, which went back to Daniel's dream of the four empires and had passed into mediaeval thought and had been renovated by the German idealistic philosophy, also offered to the socialists and the communists the frame for their picture of universal history, in which, over the course of the preceding ages, arose, as absolute finality, the palingenesis of humanity finally redeemed in the association of labour.

But these first theorists and programmists of communism, who conceived their programmes after the fashion of an economic enterprise, a hygienic reform, or an educational institution, on the one hand had faith in the propaganda carried out verbally or by the examples of a few experiences *in parvo*, and on the other, hoped to find favour in the sight of kings and despots; and Saint-Simon raised his eyes successively to Napoleon, to Alexander of Russia, to Louis XVIII. The problem was felt in a different way by those other communists who went back to the revolutionary tradition, and particularly to that of Babeuf, whose conspiracy was narrated about this time by one who had taken part in it, Buonarroti, who gained disciples. These revolutionary temperaments, in France and elsewhere, looked instead to the working-class, the proletariat, to the strength that lay in them and which, if enlightened and directed, would violently fling into the air the whole existing order, destroy capitalism, and set up the society of working-men participating in equal measure in labour and in reward. To the ends of this particular propaganda, which needed the

virus of hatred (since the vague concept of oppression and
exploitation was not enough), a new doctrine was got ready,
especially in England, under the influence of the Ricardian
doctrine of income, concerning the origin of profits derived
from labour not paid to the workmen.

As may be seen, all that flowed together into Marx's social
system existed before him, scattered here and there, and even
in part gathered together: historical materialism, thought and
art and religion as the phenomenology of economics, antiliberalism, class warfare, the succession of historical epochs
with the proletarian end, surplus labour and surplus value,
the criticism of the disorder in capitalist production and of
its crises, and so on. But Marx lent singular vigour to all
these concepts and these budding concepts, and he re-elabo-
rated them and synthetized them with the dialectic of the
Hegelian school. This dialectic, which had been universal,
formal, and hermeneutic by nature in the teacher and still
more so in his pupils, had been mingled with empiricism and
imagination, and had led to strange ethical and social concoc-
tions, notably in the so-called left of the school, to which Marx
belonged, and in Germany it had reached the desperate egola-
try and anarchy of Stirner. When a few of its rays spread to
Proudhon in France, they suggested to him the criticism of
economic contradictions, with thesis and antithesis, and the
synthesis that also in him, in his fashion, was anarchical.

Marx, developing the contradictions of the capitalist or
bourgeois age that had followed that of feudalism, and which
generated, gave birth to, and educated the proletarians as its
grave-diggers and successors, derived from it the communistic synthesis that would be accomplished by these executors
of historical necessity. On this dialectical scheme he set up
and formulated, towards the end of 1847, his *Communist
Manifesto.* In this lies his originality, not as a philosopher or
an economist (for in that respect, only a few fragments of his

thought are still useful), but as a creator of political ideologies or myths. For he gave to the communist movement, if
not a basis, at least a robe of philosophy and history, and
provided it with a book, *Das Kapital,* of great prestige over
minds not gifted with the power of criticism, over the imaginations and the passions and the hopes, a prestige that even
amid the decay suffered by all the concepts with which that
book was interwoven, still lasts and operates. At the same
time, he made an end of moralism and sentimentalism, and
turned to more elementary and facile motives. If Weitling
had given to his "Federation of Tastes" the motto, *All men
are brothers,* he gave the other, *Proletarians of all the world,
unite*—unite in hatred and in destructive warfare. But with
the dialectics introduced by him, although it seemed as
though the rational certainty of the future was obtained, he
profoundly modified the method of actuation. And he not
only did away with that of the first communists, whom he
defined as "utopists," but with that of insurrection and *coups
de main* as well, both of them equally puerile in the eyes of
the philosophical and dialectical method, which demanded
that the objective historical process be accompanied by
thought and action, and that its consecutive phases be truly
lived, and which wanted violence to intervene only at the
right moment, to pluck the fruit when it had reached maturity. The end was communistic and materialistic, but the
method, on the contrary, aimed at being historical. In practice, so far as it did or did not succeed in being seriously
so, it expressed itself either in a form of concrete and gradual political activity (and therefore substantially liberal), or
else in a naturalistic fatalism, a negation of historicity and
activity. And these disagreements between ideal and method,
which were then invisible or unseen and are even today not
clearly recognized, were to express the later history of com-

munism and Marxism in its divergent aspects and in its varying vicissitudes.

That communism was the "novelty" which stood out before
all others in the general spiritual interest is confirmed by
literature. Although among the nations that were still struggling and striving for liberty this centred around corresponding themes of patriotism and heroism, and sentimental
romanticism, among the nations that by this time possessed a
free régime it was gradually detaching itself from these
themes or was pursuing them only in an extrinsic or ornamental fashion—as was the case in the greater part of French
romanticism after 1830—and filling itself, instead, with the
images and emotions of various sorts that corresponded to
the new social anxiety and unrest. Georges Sand passed from
the story-telling defence of the rights of love and passion to
Les compagnons du tour de France, to *Consuelo,* to *Le meu-
nier d'Angibault,* and so forth; Balzac gave ample space in
the scenes of his *Comédie humaine* to the plutocracy, the bankers, the speculators, and to the conflicts of the social classes,
and conferred on himself the title of "doctor in social
sciences." Drama and comedy were also dealing with social
problems. Eugène Sue was ladling out *Les mystères de Paris*
and his other novels, which, although quite destitute of any
artistic qualities, were avidly read. In Englànd, Dickens was
writing *Oliver Twist,* and *Hard Times.* In *Sybil or the Two
Nations* Disraeli provided the novel of two foreign and hostile
nations on the same soil, the "rich" and the "poor," describing the conditions of the workmen in Lancashire; Mrs. Gas-
kell narrated in *Mary Barton* the weavers' strike in Manchester; similar subjects were handled by Kingsley in his dramas
and novels; Thomas Hood and Elizabeth Barrett sang humanitarian songs; Carlyle set himself up against liberalism
and democracy; and a few years later was to appear *Uncle*

Tom's Cabin by Harriet Beecher Stowe, concerning the sufferings and the tragedies of the Negro slaves in America.
Philosophy, particularly in the Hegelian school of the left
that we have already mentioned, took up the concepts of Saint-
Simon and Fourier, and endeavoured to translate them into
speculative and dialectical terms. The discussion of political
forms gave way to that of social problems; and Auguste
Comte invented the word "sociology" and tried to give body
to the science baptized by him with this name. Quételet published *La physique sociale,* and there followed a series of
pictures of the conditions of the working-class (one of these
relating to England was the work of Marx's comrade, Fried-
rich Engels) and of disquisitions concerning the "social question," to which everyone brought his great or small contribution in thoughts and words. Even the future author of the
history of Julius Caesar, Louis Bonaparte, inspired by the
nature of his humanitarian spirit, wrote a dissertation on
L'extinction du paupérisme. Communism is in the background of De Tocqueville's preoccupations and is the tacit
point of recall of his heartfelt inquiries concerning liberty,
which he loved with an infinite love, and equality, which he
both admired and feared. He saw, during the last seven hundred years of history, society rushing madly towards equality,
and in this contemplation a sort of religious terror pervaded
his spirit. After crushing the society of feudalism, will the
urge towards equality stop before the bourgeois and the rich,
and respect the rights of property? And none the less this rush
towards equality, even if it seems to be pointed to by the
finger of God, threatens human society with anarchy and in
its train despotism and servitude. Will it be possible to maintain or to reconstruct local institutions in defence of the
ever growing centralization and equalization, and, as it were,
a school of liberty? Shall we be able to face and overcome
the danger by educating the democracies, reviving their faith,

purifying their ethos, supplementing their inexperience by instructing them in the science of human affairs?

All the same, these fears and hopes, these desires towards opposite things, these previsions of varying nature, these fancies and these calculations, these manifold proposals, if they impressed people differently and divided public opinion were still very far from being a political party, which means a determined action on the government and for the government, whether it be to overthrow the form of the state by means of a revolution, or to operate within the existing possibilities in the effort to effectuate party aims. The communist colonies were in fact tried, and not only by Owen, but by the Fourierist Considérant, who in 1832, with the aid of a rich Englishman, founded the phalanstery of Condé-sur-Vègre and in 1849 that of Réunion in Texas, and by Cabot, who in 1848 founded the colony of Nauvoo in Illinois. But they all failed wretchedly and amidst violent quarrels, and even if they had not ended in this way, they would only have influenced opinion and not operated in the political field proper. The different excogitations of Louis Blanc on the *ateliers sociaux*, that is, workers' producers associations with the state as a limited liability partner, even if they had been established by law, would have had a similar value as an experiment, as an experiment in what later was called state socialism.

Insurrections were both preached and practised in England, France, and elsewhere, and in 1834 the workmen of Lyons rose to the cry, *"Vivre en travaillant ou mourir en combattant!"* In 1839 in Paris there was the disturbance by the Society of the Seasons. And not only were these insurrections always suppressed, but also it cannot be said that they were aimed at starting communism, which, just as it was incapable of forming a party, was equally unable to turn a chance insurrection into a social upheaval in conformity with its own principles. Blanqui, who was among the chiefs of the uprising in

1839, clearly announced that he did not have a "precise political system" and that he despised "dogmatics" and, in short, that he was aiming at revolt for revolt's sake, in the hope that from its bowels something would be born the features of which no one could foresee. After 1830 the theory of terrorism had blossomed again, or the "guillotinomania" that had already been formulated in a pamphlet by De Lezay (confuted by Constant) as a necessary method to establish revolutions and make them irrevocable. The working-men of the Parisian suburbs read reprints of the works of Robespierre and Marat, the history of Babeuf's conspiracy and Cabot's communistic *Voyage en Icarie*, and political pamphlets ruddy with flames and blood; they sang songs that were equally sanguinary and fiery; and apocalyptic pictures were painted of worlds to be destroyed and worlds to be built.

But since the paths of reality are not those of dreams, or are not equally straight and easy, and since the reality was formed by the parliamentary and elective governments, and the ruling class, which defended them, had on its side both wealth and culture, all that remained to those who desired complete social upheavals, when they passed from their theories and programmes to practice, was to demand an ever greater broadening of the electorate until they reached universal suffrage. This was done, in fact, by the Chartists in England in 1838. They asked for a charter containing universal suffrage, members of Parliament to be elected without conditions concerning the owning of property and paid for their service, the secret ballot, equal boroughs, and a yearly Parliament. But in France with such requests the communists turned into comrades or allies of the democratic and republican party, which, after co-operating with the liberals for the downfall of absolutism, demanded a greater participation of the people in the government. Because of this alliance, the latter party in its turn considerably modified its physiognomy,

and, by reflection, took on the hues of communism, and furthermore in consequence assumed various gradations, from
the most moderate, which would have been satisfied with a
limited broadening of the electorate in the present and a
greater one to be carried out with the same discretion and
judgment in the future, to that extreme which began to be
called "social democracy" or "socialism." Under this name
a union of, and at the same time a distinction between, socialism and communism was announced. The importance of this
was felt by the communists, who adopted the customary termi-
nology and called it a "bourgeois party," that is, substantially
liberal and idealistic, and not at all "proletarian," that is,
antiliberal and materialistic—as their own aimed at being.
By this means in France, to the old formula of republicanism, which had had its representative in Carrel and still
found followers, was added that which was represented by
men like Ledru-Rollin, who wished to arrive at universal suffrage, and from there to go on to all social reforms. Social
democracy was the resting-place of Lamennais, who had
already written *L'essai sur l'indifférence en matière de religion,* and now became the author of *Les paroles d'un croyant* and *Le livre du peuple,* and after the failure of his attempt to fuse Church and liberalism, was unable to remain
either Catholic or liberal, but impetuously turned himself
into a democrat and a socialist.

The terms had changed. It was no longer a struggle between
liberalism and absolutism, but one between liberalism and
democracy, from its moderate to its extreme and socialist
form. This struggle, which was the truly present and progressive struggle of the nineteenth century, was developed, as we
have observed, in the countries that enjoyed liberty. For in
the others, intent on painfully acquiring it, the effort to do
so did not permit this struggle to rise and be defeated, so that
a bare hint of it might scarcely be discerned in the varying

semblances, conservative or democratic, of the combatants, and in the disagreements concerning the paths to be followed, whether gradual reforms or revolution, and in a few sporadic manifestations. Communism, to which German publicists contributed much and finally gave the doctrinal form it still preserves, was the work of German exiles in England, France, and Belgium, for it was unable to grow in its native land, although even there a few strikes took place, as well as some weavers' and other workmen's uprisings. Marx and Engels were exiles, and in London in December, 1847, at an international congress of the communist federation, composed mainly of exiles, the *Communist Manifesto* was discussed and approved. Adepts in these extreme ideas, and in others extreme to the highest degree and which can scarcely be called ideas at all, were first furnished to the international revolutionary gatherings by the Russia of Czar Nicholas, with her hirsute refugees. In the countries that were not yet free, republicanism, Jacobinism, and above all the new words "communism" and "socialism" were grounds for uneasiness even to the numerous adversaries of the absolutist régimes, and were made use of by these régimes for purposes of intimidation and scission. Metternich insinuated that, under deceptive semblances of liberty, the war was being waged simply between those who owned something and those who wanted to own, and that the very right of property was in question. Even in Italy these scarecrows were held up, in Florence, in Rome, in the Neapolitan provinces, especially when Pius IX had set the liberal and national movement going.

There were some who were perplexed and hesitated to lend a hand to the changes in the existing order, and feared social ruin and collapse. And, speaking of free countries, our mind goes back to England and France, for there is not much use in watching the struggle in little states, where we should feel that we were looking on at a tempest in a tea-cup. Nor in

Belgium, where, because of the social and political composition of the population (partly bound to the ancient and strictly Catholic tradition of Spanish and Austrian Flanders, and partly to the more recent one of French and republican Belgium) there had at first been a necessary compromise between the Catholic and the liberal parties in the opposition to Holland and the consequent separation from her, and now the government passed from clericals to liberals and back again, and from moderate clericals to moderate liberals, and the process was not complicated until much later by socialism and social-democratic clericalism. Nor, furthermore, in Spain, where we have already noted the frequent interference of veiled or open dictatorships, which prevented the struggles between liberals and radicals from being particularly fruitful or instructive. For different reasons, the United States, which during these years De Tocqueville studied and elucidated for Europe as the typical country of democracy, offered no material or teachings for this conflict, because of its persistent character as a colonial country, in which democracy, introduced by the religious sects, had developed untroubled by absolute monarchies and patrician oligarchies and without other obstacles, in which social differentiation was neither deep nor strong, economic production formed almost the only object of activity, and the wealth of those who had grown rich circulated with notable rapidity. In this country there were not, therefore, two great parties with political programmes worthy of discussion, but groups struggling for power, each with a following of its own, while more and more importance was being attached to the conflict between advocates and opponents of slavery, which was the great American question, arising from the peculiar process of American economic development. A millennium and a half ago, Europe had overcome slavery, and was now rooting it out in her colonies, just as she had suppressed it everywhere except for residues in a few parts of the Austrian Empire and throughout Russia, in the form of personal serfdom and servitude to the glebe. England adhered firmly to the régime established with the electoral reform of 1832, which had been a first effective, though slow and cautious, revolution in her customs and in the composition of popular representation, and had brought to the House of Commons many new men, manufacturers and tradesmen, and led the old parties of the Tories and the Whigs to divide into a Conservative party and a Liberal party, with the addition of a new party of Radicals. This had changed the quality of parliamentary debates, which had been doctrinal and restricted to general principles, to technical and particular principles, and had brought with it in addition the reform of municipal administration, with uniform regulations and the vote for every man who paid taxes. No deep and irrepressible need was felt for a second revolution of this kind. Although the demands of the Chartists, their six points, contained many things that would all have to be carried out in the future—and have now been carried out—that is, which were far from intrinsically impossible, they were not adapted to the actual conditions of the country and to its mental and moral disposition, and so the petitions they presented to Parliament were rejected. The Government allowed the Chartists to hold their meetings, to publish their tracts, to carry on the most lively propaganda, but were firm in repressing any attempt at tumult or insurrection. In 1833 Owen began his agitation for the eight-hour day, in 1834 the Grand National Consolidated Trades Union was founded in London, in 1837 the demands were agreed upon that were formulated in the People's Charter in May, 1838, with a crescendo that in 1839 threatened to lead to civil war, but was stopped just as much by the military and police operations, to which the Government had recourse, as by the uncertainty of the very leaders of the movement. Although the agitation was resumed in 1840, and although in 1841 it called for a general strike, after this year it may be considered to have worn itself out and disappeared from the political arena, giving up its demands for a social democracy. The working-men realized that it paid them best to support the radicals of the middle classes, and attempted of their own initiative to found cooperative societies, some of which failed and others, formed with more experience, survived and prospered; they devoted themselves in their trade-unions to their own economic interests, which they championed in legal ways.

This result had not been imposed by a social class, armed with the forces of the state, or by a group of material conservative interests, but was, as it were, the outcome of the English spirit: the modes of thinking, feeling, and behaving of all the people—their moral sense of responsibility, their education for liberty, their devotion to their country, their sure perception of English interests in the world, their practical attachment to historical continuity, their diffidence towards all that appeared to be either abstract or excessive, their disposition to effect an equitable adjustment of all disagreements, to satisfy actual needs and provide a remedy for those evils that can be remedied, and, in short, in consequence of all this, the wide-spread political consciousness, and the quality and number of statesmen produced by England, superior to those of any other country. These virtues are the basis of current pronouncements, such as the saying that English liberalism is an "aristocracy," an aristocracy, moreover, that is always open and always being renewed, or the other saying, which seems to be an accusation and is, under a certain aspect at least, praise, namely, that French working-men are moved by "ideas" and English working-men only by "needs." This spirit was also visible in her radicals, in her social democrats, in the Chartists and socialists, and acted as a brake. For instance, when it seemed as though the cry of revolt was about to issue from the national congress of Chartists in London and in Birmingham in 1839, the chiefs rejected recourse to violence and decided on a simple strike, feeling that they were not supported either by the majority of the country, or by that of the working-men, or by their own inner convictions. Mazzini knew these limitations that the English set on themselves, and wrote in one of his letters of 1839 that he often saw his articles rejected by English periodicals, which shrank from "every idea that is too general, too systematic, too *Continental*, as they say." But the ruling political class was able not only to control and repress, or wisely to allow to scatter, all unorganized and fantastic movements, but it also knew how to set about the improvement and progress of the working-classes.

It was in these years that it undertook the wide investigations that revealed such great poverty and hardship and suffering. These were imitated after much delay by other states, and thus systematic legislation in defence of labourers began in Europe. In 1833 the first English law was passed concerning child labour, in 1842 that concerning women and children employed in coal and iron mines, in 1843 another concerning the labour of children in all branches of industry, and many measures followed for hygiene and other similar objects. The English also had the wisdom to pass measures of which the working-classes did not see the benefits that would accrue to them, and which were opposed by other classes that were offended in their particular interests, such as the abolition of the tariff on grain. This had been demanded for a quarter of a century, and after seven years of vigorous agitation on the part of the Anti-Corn Law League, was voted in 1846. The free-trade trend given in general to commercial politics did not prevent, moreover, the prudent intervention of the state wherever this was necessary. Thinkers and poli-

ticians who at this time entered the arena would have preferred more intervention and more direct state action, and
foremost among them the antidemocratic Carlyle, a romantic
after the German pattern, and the fantastic and paradoxical
Disraeli, who furthered and announced a "young generation," with a revived Toryism. This was to take to heart the
interests of the people, as the liberals and the free-traders did
not. The latter groups were, with Cobden, averse to the means
of defence that, ever since 1834, the working-men had been
preparing for themselves in their trade-unions. The monarchy finally and loyally accepted parliamentary government, after William IV, who had dismissed the Liberals and
called upon the Conservatives, was convinced, by the results
of the elections of 1835, that he had best recall the Liberal
leader Melbourne; and the youthful Queen Victoria was advised by the Prince Consort to proceed in constant agreement with Parliament.

Exactly the opposite of what was going on in England
happened in France, which, with the July Revolution and
with the replacement of the line of the Bourbons by that of
the Orléans, had raised its freely conceded constitutional
charter to a negotiated constitution, deprived the monarch of
the power to issue ordinances (which had been the incentive
for the July insurrection), transformed the hereditary chamber of peers into a chamber nominated for life by the king,
diminished the amount of property required in order to exercise the suffrage—thereby doubling the number of electors,
which rose to two hundred thousand and then grew to two
hundred and forty thousand—reinstituted the National
Guard, suppressed the article concerning the religion of the
state, and abolished the censorship on books and newspapers.
But the life of the organism thus formed was differently interpreted by the two parties that had brought it into the world,
which took the opposite names of Movement and Resistance.

For the men of the Movement, the establishment of the July monarchy was a necessary but only an initial step, to be followed promptly by others directed towards liberal reforms in every branch of society and in an ever greater participation of the people in the Government. It was to favour a similar movement in all Europe, and indeed to lead it, restoring to France in this sphere the leadership which not only would form her moral greatness, but would give her the greatness of a power, and undo or correct, in regard to her also, the treaties of 1815. These men wanted, in short, a declaration of war on the Holy Alliance, and therefore they greeted with joy the insurrections in Belgium, in Emilia, in Poland, and considered them as being the cause of France herself.

To be sure, in this programme of vigorous impetus which they strove to impart to French home and foreign politics, and which was urged and menacingly demanded by men acting outside of the Government and without its responsibilities, there were latent actual difficulties and impossibilities, and dangers of calamities and ruin if an attempt were made to take them by assault by battling against them. The men of the government were in a certain measure obliged to bridle it and oppose it and moderate the impetus, but all the same, not to suffocate it, or to dream of deviating it or to behave as though this impetus were non-existent. When they repressed tumults and uprisings, such as that of 1832 on the occasion of General Lamarque's funeral and others that arose from time to time, and when they refused to interfere in wars rendered impossible by the relations of France with the other powers and groups of powers, they were only doing their duty to their country. None the less the tendencies expressed in these desires and in these incitations, and the others manifested in the longing for a republic, for social democracy, or even for communism, however exaggerated and extravagant they may have been in their forms, were also addressed to the public good, were germs of life that were endeavouring to break forth from the ground and open in the sunshine, and it was advisable to cultivate and educate them. A liberal government is treasonable to its own character and violates the intimate law of its being if it is not a government for the acquisition of ever greater liberty; and even the political necessities that it has to bear in mind in its relations with the other states, and which oblige it to respect antiliberal régimes and even at times to ally itself with them for international ends and to allow them a free hand in their conservative and reactionary internal politics, do not justify the absolute desertion of the defence of liberty in the world, which is the animating principle of its life, a defence that must persist even in occasional retreats, in temporary renunciations, ever ready to advance again and not only to profit by the course of events but to prepare it. Otherwise the policy of a government loses what is usually called its "line," which is, in the last resort, the line of a people's history.

The men of the July Government, on the contrary, considered liberty as a *res condita* and not perpetually *condenda*, and the established régime as one that satisfied the demands of reason by choosing the golden mean between two extremes, a mean, to tell the truth, that was not synthetic nor dialectical, that is, mobile in its movement, but analytic and static and imposing a goal on movement; it was called a *juste milieu*, and became an object of disesteem and satire. This rigidity of theirs was opposed by the equally rigid abstractions of radicalism and republicanism with their persistent confidence in the facile methods of Jacobins and conventionalists, and prepared inevitable revolutionary outbursts and fearful upheavals and a dark future. It did not come, as many fancied, from a rare natural aptitude of the French people for free government, but from historical conditions and, one might say, from historical experience and at the same time from historical inexperience. During half a century France had been flung from one revolution into another, and from one dictatorship into another, from the revolution of 1789 into the Jacobin dictatorship, from Thermidor to the dictatorship of Napoleon, and then to the restoration of the monarchy with a charter of liberty, and then to the overthrow of that monarchy.

She had been waiting, but always in vain, so it proved, for this process to be closed, which was so different from her history and from that of her monarchy. These experiences, these vain hopes, induced her to cling, after so many fruitless happenings, to the régime that was established and which seemed likely to satisfy every temperate soul, and led her to look askance on innovations that might endanger it and let loose the revolutionary torrent. And inexperience or too short practice of free life had not yet permitted the formation of that sense of change and of continuity at the same time which the English people possessed, not indeed by a gift of nature, but through historical development. So that there was too much fear of conflicts, too little consciousness of the strength derived from opposition and of the utility of the alternation of parties in power, too little persuasion of the necessity to refresh, gradually, minds and spirits, and to renew the ruling political class. So these men, who were remarkable for their talent and their knowledge and their personal probity and their disinterested love of the state, rejected every demand for electoral reform that would have done away with the exclusive criterion of property, and opened a way for what were called the capacities. They even rejected the modest parliamentary reform directed towards diminishing in the chamber the number of deputies employed by the state and therefore dependent on the Government or looking to the Government for assistance in their careers. They did not wish to or they were unable to raise and educate their opponents and successors.

Men like Périer, Molé, Thiers, Guizot, and the others who presided over the various cabinets differed from them not at all or very little, so far as regards the immutable preservation of the existing order. Thiers, for instance, had a temperament very different from that of Guizot. He was more individualistic than the latter, less keen on state intervention, more disposed to alliances with the radicals and less to those with the Catholics. But Thiers, like Guizot, recognized nothing outside of the "legal country" and abhorred the principle of the "sovereignty of the people"—which after all has a moral, if not a juridical, truth of its own. In 1840 he caused the bill on electoral reform to be deferred; and again in 1845, when he was allied with Barrot and other radicals, he persuaded his allies to postpone it, and the "constitutional" opposition of his party and of his allies made a feeble and uncertain show of itself. Similarly in the other branches of the legislature and the administration, this hesitation to stir the waters and to arouse discontent in the electoral body dominated, whether it was a question of debt-conversion or of tariffs or even of slavery in the colonies. Hostile as they were in the first years to the clericals and the Jesuits, they soon inclined towards respect for religion as a bulwark of social conservation and for God as the best policeman: a Napoleonic doctrine, but one that had been rejected with contempt a generation ago by Benjamin Constant. In 1833 Guizot granted freedom to the Catholic elementary schools, for he was willing that the lower classes should be educated in this way, and asked only that higher education, in which the ruling class was to be formed, should remain independent and lay. And in the following years, Molé contented Montalembert and the Catholics or liberal clericals more generously, until the tumultuous conflict occurred between the

Jesuits and the university of the Quinets and the Michelets.
Foreign policy, which had been prudent enough, became
timid and conservative, like domestic policy. Although in
1837 Molé still announced his hatred of absolutist régimes
and pity for the nations that know their own strength so little
as to submit to them, the French Government actually accepted all that the absolutist powers desired and ended by
detaching itself from England and turning towards Austria.
And since Louis Philippe, who had gradually, with great
shrewdness and finesse, freed himself from the politicians
who annoyed him or had turned them into instruments of
his own, handled foreign affairs personally, this policy assumed more and more the character of action directed towards the sole end of maintaining the House of Orléans on
the throne. If a closed oligarchy, with a very restricted electoral basis, kept the Government for itself and excluded from
it by far the greatest part of the French people, this very
oligarchy was, in reality, overwhelmed by an extra-parlia-
mentary power. It was in vain that parliamentary coalitions
were attempted in order to remove this personal power, and
in vain that Thiers concocted the doctrine that "the king
reigns and does not govern"; it did not pass into French practice, whereas about the same time it was being thoroughly
carried out in England. The ardour, the courage, the impetus,
the faith, that had animated the liberals in the years of the
restoration, were gone; of the Doctrinaires, such as were not
dead had grown, as it were, cold and spent, almost as though
it were not possible for men to sustain in their individual life
two great struggles, one after the other, and as though they
had worn themselves out in the first. Royer-Collard, who had
drawn to one side, no longer recognized his pupils of times
past, could not bring himself to accept the things that he
beheld, and denounced the "sly attacks on liberty," the school

of "immorality" that had been opened, the policy "devoid of all greatness," and the "sleep without a dream" in which France was sunk.

And if this monarchy and its mode of government acquired the sobriquet, which it has kept, of "bourgeois," the reason does not lie, as the materialists of history theorize, in the economic and schematic nature of every government, but in this very lack of political vitality, which allowed the foreground of the picture to be filled by the economic interests of the higher bourgeoisie, the financiers and bankers, who alone had consistency and visibility. It is impossible to say of a government which accomplishes a true political task that it is aristocratic or bourgeois or lower middle-class, because it includes of necessity these and all the other classes and rises above or tends to rise above all of them, as can be seen if the English governments are brought into comparison. The impression that the July monarchy made in this regard was the same in men of the most diverse origin. With his pen dipped in poison and gall, Karl Marx described it as "a stock company for the exploitation of France's national wealth, whose dividends were divided among ministers, chambers, two hundred and forty thousand electors, and their following, and Louis Philippe was their director, a true Robert Macaire on his throne." But not very differently, that careful and just gentleman, De Tocqueville, thought that posterity would perhaps never know "to what degree the government of this period, towards its decline, proceeded like an industrial company, in which the operations are carried out for the benefits that the members can derive from them." And Ernest Renan, when he recalled those times and those men, judged that "no generation ever entered into history with more inexact concepts of its own duties and with so few ideas concerning the ends to be aimed at, and at the same time with such a greed as to cause it to fling itself upon life as upon a prey." In the midst of the country's prosperity and the accumulation of wealth, there was a feeling of emptiness. With the aristocracy vanquished, the people held back, the directing class without any opposition in its midst, in spite of the brilliant minds that filled that assembly the oratory of the parliament was aimed at nothing and wound around itself. "Our great orators," remarked De Tocqueville, "were considerably bored at listening to one another and, what is worse, the whole nation was bored at listening to them." Boredom. Lamartine launched his motto, which expressed the common attitude: "France is bored."

To be sure, discontent was rife in the other classes, in the petty bourgeoisie, in the peasants and part of the industrials; the National Guard was mainly recruited from the lower middle class and offered no guarantees in case of uprisings; juries had more than once, as a protest, acquitted persons accused of political offences; the ideas championed by the democrats did not obtain that minimum of satisfaction to which they were certainly entitled. But if the ruling class accomplished no political action, the opposition too was vague and confused and disorganized. To the unsatisfied need for political progress was added the unsatisfied sentiment of national *amour-propre*, of greatness, of *la gloire* of France. This was not only unsatisfied but offended as well, especially in 1840, when France suddenly beheld herself isolated and humiliated in the Egyptian question, in her policy of support to Mehemet Ali, and obliged to submit to what England had arranged in her separate agreements with Austria and Russia. The Napoleonic cult, which in the preceding generation had implied dislike of the restored absolute régimes and eagerness for liberty, now assumed this new meaning of longing for vanished military power and glory; and the Government favoured it as an outlet for the imagination that feeds on memories, the King caused historical pictures to be painted for the gallery of Versailles, the statue of Napoleon returned to its place on the column of the Place Vendôme, and the ashes of the Emperor were brought back to France and placed in the Invalides, while Thiers, in a spirit of opposition to this very government without glory, composed his *Histoire du Consulat et de l'Empire.* And meanwhile, in the shade, the figure of the future dictator was assuming shape, in the person of that Louis Bonaparte who in 1831 had been with the Carbonari insurrectionists in Italy and after the death of the Duke of Reichstadt was the head of the Napoleonic family, the pretender, and in 1836 had published, almost by way of a programme, his book *Les idées napoléoniennes,* and twice, in Strasbourg and in Boulogne, had tried to raise France at the cry of his name.

In 1847, while throughout Europe the waters were rising and the tempest was approaching, the Guizot cabinet, which in foreign policy wooed Metternich and enjoyed the hostility of Palmerston, obtained the rejection of the proposal for electoral reform, which had been demanded by the united opposition within moderate limits—by the increase of another two hundred thousand electors. Thus began the agitation, after the English model, of the *banquets,* which assumed a disturbing aspect, although it did not trouble the Government, to whom the elections of the previous year had given a big majority. On January 27, 1848, that unwelcome and unheeded prophet, De Tocqueville, warned of the approach of revolution, declared the necessity of electoral reform and other reforms in connection with it, but above all recommended and expressed the hope that there might be a change in "the very spirit of the Government."

The inertia and insensibility of the Government was preparing a revolution in France, and another of diverse nature was being prepared by the activity and the enthusiasm that had been kindled in Italy and in the other countries desirous of independence and liberty. And the outburst of the two diverse types of revolutions and their intertwining and mingling, and the various outcomes of both types, were the events of the year 1848.

VI. LIBERAL-NATIONAL REVOLUTIONS,
DEMOCRATIC-SOCIAL REVOLUTIONS,
AND REACTIONS
(1848-1851)

IN the connotation of common speech and in the images that
it awakens, this date, 1848, marks in the first place the
complex of liberal-national revolutions that at this time burst
out in Italy, Germany, Austria, Hungary: revolutions that
certainly received a strong impulse and new material from
the Paris revolution of February—by which the Orléans
monarchy was overthrown and the republic was proclaimed.
But it would not be exact, either in the chronological or in
the ideal sense, to attribute their origin and birth to this outburst without qualification. In fact, as early as January 12
Palermo had risen, demanding Sicilian autonomy and a parliament; and on the twenty-ninth of the same month the King
of Naples had granted a constitution, modelled on that of
France of 1830, which was approved on February 1 and
opened the series of the liberal constitutions of this year. Indeed, even earlier than this Italy, as we have mentioned, had
entered into a period of ardour and expectation and reforms,
and had asked for and obtained numerous institutions that
prepared the liberal régime; and the insurrectional attempts
in Calabria had supplied Europe with a symbol of liberty in
the "Calabrian hat," which half a century before had been a
token of reaction and of Sanfedist brigandage. So that, if
we wished to assign a chronological beginning to the na-

tional-liberal revolutions of 1848 in any particular event, the most appropriate for this purpose would perhaps be the election to the papacy of Bishop Mastai-Ferretti. The truth is that these revolutions were the prosecution of the movement begun in 1815, and the spread of the 1830 revolution to two peoples, the Italian and the German, in whom at that time the impulse had been hindered and repressed, but who had all the same not ceased to tug at the yoke and to continue the attempt, or at least to desire and to strive; and to other peoples who at that time had remained tranquil and had later, in their turn, given signs of impatience and manifested the desire for innovations. Under the ideal aspect, in short, the Paris February Revolution, notwithstanding a few similarities in psychological tone and a few coincidences of details, was far different in matter and in spirit from the liberal-national revolutions, and at once proceeded in a different direction.

This year left a mingled impression of rapture, hallucination, youthful folly, followed by an awakening and a return to reality and disillusion in its last survivors, from whose lips we have often gathered the smiling and yet melancholy admission: "In that year, we had all lost our heads." And on the other hand the pedagogico-political necessity for imparting lessons of wisdom by drawing examples from the past has led many to stress the superficiality, the puerility, the hyperboles, the rhetoric, the theatricality, of which men were guilty at this time, and their scant reflection and prudence and their overgreat temerity and their credulity in miracles, especially in those that were to be performed by speeches and laws and shouts and songs and waving of flags; although indeed sarcastic satire and mocking jests have not dared to mingle with these reproaches. They have not dared because, whatever may have been the insufficiencies and the weaknesses, and the errors that were committed, mankind then went through one of those rare moments in which it is completely filled with a happy confidence in itself and in its future, when, growing greater in the purity of this joy, it becomes good and generous, and sees brothers on every hand, and loves them. Thus it was at the beginning of the revolution of 1789, which stirred and thrilled hearts all over the world. Thus it was, and to a higher degree, in 1848, when formidable obstacles, which had been assaulted in vain for more than half a century, seemed to dissolve as if by magic, like the walls of Jericho at the sound of trumpets. The tide of enthusiasm enfolded and carried away everybody; and even the enemies of yesterday, the obnoxious absolute monarchs, the abhorred despots, the hated tyrants, no longer seemed to be the same, either because they were carried away with the rest, or because, from calculation or instinct of defence, they pretended to be so, or because they themselves at times were not clear as to which of these two orders of motives they were in reality obeying. The men who had been their instruments, often bad and cruel instruments, were generally spared or pardoned or set on one side and forgotten with the past that was vanishing.

Such, moreover, is the nature of liberal revolutions, which are by no means eager to call for the hangman and the shooting-squad, mild as they are by nature and inclined to be reconciled with their opponents. And such it proved to be in the revolutions of 1848, as in the others that preceded and followed them. Students, intellectuals, bourgeois, artisans, were their executors; and everywhere they opened and ended amidst acclamations, the throwing of flowers, festivals, frenzied joy, people embracing on the street who hitherto had not even known one another; and citizens taking up arms as National Guards, parades of these new forces and levies of volunteers; and the outburst of newspapers, broadsides, and posters in a style full of emotion, solemnity, sublimity, and willingly biblical, such as that in Italy of the monk Tosti's "psalters" and in France of the writings that re-echoed *Les paroles d'un croyant* by the ex-priest Lamennais; and prayers in the public squares; and gatherings and clubs, where eloquence again flowed in torrents and the various proposals and opinions were fiercely and passionately discussed and applauded. All these exaggerations, these flaws, these errors, which later incurred blame, were not restricted, as many Italians think, to their nation, and were not worse there than elsewhere, because things went in the same fashion and displayed the same physiognomy in Paris, Berlin, and Vienna as in Naples, Rome, and Florence. It seemed as though one and the same daemon were agitating the entire mass of Europe; and under this aspect 1848 was also one of those moments when the historical unity of European life, ordinarily concealed by the conflicts of the various states, leaps to the eye and seems to call for a political unity as well.

Nor ought the antinational and antiliberal reactions that closed the process of these revolutions lead us to consider them as a failure or as a tangle of variegated experiments negative in their results and serving only to inculcate the necessity for changing ends and means. In a general sense, every historical event is also a failure, because it never comes up to the ideal, which continues to posit its demands and to voice its criticism—and if it did not do so, history would cease. In the same general sense, the past is always an experiment for whoever operates in the present. But an actual failure, in the particular sense of the word, takes place only when a principle is abandoned because it has proved to be fallacious or because it is worn out: whereas the national-liberal revolutions of 1848 confirmed their own principles, supplied them with new and better-suited forms, and thus bore them magnificently forward on the path of actuation.

To begin with Italy, the standard under which the revolutionary process had been undertaken was the neo-Guelph idea of the independence and liberty of Italy protected by the wings of the Papacy, which, from an internal hindrance to her unification such as Machiavelli had defined once and for all, and from a natural opponent of the liberal concept, would turn into, and did already seem to have turned into, the author of and co-operator with both. In these first months a young philosopher inspired by Hegel, Silvio Spaventa, was still hunting for arguments to think the unthinkable, and said that the abstract infinite of the Church and the living infinite in nationality and the state, the infinite of religion and the infinite of society, by the work and action of a "man held to be infallible" had recognized one another in their unity, in the unity of God, "who reigns in the intellect and the heart as in His own heaven which most participates in His light." But this ambiguous reconciliation, if it had surrounded the Italian outbreak with a rosy light and had permitted it to gain ground with greater ease, was obliged, when put to the test of concrete politics, to unveil its irremediable contradiction. For the moment, it was still valid for the outburst of the revolutions; and amidst cries of *"Viva Pio nono!"* the King of Naples was induced to grant the revolutionary demands, and in this disposition of minds and spirits, and with the additional shock of the events in France, were granted the constitutions of Turin, of Rome, of Tuscany. Later, with the further shock of the Viennese revolution, the Milanese rose and in five days of fighting obliged the Austrian army to withdraw and to abandon all Lombardy, Venetia pronounced herself a republic, Charles Albert crossed the Ticino and declared war on Austria, the Pope allowed his troops to advance to the frontier, the Tuscan university-battalion and other legions of volunteers went off to fight, and last of all the King of Naples allowed an army corps to move towards the valley of the Po, under the orders of the old republican of 1799 and Carbonaro of 1820, Guglielmo Pepe. Charles Albert's distrust of republican France, especially because of her aims on Savoy, the remembrance of the way in which the Directory and Bonaparte had treated Italy, the effect of Mazzini's preaching, and the courageous impulse of the Italians caused every proposal of foreign alliances and foreign aid to be set aside at once, and called forth and made popular the motto: *"L'Italia farà da sè."*

But the insoluble knot was already revealed in the awkwardly put-together Roman constitution of March 14, a hippogriff, which tried to combine the vote of the chamber— merely consultative, moreover—with the veto of the body of cardinals, the freedom of the press with ecclesiastical censorship. So that when it became necessary to declare war on Austria, on April 29 the Pope, without the knowledge of his ministers, pronounced the allocution which reminded those who had been pleased to forget it (and one might even say himself as well) that the head of the Catholic Church cannot take up arms for one people against another people equally Catholic. There followed rapidly the corollary that the Catholic peoples and states were called upon to support him against any people that might rebel against him and threaten the security of his temporal power, as was seen in the following year in his summons to the Austrians, French, Spaniards, and Neapolitans against the Italians in the Papal States and in Rome. It was the collapse of neo-Guelphism, notwithstanding the journey to Rome undertaken in the following month by its inventor, Gioberti. And with this collapse, the Italian movement was shorn of its original point of support in a historically existent power, such as the Papacy was.

Charles Albert, who also had drawn force for his resolution from the solidarity of the Pope, saw himself reduced to a solitary alliance with the national sentiment, without any

religious chrism. He had already shrunk from negotiations
for a league with the other Italian princes, accepting their
military assistance but postponing all decisions concerning
the future organization of Italy until after the victory. Indeed, if he had opened negotiations, at the bottom of them
would have been found not agreement but disagreement. Perhaps that is what combined with his ambitions in persuading
him not to open them. The main question, in this future arrangement, was that of preponderance and hegemony; because Charles Albert would most certainly not have been able
to give up the fruits of victory, the power that would have
accrued to him from the amplification of the kingdom of Sardinia into the kingdom of Northern Italy. How could the King
of Naples, who felt himself to be the peer and the rival in
Italy of the King of Sardinia, have accepted this disequilibrium, and the Grand Duke of Tuscany and the other minor
princes have been able to resist the attraction exerted by a
kingdom of Northern Italy on the peoples of their states?
And what would have been the condition of Sicily, which
had decreed the downfall of the Bourbon monarchy and was
looking for a new king and thinking of a prince of Savoy,
and meanwhile was running the risk of falling under the rule
or under the protectorate of England?

With this refusal Charles Albert not only saved his hegemony, but promoted it *de facto*, thanks to the "fusion," proclaimed amidst many and violent contradictions, of Lombardy and Venetia with the Sardinian state. It was in vain that
the plan for a league of Italian princes, which had failed in
the spring, was taken up again in the autumn of this year
(and at a very unfavourable moment, when the greater part
of them were resorting to reaction) by Pellegrino Rossi, the
minister of Pius IX, and then by Gioberti, the minister of
Charles Albert; they did not even succeed in making it an
object of serious discussion. The federative congress, brought

together by Gioberti in Turin, was a conference academic in character, and the constituent assembly, conceived and championed by Montanelli, of representatives elected by the Italian peoples (an assembly that presupposed not only the possibility of these popular elections but the power to impose on the princes the deliberations of the assembly that would result from them) remained in the air, although it was deliberated by the Tuscan parliament. On the other hand, the national insurrection, the war of the people for independence and the republic—which Mazzini always carried at the back of his mind, although he had practically suspended it in order to leave free course to the royal war against Austria, and which he reiterated and proclaimed after this appeared to be a failure—had no effect.

Meanwhile Charles Albert, driven to an armistice, evacuated Lombardy; and in Naples, with the victory of the royal arms over the barricades of May 15 and with the recall of the Neapolitan contingent before it had reached the fields of Lombardy, the reaction had begun, and with it the agony of the parliament and the constitutional régime, while the army was beginning to win back Sicily. In the ensuing year, the resumption of Piedmont's war against Austria ended rapidly in the defeat at Novara. Tuscany, which had passed through a series of internal convulsions, returned to her Grand Duke, with a garrison of Austrian bayonets. In Rome, which, after the Pope's flight to the kingdom of Naples had set itself up as a republic, the French army set other competitors aside and intervened and gave it back to the Pope. Last of all, Venetia fell back under Austrian rule. There followed express or tacit abolitions of constitutions that had been sworn to, political trials before special courts, death-sentences and convictions to the galleys, exile, police severity, denunciations and revenge, all that is called reaction with its familiar and monotonous phenomena.

The loss of all that had been won in the first half of 1848 appeared to be great in the material field. But as regards the moral and political aspect, if a comparison had been attempted with the previous conditions of Italy, it would once more have been evident what advantages had been gained through these happenings. Italy had added to its ideal patrimony a treasure of recent feats, noble popular insurrections, wars conducted by national armies, legions of volunteers, victorious battles and others boldly fought, long defences of cities besieged by Austrian and French arms: the "five days" of Milan and the "ten" of Brescia, Curtatone and Montanara, Goito, Rome, Venice, and other dazzling memories of heroic undertakings. She looked with emotion and pride on the figures of those who had fallen for the national idea or who were living in readiness for the rally. And she had won the experience of the life of liberty, an experience that cannot be forgotten. Parliaments and ministers and debates in the political press had often proved to be up to the high level of the thoughts and the actions demanded by this form of life. The word that was spoken in Piedmont after the last disaster, "We will begin again," lay in the things themselves, which uttered it in their mute language. In the field of political thought, no small benefit was derived from the sweeping-away of neo-Guelphism, which had done all the good it could and whose survival would have been bootless stubbornness. With it went the renunciation of the other opposing fancy of a war to be declared and fought by the People against the foreigner and against the native princes for the republic; and there arose at the same time a less prejudiced attitude towards the monarchical form, and also towards the possibility of alliances with foreign powers. What is more, there had emerged a new and solid fulcrum for the resumption of liberal and national activity, in an Italian state, with a proper administration, and a heroic army that had shed the blood of its citizens to drive the foreigner from Italian soil, which alone had preserved constitutional and liberal laws.

Charles Albert, in spite of the contradictions and the flaws of his character, in not giving up the fight after the change in the Pope's attitude, in not ceding to the old *raison d'état* that would have led him to come to terms with Austria (ready, at one moment, to leave Lombardy to him), in carrying on the war in 1849 under desperate conditions and certain of defeat, safeguarded, it is true, his own honour and that of his house, but by so doing also bound the monarchy of Savoy to the cause of Italy and the liberal revolution, gave a new direction to the problems concerning the hegemony, the preponderance, and the unification of Italy, and, involuntarily and unconsciously, prepared from afar the conversion of the other problem, that of the Papacy and its temporal power, from an international question (as it had been considered and treated in 1849 and as men still wished to consider and treat it in the years immediately following) to a national and Italian question. After Novara he drew to one side, abdicated, and went to die in voluntary exile. But the work that had been his and yet not his, that is, which had belonged to so many other wills that had contributed towards it, continued its logical development. The leadership of the House of Savoy, its Italian mission, was the thesis that the antimunicipal Gioberti, formerly a neo-Guelph, proposed and defended in his *Rinnovamento;* and the union with Piedmont, the slogan that began to circulate, was accepted by many who previously had entertained a belief in the republic or had been autonomists and federalists, and who were joined even by patriots confined in prison for life-sentences, such as the chief of the Neapolitan liberals, Carlo Poerio.

A greater clarity in the terms of the political struggle and a changed relation of the forces that were to conduct it to its goal were, although with less rapidity and less clearly en-

visaged than in Italy, the results of the progress accomplished
in Germany. A constitutional basis, as we know, was not lacking in several of her states, although richer in appearance
than in reality; but (not to speak of Austria) it was quite
lacking in the greatest and most powerful of them all, in Prussia. In 1848, as an effect of the new breeze that was blowing,
indeed of the impetuous wind that was raging over Europe,
where a constitution already existed it was revived, and where
one was lacking it arose for the first time. In Prussia the
united diets were still sitting when the Government was sur-
prised by the February Revolution. Frederick William IV
hesitated to grant the request for a constitution; at first he
limited himself to promising, as he dissolved the diets, quad-
rennial sessions for them, and then, because of the growing
excitement of the people, reconvoked them for the following
month in order to consult them concerning a project for a
constitution; and only on March 18, after the news of the
Viennese revolution, did he publish a decree for the transformation of Germany into a federal state with a preliminary
representation of the assemblies of all the German countries,
and for the anticipated meeting of the Prussian diets. This
did not prevent barricades in the streets of Berlin and a
bloody conflict, which the King, when the royal arms had
already gained the upper hand, interrupted with a proclamation to the people of Berlin, removing the troops from the
city and submitting to the popular will. In spite of all this,
in November of the same year, on the different outcome in
the fall of Vienna, he reacted, and, supporting ill the over-
radical proposals made by the deputies (such as that concerning the formula of "the grace of God" and concerning
nobility, titles, and decorations), transferred and then dissolved the constituent assembly. And on December 5 he
granted of his own accord a constitution not unlike that which
had emerged from the discussions of the assembly itself, but

which was followed by a restrictive electoral law, soon after
to be modified in a still more conservative direction; other
equally restrictive dispositions concerning the press and political trials; and a constitutional practice forever quibbling
and hostile to the constitution itself. Similar treatment was
undergone by the constitutions in other states, although it was
only in a few, such as the notorious Hesse-Cassel, Hanover,
and Mecklenburg, that the statutes were revoked and a return
was attempted to the laws of the good old times.

Yet there remained in Germany, after 1848, far more
elements of constitutionalism than there had been before.
And with the mitigation of reaction, practice was also to improve, although, especially in Prussia, always in the direction of constitutionalism and not parliamentarism. In Bavaria,
Maximilian II had not the least desire to act the part of a
despot, wishing only to "live in peace," as he used to say,
"with his people," and in 1854 he allowed himself to be in-
structed in history by Leopold Ranke, to whom he put con-
scientious questions of a political character. Ranke advised
him and the other German princes to maintain without yielding the form of government *von oben*, from above, as far as
it was possible, but also to do all that was rendered necessary
by the spirit of the times and the force accruing from the idea
of national sovereignty, and not to abolish the parliaments
but to modify them. The relics of feudalism too, tithes, hunting-rights, seigneurial justice, and such things, which were
swept away in this year, were never reintroduced, except in a
few states and notably in the afore-mentioned Mecklenburg,
where the law allowed landowners once more to beat their
peasants and where, because of Lutheran zeal, the heckling
of Catholics started again.

But the great effort in which the German revolution of
1848 was summed up did not lie in the constitutional reforms
of the separate states, but in the attempt towards unification

of all of them by liberal and parliamentary means, thanks to a popular assembly. If this had succeeded, not only would the constitutions of the several states have been renewed thereby in form and in substance, but all German political life would have assumed another bent. This effort, called the Frankfort Parliament, was proposed in March by a little unofficial meeting in Heidelberg, and prepared in Frankfort in April by a gathering composed of men of letters, journalists, political ex-refugees, and members of the opposition in the various German chambers. Its members were elected by very wide direct suffrage of all the population of Germany, and it opened in Frankfort on May 18. It turned its attention, under the presidency of Gagern, to discussing, with loftiness of intellect and plenty of learning, the best methods for unifying Germany. Rising beyond the extreme proposals of the conservatives, who would have liked to leave to the princes and their governments the decisions to be taken, and those of the democrats, who aimed at a federal republic on the American model, the moderate and more numerous elements decided for the form of a constitutional and hereditary monarchy. In the formation of this monarchical unity, and in the choice of the monarch to whom the leadership should fall, the German politicians encountered difficulties similar to those which had prevented a league among the states in Italy, and equally insoluble. They had not only to overcome the reluctance or the hostility of the minor princes and of Prussia herself, but also to decide whether Austria was to enter the future unitary order—either with all her pluri-national sovereignties or only with such as were German—or whether she was to remain outside, allowing the other states to group themselves around Prussia. The first was called the "big-German" solution, the second the "little-German." In the end the latter prevailed, with the additional declaration that a treaty of union would be concluded between the two empires, the German and the Austrian.

And so they went on to the final deliberation by which the imperial German dignity was offered to the King of Prussia. But Frederick William, who received the deputation of the parliament in Berlin on April 3, 1849, refused a crown that had been presented to him by a popular assembly and therefore seemed to him to be soiled with blood and mud, reeking with revolution. He would never allow his divine right to be submerged and rebaptized in the will of the nation and to lose its "Borussism," its Prussianism, in Germanism, as was the tendency of the national-liberal movement. Differing in this from the House of Savoy, which had, in the person of Charles Albert and later with his son and successor, experienced and overcome such repugnance, the Hohenzollern was surrounded by friends and advisers and ministers and soldiers who felt as he did. And, to mention one of them, General Wrangel, scandalized, cried out, "Are we really to unite our sacred banner with the flag of the Mazzinis and the Kossuths?" Now, upon this refusal, which was a negation of its ideal principle, and sounded not only highly offensive but almost contemptuous, the national Frankfort Parliament, if it had impersonated a political force, if it had possessed revolutionary spirits and adequate means, ought to have summoned to its side the whole German nation to protect its dignity and its legitimate demands against the particular interests and the aristocratic decrepitude of the princes, ought to have imposed its own deliberations and not even to have shrunk, in the last resort, from proclaiming the republic. In a scattered way, this resoluteness to resist and the impetus to revolt were manifested in the insurrection of Dresden, which was put down after three days of hard fighting, with the aid of the regiments sent by the King of Prussia; in the less energetic and more disjointed insurrection of the Palatinate and

Baden, which was also put an end to by the troops com-
manded by the Prince of Prussia; in the surviving section of
the Frankfort Parliament, composed of the members of the
left, which tried to assemble and continue its deliberations
and issue its decisions, and was driven from the places where
it met and in the end dispersed.

But the greater part of the components of this parliament
had gradually abandoned it, and in May, 1849, its president,
Gagern, with all the more authoritative members, signed an
act of renunciation and dissolution of the assembly. These
men, in the depths of their being, were attached to the old
Germany of the principates and extremely reverent towards
the King of Prussia. For the most part they were savants and
scientists and professors, by tradition inclined and devoted
to submission. Amiable people though they were in many
ways, they were not the stuff revolutionaries are made of.
And since they were not such in their intrinsic make-up, they
were also unable to resist and to persist in the deliberations
adopted in their debates, or even to represent, by their attitude, a theoretical or even a mute protest and an appeal to
the future. For all or almost all of them changed their desires and modified even their criteria of politics and history.
A notable example of this was given by Droysen, who at this
time passed in philosophy from the theory of ethos to that of
Macht, or power, and in history, to the idolization of the history of Prussia under the aspect of sacred history, as of a
people or rather of a monarchy chosen by the Lord. To this
end he did not even shrink from twisting and bending in his
narrations the often unwilling reality of facts. Even worse
was heard from other philosophers and historians and scientists; from Stahl, for instance, the rector of the University of
Berlin, who in an inaugural speech pronounced the judgment
that German science had been guilty of entering "into a fight
with the condition of existing things, and signally against the

dominant powers" and that it must "about-face." These men, who first tried to effectuate and then disclaimed the liberal-national transformation of the German people, and substituted for this ideal another and different one, did more harm to the political education of their people than even the very monarchs of the cut of a Frederick William IV, who never disowned his own vision of the past. It is to them that must be imputed the destruction of their own work, the absolute lack of affection and regret preserved in memory for the Frankfort Parliament, where after all such great proof of sound doctrine and lofty thought had been given, and, in the immediate future, the discredit into which liberalism in Germany sank or remained as a political force or a source of political strength. We say in the immediate future, because the reasons for this stunted or delayed development, if they were undoubtedly not to be sought in a natural and racial conformation, yet lay in the ancient history of this people, in its mediaeval history, and even in that of its religious and ecclesiastical reform.

In rejecting the crown offered him by a popular assembly, Frederick William IV had maintained as belonging to him and to his monarchy the unifying mission attributed to Prussia, and made ready to actuate it in the only way that he considered legitimate and dignified—in agreement with the other princes. And so he drew up an agreement with the kings of Bavaria, Saxony, and Hanover, and after the withdrawal of the first, with the last two: the so-called Pact of the Three Kings, to which homage was paid by the imperial party (which had taken shape in the Frankfort Parliament) in a gathering, or post-parliament, held at Gotha in June, 1849. And when the two other kings also withdrew, Frederick William IV tried to carry on by himself, and convoked for the ensuing year a parliament of national union at Erfurt. But Austria, who meanwhile had beaten down the revolutions and wars in her dominions and who had already in the Frankfort Parliament opposed the imperial constitution, and had meant to show her absolute disregard for that body by having one of its members, Blum, shot for having taken part in the revolutionary defence of Vienna, Austria, who in April had called her delegates home, and had then exerted pressure on the three kings to induce them to recede from the Prussian alliance, was resolved to proceed summarily and, as her minister Schwarzenberg said, to *"avilir d'abord la Prusse et à la démolir ensuite."* So that she seized the opportunity of the revolt of Hesse-Cassel against its Elector (who had violated the constitution) and of the conflict that had broken out between him, supported by Austria in his appeal to the old diet, and Prussia, who had caused her troops to invade his country, and she threatened war unless Prussia withdrew. In fact a small skirmish had already taken place when Prussia gave way, sent her minister Manteuffel to an interview with Schwarzenberg in Olmütz in November, 1850, and recalled her troops.

In the conference of Dresden she accepted the re-establishment of the old federal constitution and of the diet that was at the head of it according to the form given to it in 1815, under Austrian supremacy. It was a disgrace, although not all Prussian statesmen felt it as such, for many of them, out of hatred towards revolutions, remained faithful devotees of Austria. It was felt above all by such German patriots as had placed their hopes in Prussia. Their shame was increased by her renunciation of her protection of German rights in the duchies of Schleswig and Holstein, whose cause the Frankfort Parliament had considered as national, and for which federal and Prussian contingents had fought. But now, under the pressure exerted by England and Russia, and because of Austria's lack of interest, these returned to their earlier condition under Danish rule. But this very sequence of failures and humiliations caused the idea to rise in other German politicians and soldiers that the unifying mission of Germany was indeed incumbent on Prussia, and that she must not let it escape her, but that it was advisable to shake off alliances with the people, get rid of all romantic and mediaeval fancies, and return to the methods of Frederick or Machiavelli, whichever name one might choose to give them. The Prince of Prussia had expressed this sentiment when he wrote in May, 1849: "He who is to govern Germany must conquer her; measures *à la* Gagern are no longer of any use. That Prussia is destined to place herself at the head of Germany is shown by our entire history; but when and how, that is the point." In a fashion very different from that of Italy, in Germany too the programme of the future was taking shape; and the experience of the three years from 1848 to 1850 and the shame of Olmütz made plain the only policy that sooner or later must be followed.

In the Austrian Empire the revolutionary process was as different from the Italian as from the German, because the principal question was neither that of independence nor of liberty nor of state unity, but that of nationalities fighting one another for the independence and power of each and, in consequence, against the unitary state that gave the supremacy to one over all the others. Once, those nations or fragments of nations had lived together in peace, Lombards and Germans and Hungarians and Bohemians and Croats, with great devotion towards their common emperor, without the spirit of revolt of one nationality against the other, for none of them were felt to be foreign or could be called foreign. The official language was Latin and for non-official purposes everyone gladly used Italian, the language of Metastasio and of so many other men of letters who, like him and before or after him, adorned the imperial court. There had been only a little trouble under the reforming and centralizing Joseph

II, with his endeavour to give the first place to the German language and German elements. But the Napoleonic wars and the romantic exaltation of nationality and the liberal leaven had changed the general attitude, awakening the demand for independence in each of these nationalities. It is true that the Hapsburg-Lorraine empire, thanks to the hegemony of the German element, performed a civilizing function, if not towards Italy (which received but little aid, even in learning to follow the new German thought, from backward and bigoted Austria, and found it more convenient to go straight to the fount or to make use of French mediation), undoubtedly towards populations like the Slavic, that were still uncultured and rude. But even this function seemed to have come to an end, and the other, attributed to it by the professors, of providing with its link an example of harmony and fraternity among the three principal races of Europe, the Latin, the Germanic, and the Slavic, was precisely an idea such as might be expected from rhetoricians and professors.

And that is what we must also hold of the theory propounded by German publicists and professors, that this pluri-national state, proprietary in character and origin, should act as a model and pattern for a future Europe. Nor was there much reason to hope that this pluri-nationalism might give birth, by a process of slow transformation and without a deep upheaval, to something like a big Switzerland, not so much because it was too big as because this empire had never been, like Switzerland, a centre of active religious reform and a refuge for the victims of persecution in neighbouring countries, nor, with the exception of its Italian lands, had it been ravaged and fertilized by the hurricane of the French Revolution (not to mention that Switzerland itself had, of late, been obliged to undergo the conflicts and the war of the Sonderbund). Its fate was, therefore, as Mazzini foresaw, dissolution, and its progress was the beginning and the progress of this dissolution, which alone could in the future be followed by a varying recomposition. There too in 1848 the revolution assumed a liberal aspect. And Hungary gave herself a new constitution, approved by the Emperor, of a very democratic character, with a parliament that was no longer one of representation by classes but formed by direct popular election, and with a responsible ministry, of which Batthyányi held the presidency and Kossuth was a member. At the same time, in March Vienna was noisily agitated, Metternich resigned and went into exile, and a parliament was summoned in that city of all the other states of the empire, which began its sessions in July. But in Vienna liberalism had no ideal preparation; it was an inspiration of the times, the principal rôle was played by students and workmen and Poles and other revolutionaries come from everywhere, and so it passed, democratically and demagogically, from disorder to disorder and from excess to excess. So that when the parliament assembled, no more heterogeneous spectacle could be imagined than that of these deputies, so different in degree of civilization and scarcely able to understand one another. In fact the most concrete result that they were able to accomplish was the abolition of persisting feudal burdens (just as, moreover, in Hungary at this time the serfdom of the soil was entirely abolished and the Hungarian clergy gave up the tithes that they were still collecting).

On the other hand, the nationalities of the empire did not all tend purely to independence, but some of them also strove to maintain or to promote particular imperialisms, especially the Hungarians against the Croats and the Rumanians, and, in different fashion, the Bohemians, who convoked a Pan-Slav conference, and, when they were cut short in their attempt to gain independence by the military force of Prince Windischgrätz, gave vent to their hatred of the Germans by serving as the instruments of the house of Austria. This Hapsburg policy for the moment saved the empire, by thus playing one nationality against the other, Germans and Croats against Italians, Bohemians and Croats against rebellious Vienna, Croats and Germans against the Hungarians, and by resorting, in order to dominate these last, to the Czar, who helped them with the resources of the Russian army. With the victory over the Hungarians, and with her other victories previous to this, Austria re-established the authoritative state in the empire, withdrew the constitution that had been granted and formulated by the Emperor himself after he had dissolved the parliament of 1848, and resumed in Germany and in Italy her rôle of restorer of legitimate princes and defender of order. But the saying of the Austrian poet that "Austria was in Radetzky's camp" supplied at the same time an exact definition and a historical condemnation of this empire, for modern civilization cannot respect a state that is a military camp, which is founded solely on the strength of its army. The refugees of Italy and Hungary, in spite of the different tendencies of the two nations, were made brothers by their common enemy and by their common exile, and awaited with confidence the total or partial dissolution of the empire, a dissolution that was substantially initiated in 1848 and that was temporarily stopped in its effects by the ensuing reaction without its being able to remove the causes.

In this year the Irish meditated a national uprising, the proclamation of the Republic of Ireland and separation from Great Britain. After the February Revolution the association called Young Ireland changed its character from literary to political. It became necessary, in April, to vote a law of safety of the realm, in July, to suspend *habeas corpus*, and repress with severity O'Brien's attempt at revolt. Famine, rapine, theft, murder, bloody conflicts between Catholics and Anglicans, did not cease on that account; and conciliatory measures, assistance to the poor, and drainage works proved to be insufficient. But except for this chronic affliction, which was destined to drag itself on for a long time, England was able to look on at the revolutions of the Continent like one who watches the stormy sea from the shore: with a feeling of participation but at the same time one of self-satisfaction and noble pride, expressed at this time by Macaulay in a famous page of his history. Chartism gave out its last flare, which was consumed and went out with the petition, signed by several million names, that a procession of a hundred thousand demonstrators attempted to present to Parliament on April 10, 1848, but which was declared to be illegal in this form and, when it was submitted to the scrutiny of Parliament, ended in ridicule. In 1849 free trade reached full realization when the Navigation Act was abolished; and whereas through its instrumentality the cultivation of grain was greatly encouraged in foreign countries and in the colonies, English traffic was greatly increased. The first world's fair, opened in London in 1851, was the formal celebration of the new industrial and commercial life that had been inaugurated. The last opposition of the Conservatives fell in the Parliament and the elections of 1852. The old parties underwent a change, and now Disraeli and Gladstone were seen face to face for the first time: they were to lead the Conservatives and the Liberals for thirty and forty years.

Belgium, where the government was held from 1847 to 1852 by Rougier's liberal cabinet and then by Brouckère's coalition, was not even touched by the general revolution. None the less she reformed the electoral law, lowering the amount of property required, and introduced regulations concerning parliamentary incapacities, reforms that in France had been imprudently but constantly denied. And she attempted to regulate child labour in factories, which was prevented for the moment, together with the freedom of trade-unions, by the very powerful industrials. In neighbouring

Holland, in 1848, the passage from the semi-absolute to the constitutional régime was finally achieved with the formation of two chambers, representing greater and lesser taxpayers, and the lower one chosen by direct suffrage.

Equally untouched by insurrections, but because of conditions diametrically opposed to those of English life, was Russia. Nor did Poland, held by her iron hand, move either, although the Poles of Posen rose and fought the Germans, and Polish refugees fought in all the revolutions of Europe, sometimes at the head of their legions of volunteers or their regular armies. The Czar had said that the revolutionary tide would die down at the frontier of his states; and so it did. Vigilance within the country was rigid and extremely sensitive; books that had already been censored were censored again; the circulating libraries were purged and repurged; the chair of European public law was removed from the universities, philosophical instruction was restricted to logic, philosophy, and psychology and entrusted to professors of theology, and classical instruction was almost entirely abolished. Under this enforced tranquillity, a generation of extreme rebels was being prepared, because the lack of every liberty, which hinders the formation of a culture that implies discernment and criticism, turned the minds of students either to turbid day-dreams, mystical in origin, or to abstract and simplifying rationalism, or to a mixture and jumble of the two things; it caused men to confuse the ill-understood, universal explanations of philosophy with practical programmes, and created the mania, as was said then, for applying them.

In addition, if in Alexander I's day those who later became the Decembrists used to read the works of Constant, Destutt de Tracy, Bentham, the new generation fed secretly on the doctrines of the materialists and the French and German sociologists and utopists. Russia's great question, which was the agrarian question, seemed to stress communism there in preference to economic freedom and political liberalism, which were exceeded before they were born; and the idea began to be formulated that Russia, unlike the countries of Western Europe, would shorten the path of history, joining the communistic future because of her ancient agrarian communities, and thus skipping the bourgeois and liberal era. But unfortunately she had also skipped the long religious and philosophical travail of Europe and the centuries of training in logically correct and rigorous thought and in criticism and caution, and all the cognate and complex experience, rich in humanity. Her intelligentsia, as it was called, her cultured class, did not even suspect the finesse and the complexity of European intelligence. Legal sentiment in Russia was weak or absent, even in the class of big landed proprietors, the only one of any importance alongside the immense number of peasants still tied to the soil. This made Herzen (who is responsible for the theory mentioned above concerning the future of the agrarian communities) say that no country was so well fitted as Russia for an integral revolution and for a radical "social regeneration," since all that was needed was a *coup de force.*

Meanwhile, what counted in Europe was official Russia and her Czar, who was always in the vanguard in defence of the good cause. In the course of the revolutions of those years, in which he had preserved his peoples from the contagion, he had sent his army to Austria to put an end to the Hungarian insurrection, thwarted Prussia in her pan-Germanic ambitions, supported Denmark's claims to Schleswig-Holstein, broken diplomatic relations with Charles Albert because of his betrayal of legitimism and absolutism. He had distributed eulogies and praise to all the men of the reactionary cause, from Windischgrätz, the subduer of Prague and Vienna, and Filangieri, the subduer of Sicily, to General Cavaignac, who, although an ardent republican, still possessed in his eyes the merit of having beaten down the Parisian working-men in the events of June. In the midst of the general hatred of his tyranny and harshness, the fervid religious faith, the firm political conviction, the straightforwardness, the loyalty, and the disinterestedness of Czar Nicholas—this last intransigent champion of the absolutist cause left among the princes of the world—were often recognized even by his adversaries. None the less, the reactionary efficacy of Russia in Europe had diminished from 1815 to 1830 and from 1830 to 1848, although publicists were still concerned, even afraid, lest this vast empire turn loose millions of armed men on the West in an Attila-like invasion. But before much time was to pass, this menacing military power too was to reveal the limits of its strength, and that efficacy was to vanish altogether.

Although the revolutions of 1848 were almost completely lacking in anti-Catholic and antiecclesiastical tendencies, and the clergy often took part in patriotic ceremonies, and even the Roman Republic, which had risen on the ruins of the Pope's temporal power, was careful not to touch religious beliefs, as soon as the reaction began the Catholic Church hastened to offer and to give her own co-operation, to divide the booty with the absolutist governments, to accept salaries and rewards for her services. And so an assembly of Austrian bishops in Vienna was seen to brand liberalism as "impious," and to qualify as "paganism" the value attributed to nationality, the origin of which (so they claimed) was solely in the chastisement of God, who diversified the tongues of men at the foot of the Tower of Babel. The concordats negotiated by the Church at this time restored to her or gave her what it had seemed madness to hope for. In that with Austria in 1855, which was called a "printed Canossa," the state wiped out all the work of Joseph II, gave up its *placet* and its right to intervene in the training of the clergy and in the penalties

inflicted by the Church, handed over to the bishops the supervision of public and private schools, excluded all non-Cath-
olic instructors from the gymnasiums and middle schools, recognized ecclesiastical jurisdiction in all matrimonial questions, in accordance with the canons and the findings of the
Council of Trent, engaged itself to prohibit all irreligious
books by every possible means; it granted absolute liberty
for the foundation of new religious orders and associations
and permitted the acquisition of property on their part, guaranteeing the present and the future inviolability of ecclesiastical property, and as regards all other cases concerning
things and persons of the Church not expressly contemplated,
submitted to the doctrine and the discipline of the Holy See.
Of an identical nature had been also the concordat of 1851
with Spain, in which, furthermore, the Catholic religion was
declared to be the only religion of the country. Those concluded with Baden and Württemberg were, because of their
enormity, rejected by the respective chambers. In Prussia,
Frederick William IV abandoned all the rights that the state
had maintained over the Catholic Church and gave a free
hand to her and to the Jesuits.

At the same time, the Church took care to set far
away from herself every suspicion of any compromise at all
with modern civilization: the Jesuits founded a periodical
called *Civiltà cattolica* (*Catholic Civilization*). The dogma
of the Immaculate Conception (which assumed a reactionary
tinge almost by way of exchange for the help given by the
Madonna against the recent and successfully suppressed revolutions) was soon followed, in 1864, by the syllabus of the
century's errors, with liberalism as capital and fundamental
among all those errors, and later by a council that decreed
(what had already been foretold by these acts) the other
dogma of papal infallibility. With absolute unconcern, men
were canonized who had been inquisitors of the Holy Office

and had for this reason acquired the peculiar odium, in their historical significance, of the civilized world. Her exultation over the disasters that had overwhelmed her opponents and the favour that she had found in the eyes of the governments caused the Church to hope that she might soon supplant Protestantism in Germany with the aid of the Jesuits and the societies of Pius, St. Vincent de Paul, and St. Boniface. In England, Lord John Russell defined as "arrogant" the procedure by which the Roman curia had instituted there twelve dioceses and an archbishop, and in 1851 a law, called the Title Bill, was passed to stop this movement. The law was not applied and was in the end abolished as not being in accordance with liberal sentiments.

For indeed the possibility of such arrogance and audacity, her independent state, and in general her supernatural and international power, or ultramontane power, as it was called, were derived by the Catholic Church from nothing but the nature of the modern state and that liberalism from whose strength and from whose weakness, from whose life and from whose death, she, without scruple, in turn gained her advantages. But the danger of this double game was perceived by such Catholics as Montalembert, who in truth had played it himself sometimes, but began to be troubled by the growing unpopularity of the clergy and the antireligious revolt that was smouldering in the minds of the young men, the intellectuals, and also the working-men. He branded as "cynical" the theory that was professed and practised by the Church and which he summed up in these words: "When I am the weaker, I ask you for liberty, because it is your principle; but when I am the stronger, I take it away from you, because it is not my principle." He feared that at the next vicissitude she would be blamed for this cynicism and treated with a not undeserved severity. On the other hand, notwithstanding the practical capacity that she had acquired through the disci-

pline that she was able to give to the clergy, now relieved of
state control and dependent only on her, notwithstanding the
liberties and privileges that she enjoyed, the Church gained
no ground in the realm of the spirit. And she seemed to be
taking on more and more the aspect of a sort of industrial
concern, which, according to the conditions of the market,
now makes big profits and extends the field of its production,
now suffers losses and restricts its activity, waiting for the
market to improve. Her returns of prosperity were brought
into relation with the periods of society's mental and moral
depression, and with the necessity that the governments may
feel, in certain cases, for an alliance with the not always distinguished forces the Church has at her disposal.

No matter how obnoxious and irritating and burdensome
the reaction was in all the countries of Europe, no matter
how much suffering it created, and torments in its prisons and
desolation of exiles, no matter how much anger and rage
it aroused in the hearts of all, it was felt to be lacking in
that seriousness which even reaction has if it is animated
by an aged but still tenacious and deep-rooted faith that
can be respected for its sincerity when it is guided by the
mysticism, the fanaticism, the inflexible coherence of a Nicholas I. Too much had been altered and realtered, sworn
and forsworn, by monarchs and other absolutist leaders; too
often had these kings and princes been seen, at the windows
of their palaces, in the streets, and in the churches, decorated
with national and liberal cockades, flattering and cajoling the
revolutionaries, with good or bad will, following their paths
and persevering in them. Too familiar was the news of the
death of liberalism and of the national desires of the peoples,
which was always followed by their rising again, younger
and more vigorous than ever. The joy of these momentary
triumphs was fleeting, and the rhetoric of these servile eulogies was quickly silenced. The spirits of the vanquished were

not discouraged, and their faith in the future kept them eager
and ready for action, the hour for which would strike at no
distant time. They did not feel alone or overwhelmed in the
world, because the consciousness of European civilization was
never felt more keenly than at this moment, nor was Europe's
opinion ever more concordant and active. Its principal centre
was England, who did not shut herself up in the egoism of
her firm liberal structure, elaborated through the centuries,
and of her security and prosperity, but made use of her politically happy conditions to speak and work in favour of the
liberal cause against absolutism. Her cities offered hospitality
to refugees from the countries wilting under reaction, who
formed their national and international clubs there. Her
writers and publicists attacked and discredited these governments and covered them with blame and ignominy. Private
English citizens provided agitators and conspirators with
every kind of assistance. The crowd hailed Kossuth, and followed General Haynau, the "hyena of Brescia and Arad,"
with imprecations and worse when he dared to visit London.

Palmerston, who had furnished arms to the Sicilian rebels,
in office continued undismayed his demonstrations against
the authoritarian régimes of all countries. Once he was
blamed for this behaviour by Peel, to whom this function
of judge and mentor of foreign governments seemed excessive, but he was greatly admired and applauded by the
English people, who gave him the sobriquet Lord Firebrand.
He followed up his demonstrations of opinions and words
with deeds, and made the emperors of Russia and Austria toe
the mark when they asked Turkey to hand over the revolutionaries that had taken refuge on her territory; and although
he was unable to avoid offering a formal apology to the Austrian ambassador for the treatment that Haynau had received
at the hands of the London populace, even on this occasion
he did not refrain from showing how much he loathed the

man. Gladstone addressed to the cabinet minister Lord Aberdeen his letters on the Bourbon government in Naples, sending broadcast through the world the name that had been given it—"negation of God." It was not without justification, therefore, looking at history from above, that Gervinus, in his *Einleitung in die Geschichte des neunzehnten Jahrhunderts,* published in 1853, exhorted men to curb all impatience and to preserve the living certainty of a not distant relief. He showed that absolutism was falling back more and more on the defensive, which was showing greater and greater weakness, and he scattered the gloomy fancies of pessimism, which even then was discovering signs of the "decadence of Europe" —of that Europe so rich in intellectual and moral lights, in addition to economic productivity, and whose greatness was not any longer in single personalities but in the diffused and growing civilization of the multitudes, and whose history was therefore not any longer biographical and confined to rulers, but a history of entire peoples.

In one country alone the collapse appeared to be serious and the retrogression of the liberal cause to be undeniable, because it seemed as though the fruit of more than sixty years of history had been lost and a régime of liberty destroyed that had not been enjoyed for a few months only but asserted and deepened and widened during thirty-five years: in France. Here the short-sighted conduct of the Orléans monarchy and its ministers, in not permitting a modest or gradual enlargement of liberty and the extension of the franchise to a greater number of citizens, had provoked the revolution and, with the fall of the monarchy, the proclamation of the Republic and, with the Republic, had opened the gate to democratism and demagogy, which went back to the traditions of the Jacobins and the conventionalists, and were thereby imperilling liberty itself. And since the democracy that was entering upon the scene, unlike that of former times, did not

encounter a feudal system to be extirpated and an aristocracy
to be abolished, nor even a threatened restoration of absolutism, and was not offered the glory of a Europe to be awakened and urged on to revolution because Europe was already
awake and stirring of her own accord, all that was left to do
was to fill its own emptiness and nourish its impetuousness
with the confused idea of a radical reform of society in its
economic and civil regulations for the happiness of the People and, with all its loathing of communism, to present itself
as social democracy and social republicanism. After so much
talk about communism and socialism during the last twenty
years and such great desire that had been excited to actuate
it altogether or in part, in one way or in another, and in any
case to try it out, it was inevitable that the revolution in
France should attempt this experiment, and already in 1842
Lorenz von Stein had prophesied it with certainty.

In other countries of Europe too, during the course of the
events that we have been describing, democracy of a Jacobin
and social or socialistic bent had shown its face here and
there, from time to time: in Italy, in Austria, and still more
in Germany, where in April, 1848, it attempted a first insurrection in Baden. And with its untimely and excessive claims,
with its provocative and at the same time feeble methods, it
had contributed to detach those who feared a catastrophe from
the liberal régimes and to reconcile them with the reactionaries, and had supplied these with opportunities and facilities
which they did not hesitate to snatch. In this way they helped
to return to their seats rulers like Ferdinand of Naples, Leopold of Tuscany, Frederick William of Prussia, and Francis
Joseph of Austria, and won toleration in Spain for the dictatorship of Narváez and Bravo-Murillo. But in general where
the struggle centred around national independence and unity
and constitutions, the liberal parties prevailed, variously tempered and stressed, and the defeat was due not to solicitude

for social conservation, but to adverse fortune in battle and to political and military strength, which was still in the hands of the absolute monarchies.

In France, on the contrary, this poorly filled emptiness of political concepts, which was not only denounced by conservatives and moderates, but placed in the pillory by Marx with his satire on the word "People" that was its exponent, had at its side the passion of the working population of Paris, which for years had been inflamed in the expectation of a social palingenesis, had shed its blood in July, 1830, and had come to the conclusion that the common victory had benefited another social class. Since then it had tried its hand at more than one uprising and now, in February, had again fought and conquered, and did not intend to be once more cheated of its efforts and disappointed in its hopes. And if the communist theories, in their logical foundation, do deserve the accusation of materialism, these working-men were not materialists. It is true that they were spurred by a human longing for a better mode of life or even by the need for food and the lack of work, but they were also profoundly moved by an ideal of justice and happiness, for which they were ready to give their lives. This was an ideal that they were to prove unable to translate into vital institutions and acts leading up to them, into facts or into a serious political programme; and it was still less within the abilities of the men whom the revolution had carried to the head of the government, least of all of the noisiest among them, the social democrats. But no one was willing to confess this incapacity and impossibility, and in the first week it was not necessary, because even in Paris the psychology of 1848 was reigning, and enthusiasm overwhelmed all men and carried them away. The young, says a contemporary, were absorbed in the pleasure of feeling themselves to be free, and *"ils marchaient d'un air insouciant, d'un pas dégagé et léger"*: joy and confidence created a disposition to generosity, to reciprocal concessions, to agreement and harmony. So the right to work was proclaimed, the working-men consented to give up the red flag and accept the tricolour, a commission of workmen was instituted and established, the *ateliers nationaux* were opened, the abolition of taxation was promised; and in rapid succession came humanitarian laws, the abolition of the death-sentence for political offences, of corporal punishment, of imprisonment for debt; and universal suffrage in one bound raised the number of voters from two hundred and fifty thousand to nine million.

But soon men realized that they were moving in a world of imagination and dreams, and that they could not go on indefinitely in this phantasmagoria. The commission of workmen drew up on paper a pacific social revolution, which a ministry of labour was to execute, transforming the state into a great manufacturer, which with the products of its own concerns was to buy up privately owned factories, create co-operative agricultural colonies, ensure work to all, sell goods at cost except for a mere increase of five per cent, and so on. The *ateliers nationaux* in no way resembled a serious economic enterprise and did not even answer to the ideas of Louis Blanc, but resolved themselves into a mere expedient for the temporary occupation of unemployed workmen in unrequested or useless or scantily useful labour, and therefore at great and unproductive expense. And the number of those who crowded to them and who could not be rejected multiplied from one month to the next. The popular newspapers seemed to have made up their minds to frighten all those, and they are never few, who love their own tranquillity and behold rapine, rape, fire, and a rain of blood in every outpouring of big words. But the men who were in power lacked the ability to create forms, and means to actuate what was capable of actuation in the social-democratic demands and to set unsurmountable barriers against all the rest, restoring order and leading people back to measure and common sense. They followed every impulse aimlessly or avoided coming to any decision, and prolonged the mad whirlpool of hopes and ambiguities, incapable as they were of unravelling the tangled skein, and so left the solution to the course of events.

The solution did not make them wait long, and since Paris and the Parisian workmen were not all France, and the course that events had taken was not pleasant and gave no promise of good to come to the greater part of the population, and the peasants in particular could ill support the increase in land-tax, which fell mainly on their shoulders, the elections by universal suffrage of the Constituent Assembly (elections that the Parisian extremists, who scented the wind, had attempted to postpone) returned a chamber preponderantly conservative or moderate; and, since a chamber of this sort was not welcome to the working masses and their agitators, on May 15 the crowd invaded the assembly and tried to disperse it with violence and to proclaim a new provisional government. The movement did not succeed, and led to the arrest of Blanqui, Barbès, and the other communist leaders. The next step was to face the calamity and danger of the *ateliers nationaux,* where there was no longer any work and no one knew how the unemployed and the idle were to be paid, although the wretched daily wage had been cut in half. The vote decreeing the suppression of the *ateliers nationaux* unchained the battle of June in the streets of Paris against the rebellious working masses, with desperate rage on both sides, and ended with the bloody defeat of the workmen, sealed by death-sentences, imprisonment, and deportation.

But not even this ended the revolutionary process and became the beginning of a stable organization of a republic such as might guarantee the greater liberty demanded in earlier years, the failure to grant which had caused the downfall of the Orléans monarchy. The fear aroused by the events of June had been great, and, when the danger was passed, was felt to have been even greater, and a still louder cry of alarm was raised for the defence of the home, women, children, property, morals, religion. Once more the Church and the priests were looked upon with less hostile eyes; they were seen as a safeguard of order, their control was accepted once more, and the children were sent to their schools. The more the democrats, or Montagnards, as they were called, insisted in their threatening demands for social reforms and in their turgid phraseology, the more the conservative and moderate groups clung together, and reactionaries of every sort, clericals and legitimists, grew bolder, and all the more, amidst these exasperated factions—one of which, the champion of the social order, felt more and more sure of its strength every day and resolved to make use of its strength—did the possibility of liberal mediation diminish. This could and should have been attempted, but without hope, as at the outburst of a disease that one tries to arrest even though one knows that in any case it will have to run its entire course.

When the labours of the Constituent Assembly were ended and the election of the president of the Republic by direct and universal suffrage was undertaken, the success, by an immense majority of votes, of Louis Napoleon against the republican Cavaignac showed that the revolutionary process had already begun to be converted into its opposite, reaction. During these years France, without any peace at home and reduced to impotence in her foreign relations during the revolutions on the Continent, gained no credit either among the peoples or among the governments, and exerted no influence whatsoever. And her solitary and inglorious undertaking, the expedition against the Roman Republic, was rendered obligatory by the absolute necessity not to let Austria intervene alone in Italy, and, at the same time, by her internal weakness—to such a degree that, in order not to arouse discontent in her own clericals, she had to allow the Pope, whom she had brought back to Rome, to reject every suggestion of reforms, fall back into his own wretched forms of government, and rule even worse than before, almost as though he wished to defy and mock the French democrats. The latter, irritated by that expedition which had been ordered by the Prince-President and the cabinet against the vote of the assembly, rebelled and called upon the people to rise, which it failed to do; and this was the defeat of their party, depriving it of its chiefs, who escaped by flight. But the conservative majority of the assembly, although it voted a series of restrictions concerning associations and newspapers and martial law, re-opened the door of the schools to the clergy with the Falloux bill, and in practice had abandoned parliamentary procedure by continually increasing the power that the Prince-President claimed as the chosen candidate of the French nation, still allowed constitutional law to survive in the assembly. But this last liberty could not continue, because it was not con-ceded by the Prince-President, had lost the esteem of the public, who looked upon it with repugnance, and when in danger would not be defended by the public will. The *Coup d'état* of December 2, 1851, was foreseen, expected, and even feared, but not opposed. It was not the ruse of a tyrant vio-lently seizing hold of a reluctant people, but rather a surgical operation that brought to light what France had formed and nourished in her body during those four years of democracy and antidemocracy: the Empire of authority, with that com-plex of laws and customs which are the same in all authorita-tive régimes, whatever their origin or occasion may be, and which are reduced to the simple operation of binding hands and gagging mouths in order to impose their own unilateral will.

And identical with those which follow the termination of

every liberal régime (and which it is useless to describe in
detail, for Tacitus has once and for all analyzed and rendered
in classical prose the *ruere in servitium*) were the effects
then seen in France: acclamations, flattery, voluntary servitude, perjury, the rapid conversions of heated democrats—
which would have been comic if they had not been humili-
ating—mental restrictions, compromises, and fears and ter-
rors and desertion of friends and cowardly denunciations,
insensibility to the violation of justice and to daily wrongs,
the pretence of not seeing and not knowing, in order to silence
the pangs of conscience, what everyone saw and knew perfectly well, ignorance concerning the conduct of public affairs with accompanying and ceaseless whispering of scandals,
supine applause for every statement or assertion coming from
above and at the same time incredulity for all news of an
official character; and, in the midst of this general timidity,
the boldness of the bold in taking fortune by storm, the readiness to seize private advantages or to satisfy private hates
under the semblance of political zeal, without anyone's dar-
ing to oppose or to protest—all those things, in short, which,
when they were practised even by men to whom society does
not refuse its esteem, caused the novelist who described those
times to exclaim: "What *canaille*, these respectable people!"

Not that these people were not, for the most part and in
other respects, honest and rich in many virtues; but humanity,
in its average ranks, is so created that it must not be submitted to too difficult tests and asked for too hard sacrifices,
such as the renunciation of a quiet life and the care of one's
own affairs and family; it must not be made to cut too bad
a figure, indeed it should be helped not to do so. Once more
might be heard the sophisms of those who professed the "*en-
chaînement nécessaire des choses humaines*," their "*déve-
loppement inévitable dans un certain ordre*," in an order
which it is wisdom to recognize and to submit to. And, on

the contrary, terrible were the hatred and the rage that burst forth against those who refused to submit, and against the many who preferred to go into exile and produced ferocious attacks such as the *Napoléon le petit* and the *Châtiments* of Victor Hugo. Sorrow and sadness, on the other hand, overcame nobler and more meditative spirits, such as are wont to consider things rather than persons, and to seek an explanation for events in the currents of ideas and sentiments rather than in the faults of individuals. These were still unable to resign themselves to the loss of liberty, and they felt a profound and painful mortification for themselves and for their country, from which, even if they had so wished, they would not have been able to detach themselves. We are still moved today by the pages written at this time by De Tocqueville, Quinet, Prévost-Paradol, and other men of their type. But liberty is a divine gift, and the gods sometimes take it away from men, who are eternal children, and remain deaf to their supplications, and do not give it back until they have once more become worthy of it.

And yet, if the reaction of the old absolutist monarchies that followed the revolutions of 1848 was not profound, neither was this one of the Second Empire, which was effectuated by a nephew of the Corsican adventurer, himself an adventurer. Those monarchs and the other champions of absolutism greeted the new-comer joyously when he took his place at their side; and first of all the Pope, Pius IX, who as soon as he heard of the *Coup d'état* remarked that "Heaven had paid the debt that the Church owed to France," and was the first to send his congratulations. He allowed his bishops to call Louis Napoleon "the man sent by God" and would have gone to Paris to crown him (as he later acted as godfather to the Prince Imperial) if an agreement could have been reached concerning the price, which was the abolition of civil marriage and of the organic articles added to the

Napoleonic concordat. But Louis Napoleon did not really belong to the absolutist association of old monarchs, for he was
profoundly aware of the meaning of the seven million votes
that had raised him to the imperial throne, and sincerely full
of concern for the lower classes, and desired, as was remarked, a "democracy without liberty." He had cherished,
moreover, no illusions that with the imperial constitution he
had opened a new path to human society and to history. Intolerant as he was of parliaments, he possessed no clear ideas
concerning the form of state that might profitably take the
place of the services they rendered. He stated that he "had
closed the age of revolutions by satisfying the legitimate
needs of the people," and that he had aimed at "creating
institutions that would survive him"; but he was not content
and easy concerning the basis he had given to the state, and
on another occasion he remarked that "liberty has never been
able to found a lasting political edifice, but it crowns it when
time has consolidated it." He announced with a solemn promise that "the Empire was peace"; but this intention, which is
that of conservative monarchs, could not be that of Napoleon's
nephew, the heir to the imperial title and to the revenge
against the treaties of 1815, and war, which he brought with
him, necessarily implied a change in the political situation
and therefore a reopening of revolutions.

His character was amiable and mild; he had accomplished
the *Coup d'état* joylessly, as though in obedience to the destiny that he believed to be his and which had given him this
rôle. And although he could not succeed in cancelling the unreasonable and at the same time reasonable condemnation
that falls upon those who in order to carry out such historical
operations violate legality and break their own oaths, he
showed how sensitive he was to what was thought of him by
honest men, and tried to gain their approval, and it was to
be foreseen that when the first test had been passed and the

first years of his authoritarian government were over, he
would necessarily lean towards liberty. And there were liberals or friends of liberty among those who surrounded him,
even among the authors of the Second of December, in his
own imperial family, such as Prince Napoleon. So that the
state as he had reformed it not only could not be considered
an original creation and did not transcend and comprehend
the liberal state, but also bore in every part the imprint
of something that is transitory and provisional. To make it
ever more so there collaborated with words or in silence those
who had kept their faith to the cause that for the moment
was defeated, and the many others who little by little laid
their fingers on the evils of authoritarianism and judged the
disadvantages of liberalism with greater equity, gave back
their affections to it, and once more recalled it with longing,
thus stripping it of the discredit and scorn that had been
brought upon it and refreshing it and rejuvenating it in their
hearts.

Nor is it true that the great prosperity enjoyed at this
time by France in industry and commerce and business and
speculation (which, if it was not actually the work of the
Empire, was accompanied and assisted by it with the resources of free trade and commercial treaties) had the effect
of putting her political wants to sleep and preventing the revival of all efforts pertaining to them—whether because such
is not, as a rule, the effect of prosperity on men, or because
the facts showed that this prosperity held back a political
revival. The working-men, of whose welfare the Emperor had
been solicitous, providing asylums for those who needed rest
and care, establishing funds for the disabled and pensions for
the aged, and so forth, but to whom he refused the right of
association and political activity, were not grateful to him
for these provisions for their benefit, since the refusal rankled
all the more because of them. And if in the first years they

had felt a malicious joy at the oppression of the republicans who had beaten them during the days of June, they now began to forget these sentiments and began in their turn to sigh again for liberty.

In truth, the movement for liberty is bound to the destinies of that complex of multifold demands always changing and developing which is called the "social question"; and just as the destiny of liberty was by no means submerged and permanently lost in the reaction that followed 1848, neither were the hopes of the social reformers and innovators. Marx wrote, about this time, that the Parisian workmen's commission, called "of the Luxembourg" from the place where it had its seat, "still had the merit of having revealed from a public tribune that the secret of the European revolutions of the nineteenth century is the emancipation of the proletariat." But let us ignore this exaggeration which impoverished and materialized the history of a century and of its revolutions, which always integrally embraces the problems of culture and civilization and all the aspects of the human spirit. This episodic gathering was not needed, indeed, to reveal a thought that lay in the minds of all political men and all writers on political matters; and without quoting here, among so many others, the profoundest of all, De Tocqueville, and without referring to what Gervinus wrote, and what was meant by John Stuart Mill's *Principles of Political Economy* (published in the very year 1848), we will limit ourselves to a few Italian names. It will suffice to recall that Gioberti, in the *Rinnovamento*, summed up in three points "the principal needs of our age," namely, "the predominance of thought, the independence of the nations, and the emancipation of the populace, that is to say, of the greatest number"; and that Camillo di Cavour thought that the problem of the relations between capital and labour and the conditions of the working-class was reaching maturity, and confessed in 1858 that if he had not had the national problem of Italy on his hands, he would have devoted himself to the other, recognizing in this way, in his turn, the close link of succession that existed between the two orders of demands.

Marx knew perfectly well that the insurrections like that of June, which were not preceded by any social preparation or by a ripening of economic institutions, did not provide the means for setting up communism, and he had already laughed at the ingenuous utopists and rejected the theories of the Saint-Simonians (who abandoned themselves with Enfantin, as has been said above, to the Second Empire, declaring that "authority alone was capable of actuating human and individual happiness"); and the events of 1848 strengthened him in his convictions. The articles and pamphlets that he composed at this time on the history of these revolutions and reactions, clairvoyant as they were even in the narrowness of their visual angle and in their total lack of historical and human sympathy, in their universal satire did not spare the proletarians and their leaders. This lack of sympathy, this "greater element of anger than of love in his heart" that Mazzini noted in him together with "dominating temper," this lack of human kindness, and the sarcasm against his own followers, and the admiration that he felt only for the "aristocrats," his rivals and his models—according to the impression that Marx made upon the democrat Techow—prevented him from approaching not only the democracy at which he mocked but any liberal form whatsoever. His materialistic and deterministic metaphysics, which was suggested to him by the gross interpretation of the revolutions of 1848 as an effect of the commercial crisis of the previous year, and by the other more simplifying one of the Second Empire as a "reaction of the country against the city," induced him to judge that another revolution demanded as its necessary condition a new general crisis in commerce and industry, and to foresee this crisis as imminent.

But this did not happen, and instead the crises assumed a different form and a less wide extension—and then he recanted his prophecy. Meanwhile he concluded that nothing could be done in a society of economic prosperity, and that, in waiting for the crisis, the communists ought to cling rigidly and intransigently to the side of the democrats and liberals and help them, indeed, to seize power, but with the tacit understanding that immediately after that they would assault and overthrow and destroy them, as they had done with their common opponents. A rather complicated and rather literary idea, and so it appeared to the surviving German social democrats, such as Willich, who had fought in the Baden insurrection and who was now also living in exile; and this dissent produced the schism in the Communist League, the separation of the men of action from Marx and from his faithful Engels and from their followers. Marx devoted himself to the doctrinal elaboration of the economy and historiography that he had sketched in his *Communist Manifesto* and began that series of works which led him through the *Critique of Political Economy* to *Capital*. Practically, the doctrine that for the moment prevailed in him was determinism or naturalistic fatalism; and the other alternative of his historical materialism, the formation of a socialist or communist political party that would take part in parliamentary battles and render itself capable of taking over the Government, was to be actuated later and under different conditions and thanks to the labour of other men.

VII. THE REVOLUTIONARY REVIVAL
AND THE GENERAL LIBERAL-NATIONAL
ORGANIZATION OF EUROPE
(1851-1870)

THERE was in Europe, as we have seen, a small state, Piedmont, in which the liberal and national movement had not suffered any interruption, and indeed in the midst of the reactionary hurricane seemed, as it were, to be cleansed and purified, to become clearer in its concepts and surer of the path it was to tread. Elsewhere, liberalism was hiding in the catacombs; and in free countries, where it spread openly and without obstacles, it lacked the pungent stimulus of war and revolution to be prepared and provoked and faced. But independent and liberal Piedmont was at the same time living the life of enslaved and oppressed Italy, from whom, long before such a word re-echoed in official speeches, she had received the "cry of sorrow." And so, making use of what she possessed and preserved and increased as a means towards a loftier end, she was the only country in Europe that was actively revolutionary. This possibility for action was certainly partly owing to her geographical situation, which had permitted her to live and grow amid the wars of France and the Empire, and now had concurred to protect her from being crushed or subdued to vassallage by triumphant Austria.

But just as in the dangers of her long history she had been strengthened by the virtues of her princes and her people, now she was guided towards her present condition, to the honour of being the vanguard of *Italianità*, by the wisdom of her statesmen. They assisted and directed her in her new life of liberty in such a way as to win fame and esteem for moderation among all the other countries in revolution, we may say after her first constitutional cabinet of 1848, under the presidency of Balbo, which included men of radical bent and conservatives and moderates, men like Pareto with men like Thaon de Revel and Sclopis. Moderate was the cabinet that was formed in 1849, that of D'Azeglio, who was conscious of the revolutionary flame that Piedmont enclosed in her heart and which must not be allowed to die out but had indeed to be encouraged, and who succeeded in bearing himself with firmness towards the impatient and the foolhardy, or the democrats, as they called themselves. He caused the King to issue to his people the severe proclamation of Moncalieri, he did not hesitate to remind the voters that civilization is sometimes saved by military force and courts of justice, and he obtained a chamber with a conservative and moderate majority, which approved the treaty of peace with Austria. With this chamber he undertook a courageous process of reform, notably in the ecclesiastical field, in which he gradually removed all that remained of clerical privileges and subjection of State to Church, with the result that he rendered the Roman curia hostile, but entered resolutely upon the projected actuation of a free church in a free state.

The work of innovation, which in a few years carried old Piedmont to the rank of a country absolutely modern and truly civilized, and therefore capable of higher destinies, was pursued and introduced into every branch of the administration by Cavour, the man of genius whom Italy had produced from her midst, and who, after a long preparation of political studies and practical life, and after having participated in

the events of 1848-49 as a publicist and journalist, now felt
that his hour had arrived and came forward to assume the
post of command, not, to tell the truth, *"pensif et pâlissant,"*
like the man called by God to be the leader of peoples of
whom the poet speaks, but active and gay like one who knows
what he is called upon to do and knows that he is able to do it,
and flings himself without reserve into the task and the fray.
He truly loved liberty, from the depth of his soul, as much
as he had always hated absolute power, and he loved it not in
an idyllic dream, but with the clear consciousness that liberty
meets and always will meet with difficulties and dangers, and
always asks for struggle, but a struggle "in which men meet
face to face" and in which "a man of powerful intellect does
not fear to fight," diversely from what happens in the absolute governments, in which a minister must forever defend his
shoulders from little cabals, a thing that is not only irksome
but intolerable for a man of honour. Fundamental was the
formation, to which he then devoted himself, of an orderly
parliamentary activity, with parties that represented needs
and collected their forces, and were able if necessary to unite
for certain common ends, as he did by forming with Rattazzi
and his men of the left the so-called Connubio. The debates
in the subalpine chamber and senate, the legislative and political activity that was carried on there, the speeches of
Cavour, the parliamentary combinations, the resolutions of
the crises, offered examples of a correct and fruitful constitutional life, and served as a model and a school to the rest
of Italy, towards whom Piedmont, during the ten years between 1850 and 1860, exercised a function analogous to
that which, as we have seen, was performed for continental
Europe by France during the fifteen years of the restoration
with her charter, her constitutional struggles, her parliamentarians and Doctrinaires.

The monarchy of Savoy, that of the most ancient sovereign

house left in Europe, which had accepted the modern ideals of liberty and nationality; the royal army, admirable for its constant fidelity, discipline, and valour, become national by the national war recently waged; the mediaeval tradition and that of the era of absolute monarchies, which offered their ancient and well-tested strength to the new Italy and developed as it were a youthful vigour—all these seemed to assert in fact that historical continuity the lofty significance of which had been discovered by the minds of the century and of which political sages well knew the serious and beneficent effect, and over which poetry and literature had spun so many of the pleasant fancies of their historical dramas and romances. The land of Piedmont, with the epic memories of its feudal and royal past in its scattered castles and its cities, and its capital, Turin, with the peculiar character of order and regularity given to it by its dukes and kings, now animated by the lively activity of the ministries, the parliament, the newspapers, held up before the eyes of all the confluence of the past with the present, the harmony of the present with the past.

And in Piedmont, who from local importance had risen to represent the entire nation, Italy was present not only ideally but also with many of her sons gathered together there, in an exile that had none of the bitterness of exile because it was no longer undergone in a foreign country but on Italian soil, rich in promise. And there were in great numbers, besides the Lombard refugees, the Southerners, some of them officers who had directed the defence of Venice, mainly men of culture, economists, men of letters, philosophers, critics, historians, hostile to the Bourbons and persecuted by them, audacious spirits that contributed greatly towards the invigoration of Italian studies and Italian culture. After 1848 was renewed in Turin what had happened towards the end of the eighteenth and the beginning of the nineteenth century in Milan, in the

Cisalpine Republic, among the refugees from the South, when that gathering of men from the various parts of Italy had produced the first sparks of a national political consciousness. Among those Italians, the neo-Guelph idea of a few years back had been completely forgotten and seemed to belong to a remote past; the republican idea appealed no longer; nor was a great need felt, as had been the case before 1848, to form plans for the future organization of Italy, for truly, in certain cases, "the movement is an end in itself and the end does not matter," that is, the movement itself contains the end, which in its time will choose the practical paths that are open to it and concerning which it is useless to hazard prophecies. So completely did the end lie in the movement itself that when a project was put forward which, it was thought, might obtain the support of Louis Napoleon, and of which Cavour himself did not show any disapproval, for the liberation of Naples from the Bourbons, to be replaced by a King Murat, even from the Southern exiles issued a voice of reprimand, giving warning that the path of salvation and honour was one alone, to proceed in close union with Piedmont and her policy. And the Piedmontese policy was adhered to, about the same time, by the republican and former dictator of Venice, Manin; and the defender of republican Rome in 1849, Giuseppe Garibaldi, who had returned to Italy in 1854, saw and declared that the unity of Italy was not to be reached in any other way.

So that he who keeps his eyes on the development of the moral history of the time cannot but perceive in the activity of Piedmont after 1848 the continuation and at the same time the resumption of revolutionary action in Europe. Nor is this statement irreconcilable with the other that, if we look instead upon the equilibrium and disequilibrium of the great political forces and the effects that arise from them, we must look for the origin of this revival in the Crimean War—a war that upset existing relations, weakened the conservative union, and by force of reaction raised the hopes of the innovators and supplied them with opportunities of which before they had not dreamed. The Crimean War was, in fact, a political event, dictated by England's interest in preventing Russia from extending her dominion or protectorate over Constantinople and the Balkan peninsula, to the detriment of commerce and with danger to England's sea-power; and, correlatively, by Louis Napoleon's interest to break the union that had been formed against France in 1814 and to restore her to a place in European politics, winning for himself and his dynasty a prestige that was still lacking. Moral idealism was found, if at all, in the opposite camp: in Czar Nicholas, highly religious, as we have said, and a zealous defender of the faith, who considered a disgrace to Christianity what still remained in Europe of Turkish rule, and was sincerely convinced of the justice and sacredness of his mission and of his undertaking. He set out on a sort of crusade; he was overcome by equally sincere indignation when he beheld the Western powers take up arms against him in alliance with the enemy of Christianity, and was wounded in his feelings of chivalry when Austria (who had no choice of any other policy) not only did not give him assistance but showed hostility and addressed him with threatening intimations—that Austria to whom he had, out of fidelity towards the monarchical cause and to keep a promise given many years before, granted such effective aid in 1849 against the Hungarians. He was a moral idealist in his own way to such a degree that when the war went badly, despairing of victory and saddened by what seemed to him desertion and treason, he died or perhaps took his own life in tragic fashion. England obtained her ends; Louis Napoleon acquired that splendour and authority which he desired; and far more than he gained in prestige was lost by Russia, who had been considered invincible, who still enjoyed the glory won in the campaigns of 1812-14, and who for more than forty years had weighed on all Europe.

The group of the three conservative powers was broken up, for full light was now cast upon the incurable divergence of interests in the Balkans between the Russian and the Austrian empires, a divergence poisoned by ill feeling and turning into hatred, which dominated their history during the following sixty years. Men like Windischgrätz and Radetzky might weep over this breaking-up of their brotherhood at arms; but the thing was irreparable. Turkey, whom Czar Nicholas had been the first to define as the "sick man," showed enough vitality to merit the support and alliance of the civilized powers, and men like Cobden and Bright wearied themselves in vain in their efforts to remind the world what it knew perfectly well concerning the barbarism of that country, but which it wanted not to know or to forget. And it succeeded, just as it had succeeded several times in centuries when the conflict between Christianity and Islam had been more alive in men's consciousness. Even the progressives and democrats wanted to forget and did forget, for they wanted to give the interpretation of a crusade to this war, but in a sense opposed to the Czar's crusade, that of one for the liberty and independence of the nations. That is, they presented as its goal what was only a probable and ulterior event, and therewith they inserted their own goal and meanwhile regarded the war favourably. This explains the circular of Mazzini, in union with Ledru-Rollin and Kossuth, to the republicans of the world, asking them to operate in this sense, and other such manifestations, even that on the part of the communist Barbès, who was still in prison. Palmerston, once more in power, anxious to serve the interests of his country but including among these interests the communication to the other nations of the institutions that were England's pride, contributed with indefatigable audacity to the strengthening of this interpretation, and to the inflaming of these hopes.

Now, to take up our thread again, where do we once more see the independent, uninterrupted tenacious and guiding activity of a moral conscience, if not precisely in Piedmont? Among the other peoples and states of Europes, she was the first and the readiest to profit, for the national cause, from the new condition produced by the Crimean War.

Piedmont—or rather the kingdom of Sardinia—in 1855 had, through the sure intuition and resolution of Cavour, made an alliance with England and France "against the colossus of the North, the worst enemy of civilization," so said the author of the treaty in the subalpine parliament, adding that this participation in the battles of the East would serve the future destinies of Italy far better than speeches and literature; and, indeed, his expeditionary forces gained glory on the Tchernaya. And although the hopes of a continuation of the war and of a manipulation of the Austrian states by the acquisition of Danubian principalities and the corresponding cession of Lombardy were not fulfilled because after the fall of Sebastopol the business world urged for the conclusion of peace, Cavour, in the Congress of Paris, succeeded in carrying, if not into open discussion and deliberation, at least into an exchange of ideas and declarations all that concerned Italy: the foreign domination in Lombardy-Venetia and the foreign garrisons maintained in the lands of the Pope; what the Bourbon government in Naples and the papal government in Rome really were, qualified by Lord Clarendon as a "disgrace to Europe"; and, in short, the pressing urgency of the Italian problem in relation to the peaceful settlement of Europe. Over the protests of the Austrian minister against such interference in the affairs of independent states and the reservations of the Prussian and Russian ministers, who objected that they had no instructions dealing with such matters, he succeeded in getting his declarations inserted in the protocol. Some months later, France and England sent remonstrances over the methods of his government to Ferdinand II in Naples, and the rupture of diplomatic relations ensued. On March 18, 1856, Austria, who had felt the force of the blow, sent to her diplomatic representatives at the courts of Rome, Naples, Florence, and Modena a circular, which was made public, denying with energy "the mission of the Sardinian court to raise its voice in the name of Italy" and reaffirming her own right to "intervene with arms when she was called by one of the Italian governments to give aid against disturbers of the peace." But it was no longer a question of an asserted right, derived from old treaties and old international congresses, but rather one of moral force and of facts; and the fact was that the seed sown by the war of 1848 and by Novara had grown into a robust tree, and that Piedmont henceforth represented Italy, spoke in her name, and was making ready to break Austria's prevalence and domination in the peninsula.

As to this Cavour had not only placed himself on the right ground, but he had also found the man he needed in Europe. Louis Napoleon, in his divided, wavering, and often nebulous mind, had one clear and immovable point, the idea of overthrowing the treaties of 1815, and, since these treaties had trampled on the principles of nationality (was this the motive or the consequence of his aversion?), the duty of assuming the defence of that principle, modifying the arrangement of Europe in accordance with it, united with the ambition, not discordant with his humanitarian and romantic ideals, of "waging war for an idea." The Crimean War had helped him to weaken the principal bulwark of the *status quo;* but during this war he had caressed the idea of procuring the independence of Italians and Poles and Hungarians, and even of Finns and Circassians. When England wanted to go on with the war and he was drawn into peace by the financial world, he put forward the adoption of these ends for the possible continuation of the war; and in the Congress of Paris he would have liked to propose and discuss the same problem, but Clarendon pointed out to him that that was not possible without a preliminary understanding between three or four powers. This did not prevent Paris from becoming, as has been said, an "immense centre of conspiracies" for the wars and revolutions that were being planned; and Cavour profited not only from the part that he performed in the congress, but from the acquaintances and friendships and relations of all sorts that he gained in Paris and among those who surrounded Louis Napoleon. The latter had asked him, in the winter of 1855, what he could do for Piedmont and for Italy, for that Italy in whose plots and conspiracies he had been involved in his agitated and adventurous youth, and towards whom he had assumed an engagement of which, a few years later, Felice Orsini, in his own fashion, was to remind him.

With this approach to Louis Napoleon, the rift between the Conte di Cavour's policy and that which Mazzini recommended and tried to effectuate became deeper and more difficult to bridge. The Genoese, after the prominent part that he had taken in the short-lived Roman republic, during which he had given proofs of practical ability, had gone abroad again and returned to his propaganda by word and deed, and began to appear as a man of the past, no less because of his mental outlook than because of his political programmes and methods. The Italy of 1850 was no longer that of 1831; and the "national initiative," which at that time it had been necessary to awaken and to form, had in 1848 become a fact that was living in and operating on men's minds. The "war of the people," which even then had not been waged, now found its true form in a state that represented a nation, in an army that was to grow into the army of this nation. The con-

spiracies, the disorders, the attempted insurrections, although
they tended to prove that the Italians were not resigned and
to lengthen the already long national book of martyrs, sacrificed precious lives and awakened fear, which it is not advisable to awaken, in the governments and in the lovers of
order, who are afraid of the blind violence of disorder. His
central democratic European committee and the appeals that
he issued over his signature and those of French, German,
and Polish refugees, such as that of July, 1850, to the "peoples of Europe" as to "individuals of humanity," exhort-
ing them to elect national parliaments from which were to
issue the "representative congress of free nations," remained,
as is natural, without effect, and even without an echo, and
attracted the mockery of Marx, who, like Mazzini, was living
in exile in London. Not that this congress of the future was
not a noble desire and even a serious idea, but it belonged
to another aspect of Mazzini, that of precursor, and the precursor is of necessity an anachronistic personage, without
efficacy in the politics of the present. The time was to come
when this idea would sprout and throw out strong roots; but
for the moment even Richard Cobden, who had demonstrated
his power to convince and persuade, was jeered at as a utopist
and found supporters only among the Quakers and the Dis-
senters, and at best had to content himself with praise for his
good intentions when he undertook propaganda for disarma-
ment. And Clarendon, who was a statesman, saw the failure
of his proposal at the Congress of Paris for the institution of
mediation to be tried by the conflicting states before resorting to arms.

Cavour by temperament and education had never been a
Mazzinian; he was incredulous of the virtue of dictatorships,
nourished equal incredulity of the miraculous virtues of the
masses in politics, and detested in Mazzini the dictator and
the demagogue combined. He was, on the contrary, firmly

convinced that the Italian undertaking was to be carried out by a regular war between armies and armies, between governments and governments, and that "if revolution interfered once more, there would be danger of shipwreck for the second time." Mazzini did his best to arouse prejudice against an undertaking on these lines, and created obstacles and difficulties in the manner that we have outlined above. It is true that when the moment for action came, Mazzini used to advise his followers to co-operate; but with the reservation, not only mental but outspoken as well, that they would later come to a reckoning with the monarchies in favour of the republic; this deprived their co-operation of sincerity and vigour. And he persisted in his systematic obstinacy, which prohibited alliances with foreign states; so that he was willing to allow Victor Emmanuel II to wage war, but on condition that he did so with purely Italian forces. It is easy to imagine what shrieks of horror, worthy of a cursing prophet and an apocalyptic seer, he raised when the foreign ally was seen to be the very "man of the Second of December"; and already in 1855, when Piedmont's participation in the Crimean War was announced, he had accused Cavour of wishing to become "the ally of Austria and Franco-imperial despotism."

Cavour was unable to agree with him concerning studied abstention from alliances, and as to the quality of these he replied: "I am resigned; there are in Europe three powers interested in undoing the *status quo,* France, Russia, and Prussia, and two interested in preserving it, Austria and England: I regret that the former are not the more liberal, but what is to be done? I cannot stand with the other two." The new undertakings promoted, inspired, or approved by Mazzini in Southern Italy proved to be as vain and disastrous as the national loan in 1850 and the uprising of Milan in 1853; and worse than inopportune was the attempted insurrection in Genoa in 1857, which added to Cavour's abhorrence. And yet he certainly had no scruples in negotiating with, and agreeing with, revolutionaries and men of action who professed ideas very different from his own, and he came to an agreement with Garibaldi, but he was unable to do so with Mazzini, as he was unable to do so with the Pope. And when it is said that he made use of Mazzini as a pawn in his game, and waved the scarecrow of Mazzinianism and revolution—in doing which it may be noted that he would have been following the example of Charles Albert in 1848, who justified in this fashion, in the diplomatic notes of his minister Pareto, his entry into the war—when the saying of the Russian minister Gorchakov and others is repeated, that under the pretence of combating anarchy, the Sardinian government did nothing but "proceed by means of revolution in order to gather in its inheritance," then we do not so much admire or blame Cavour's shrewdness as recognize a very simple truth: that there does not exist, or that no one has yet discovered, any other way to overcome an error in philosophy, and in practice to avoid a dangerous and disastrous policy, than by accepting the one and the other, that is, the legitimate needs that impose the one and the other, and by satisfying them in a better and more adequate fashion. It is impossible not to admire Cavour when one looks through his life and his letters, and sees what genius, what versatile labour, what discretion and courage, what passion and poetry, what suffering and rage at times, what terrible tension of soul and mind—even to the breaking-point, with the breaking of his physical life—this labour cost him to which he had been called by history.

And so the war of 1859 was reached, which Louis Napoleon wanted to be provoked by Austria, and which Cavour, by his own provocations, succeeded at last in getting provoked by Austria, the object of which was the expulsion of the Austrians from Lombardy-Venetia and the constitution of a kingdom of Northern Italy—to include the Legations and

Romagna—under the House of Savoy. Louis Napoleon added to this the project of a division of Italy into four states, leaving the Two Sicilies intact, forming a kingdom of Central Italy with Tuscany, with the addition of the Marches and Umbria, under the Duchess of Parma or some other prince, and leaving Rome to the Pope, who was to be the president of the Italian confederation. There was not much to be said about this project, since in fact it depended mainly on the will of others, especially of the King of Naples and the Pope, who would have to adopt it or bow to it. The unity of Italy, that is, the formation of a great state adjoining France, did not enter Louis Napoleon's head, nor was it in France's political interests. Not even Cavour harboured in his mind the idea of Italian unity, and he has often been reproached for this. In particular the words of one of his letters have been recalled, a letter addressed to Rattazzi in 1856 about Manin, that "he wanted the unity of Italy and other tomfooleries"; and it has been observed that Mazzini saw more clearly than he, and that it was Mazzini's idea that was carried out and not Cavour's. But seeing that politics is neither prophecy nor guesswork, politically Cavour saw better than Mazzini, that is, he realized that before the problem of the unity of a national state came the problem of independence from foreign control and that of the free régime to be established in a big state of Northern Italy; this task was enough for him and kept him busy and made him consider all the rest as an idle toy of the imagination. Certainly, Mazzini had not spoken and worked, and was not then speaking and working, in vain, and was aiding, in positive and in negative fashion, Cavour's own labours.

And his other wider problem would not fail to present itself. But the solution might be various and might pass through various degrees and take more or less time. Except that history, as Cavour loved to repeat, "is wont to improvise";

and when the war had begun, after Austria's first defeats the population of Tuscany and Parma and Modena rose, and the Grand Duke and the dukes fled, since they no longer had any moral authority to give a new form to their states, or any forces to maintain themselves there. And the inhabitants of the Papal State rose, driving out their governors, except in Umbria and the Marches, where the rebellion of Perugia was repressed by Swiss mercenaries. And throughout these lands the cry was for annexation to Piedmont. This was the improvisation of history, the new element, "Italy acting for herself," without heeding treaties, diplomacy, and congresses. None of the powers had justification or power to interfere, except France. But France was Louis Napoleon, bound to the consequences of the war he had wanted and waged, psychologically compromised because of the position he had assumed as protector of the Italian people's legitimate will; so that the first part of the drama closed with annexations and plebiscites—beyond a doubt a sort of legal fiction, or symbolical ceremony, but symbolical of the principle of nationality—and with the cession to France of Savoy and Nice, which was another consequence of accepting the principle of nationality ("We cannot," honestly remarked D'Azeglio, "be for nationality on this side of the Alps and against it on the other") and had been a condition of the Franco-Sardinian alliance, suspended for a while because the war had stopped after the battle of Solferino without liberating Venetia.

The further annexations of the rest of Italy were manifestly of a different order of difficulty. Certainly the Bourbons of Naples were also without moral authority to grant new constitutions, since the old ones had been twice sworn to and forsworn, and the coldness and hostility of the intellectual class towards the dynasty (for they had never forgotten the scaffolds of 1799) had now lasted tenaciously for seventy years; and they were, moreover, quite without under-

standing of any national idea. The Pope, even if he had desired, or once more desired, to attempt a liberal reform in
his state, was unable to do so because of its theocratic nature,
and because in 1848 he had learned from experience by what
contradictions this was made impossible. But both had material forces for their defence, the Pope international troops
supplemented by legitimist and clerical volunteers, especially
from France, and the King of Naples an army which in the
upheavals of 1848-49 had remained faithful to him and had
won back Sicily. This knot was not untangled by Cavour, but
cut by Garibaldi, and by Garibaldians like Crispi, with the
expedition known as that of the Thousand, which in 1860
in a few months liberated Sicily, passed over on the Continent, and arrived almost as far as the northern frontier
of the kingdom of Naples. Here too we have an unforeseen
event, prepared by Mazzini's thirty years of education and
by Cavour's own action against Austria and on behalf of annexation. But it spread beyond the framework of the battle
between armies and armies, governments and governments,
within which he had moved. And there was once more the
danger of a dualism of political tendencies, all the more so
since Mazzini was striving to introduce his republican programme into Garibaldi's exclusively and loyally national
work. This dualism was rapidly eliminated by Cavour by the
expedition to the Marches and Umbria, which liberated these
other provinces too from papal dominion, lent a hand to Garibaldi's volunteers, and took over the prosecution of the task
until the siege and fall of Gaeta, to which the King of Naples
and his army had been driven for their final resistance. All
that remained was a remnant of guerilla warfare that dragged
on for several years, which the legitimists and reactionaries
tried to transfigure in European opinion and imagination into
a civil war of conflicting ideas, a sort of second Vendée—a
complete transformation of its substantial reality, which was

that of military operations and police work against flagrant brigandage.

If it were possible in political history to speak of masterpieces as we do in dealing with works of art, the process of Italy's independence, liberty, and unity would deserve to be called the masterpiece of the liberal-national movements of the nineteenth century: so admirably does it exhibit the combination of its various elements, respect for what is old and profound innovation, the wise prudence of the statesmen and the impetus of the revolutionaries and the volunteers, ardour and moderation; so flexible and coherent is the logical thread by which it developed and reached its goal. It was called the Risorgimento, just as men had spoken of a rebirth of Greece, recalling the glorious history that the same soil had witnessed; but it was in reality a birth, a *sorgimento,* and for the first time in the ages there was born an Italian state with all and with only its own people, and moulded by an ideal. Victor Emmanuel II was right when he said, in his speech from the throne on April 2, 1860, that Italy was no longer the Italy of the Romans or of the Middle Ages, but "the Italy of the Italians."

Nor was this character, at once bold and moderate, lacking in the work of legislative and administrative and economic and financial construction of the new unitary state, which was carried out by excellent parliamentary work, principally between 1860 and 1865. And the enthusiasm was shown especially by the determination to solve the problem of the temporal power of the Papacy, of which the last but most precious remnant remained in Rome, and which was equally offensive to the national principle, as a wedge in the midst of the new state, and to the liberal consciousness, as incapable of change to civilized government. That the Papacy did not give in to these obvious national and civil arguments could not be a cause for astonishment, because the Church, a perfect society, embraces the temporal with the spiritual, and in her day extended her power far and wide, and invested and crowned the princes of the earth and excommunicated and deposed them, and if she now beheld herself reduced to ruling over a single fragment of Italy, had not for that reason given up a right that she was unable to give up without at the same time contradicting her own doctrine and nature. Not equally reasonable, nor altogether exempt from hypocrisy, were those Catholics, citizens of other states, who furiously defended the relic of temporal power in Rome—notably those French priests and bishops who used against Italy the eloquence of their pulpits as well as the attacks of their newspapers—because, in the last resort, they demanded that one single people should accomplish a duty which belonged to all Catholic peoples equally. They expected, with unchristian injustice, this one people to sacrifice its vital principles, which neither French nor Belgians nor Germans had ever sacrificed. But even in the Papacy, except for its doctrinal premises and traditional formulas, the spirit of a Gregory VII and an Innocent III was no longer alive, and least of all in Pius IX, of whom it was said that he was decidedly lukewarm about the political thesis that he was obliged to sustain until the end by every sort of means. In diplomatic circles it was told during these years that after listening to and accepting, with the expression demanded by the occasion, the condolences and protests conveyed to him by a great German personage because of the Italian onslaughts, he had turned to someone who was standing beside him and murmured: "This German imbecile does not understand the greatness and beauty of the Italian national idea!"

The Italian parliament, cutting short the hesitation of the doubtful, defying the opposition of clericals throughout the world, with a solemn assertion of its will proclaimed Rome the capital of Italy. And through provisional transactions

with France, and the renewed attempts of Garibaldi to solve
the still unsolved national difficulties by the same method as
that which had been used for the Two Sicilies, and the revival of the old diplomatic scheme of Louis Napoleon (from
which the Italian conscience and Italian public opinion
shrank) of inducing Austria to give up Venetia in exchange
for Rumania, then in a grave internal crisis, thanks, last of
all, to the two European wars of 1866 and 1870, the new
state rounded itself out with Venetia and Rome. And here the
intransigence of the Papacy permitted Italy, in the act of
winning the Eternal City and making it her capital, to pull
up the temporal power by the roots, not leaving to the Papacy
even that little plot of ground, that minimum of a body,
which, as has been observed with a Franciscan metaphor, it
seems to need in order to attach its soul to it, and regulating
the relations between the kingdom of Italy and the Holy See
by means of a law, a monument of juridical wisdom, called
the Law of Guarantees. Politically, the end of the temporal
power took place amid general indifferènce and did not touch
the other governments, of whom only a few later voiced any
objections, not indeed in defence of the Papacy, but, on the
contrary, because through this forcible process of spirituali-
zation inflicted upon it by Italy, it had lost the possibility of
exerting pressure upon her, in case of quarrels and conflicts.
But ideally this event was, in the history of world civilization, the cancellation of the last trace of the mediaeval theocracy of the Church of Rome.

The Italian Risorgimento had been accompanied by the
sympathy, the anxiety, and the admiration of the whole civilized world. The men who guided and impersonated it in the
two years of the miracle, Victor Emmanuel, Cavour, Garibaldi, made a strong impression on men's imaginations, like
everything that is great and extraordinary, but they also
spoke to men's hearts because their significance was lifted

above the particular passion of a people and stirred mankind
—particularly in the poetic figure of the fighter in America,
the defender of Rome, the captain of the Thousand, on whose
lips the brotherhood of peoples, the peace of the nations in
liberty, justice, and harmonious labour, seemed to be a living
reality. To the peoples that were still labouring in difficulties
and conflicts similar to those which the Italians, after so many
hindrances, obstacles, and disappointments, had happily overcome, to the Germans and the Hungarians and the Poles and
the other Slavs, the Italian example appeared, as may well be
imagined, as a lesson, a stimulus, a renewal of sorrow, a hope,
an impulse to action. The revolutionary Bakunin, echoing
what they all felt and thought, wrote at this time in one of his
manifestos that "from Italy's victory over Austria dated the
existence in Europe of a number of nations anxious for their
liberty and capable of creating a new civilization founded
upon liberty." In addition to this, the fall of the old political
system, in the very country where Emperor and Pope and
Bourbon and Lorraine princes clung fast together in order to
maintain it, and the formation of the new kingdom without
disorders and revenges or other shameful and cruel things
(for, as Cavour had said, liberty scorns the use in her favour
of "the arms of despotism") shook the convictions of the
refractory, calmed fears, relieved all tension, persuaded opponents not to persist in unwise denials, and inclined everyone to conciliation and to looking upon the liberal system with
new eyes. The kingdom of Italy was recognized by the other
states, even by those which were particularly conservative and
authoritarian; as it was by Prussia as soon as the new king,
William I, had overcome his instinctive reluctance, and in
Russia by the son of Czar Nicholas, who would never have
conceived the possibility of such a happening or of such
recognition.

The effects of all this made themselves felt in the fresh beginnings that were to be noted everywhere, even in Germany, for whom, after the Congress of Paris and with the opening of the age that may be called Cavourian, there now opened what was greeted as a "new era." The troubled and perplexed but not ungenerous Frederick William IV retired because of mental infirmity, and Prince William became regent and then succeeded him. For some time an attempt was made to pick up the threads of the Frankfort Parliament, and to try once more the unification of the German fatherland, with the support, to be sure, of Prussia, but with liberal and popular means. In September, 1859, was founded the German National Union, modelled on the Italian National Society with which in 1857 La Farina, Pallavicino, and Manin had devoted themselves to assisting Cavour, and which, indeed, took steps to enter into relations with its German sister. It is also well to remember that when the Prussian ambassador protested against what was happening in Italy, Cavour replied that soon Prussia would be grateful to Italy for the example that she was affording. The French newspapers spoke of the "Piedmontese mission" of the Hohenzollerns. Even Louis Napoleon believed in this mission of Prussia, standard-bearer of the future in opposition to Austria, who represented the past, and in 1858 he had tried to gain her alliance in order to remodel the map of Europe. There was a lively sympathy between Italians and Germans, in spite of the difference of their mental attitudes, or better, because of this very difference, and the wish was voiced for a reciprocal exchange between the two peoples and their cultures, *"entre la grave et profonde Allemagne,"* as Cavour himself had written before 1848, *"et l'intelligente Italie."* The German National Union, which was not tolerated by the federal diet in Frankfort, obtained the protection of the Duke of Coburg-Gotha, spread rapidly throughout Germany; it was prohibited in several states, but permitted in Prussia. In the Prussian chamber was formed, in 1861, the German progressive party, which in accepting the national programme tended to rejuvenate Prussian political life and demanded ministerial responsibility, the greater independence of municipal, district, and provincial administration, the abolition of seigneurial justice, the introduction of civil marriage, and other elements of the liberal order. The ensuing elections returned the liberal party to this chamber with increased strength and authority, so that it was able to put up a moderate but not feeble opposition and, amidst lively conflicts with the house of peers, obtained various advantages. At the same time, in the rest of Germany the scandals of constitutional violations also ceased; the eternal Elector of Hesse-Cassel was forced by Prussia to reinstate in 1862 the constitution of 1831; parliamentary activity increased with varying intensity and, in conformity with precedents, in Baden more than elsewhere.

Certainly after swearing to the constitution (disobeying the advice that Frederick William IV had in his will given to him and to his successors), William I was not the man to break his oath. But, soldier as he was by vocation and by training, a hater of disorder and revolution, he had not bowed without inner resistance to the constitutional idea, so that when, now over sixty, he acceded to the throne, he stuck firmly to the idea of the divine right of kings, to whom the chambers are required to give advice but whose authority they cannot replace nor, with it, the responsibility towards God. Others in his entourage, officials and nobles, held the same views; and the conflict that rose between him and the chamber of deputies was always that between liberalism and the Prussian spirit. This was also true of the question of military reform. The chamber, which caught no signs of overgreat enthusiasm on the part of the King and his friends for the cause of national unity, had good reasons for suspecting that the desire to maintain a big army was dictated by internal politics, and it was not led by bad motives when it proposed to reduce expenditures by lowering military service from three to two years, a measure not in agreement with the personal ideas of the King, but one supported by other politicians, and one against which Bismarck himself did not raise any absolute objections of a technical nature. But since this conflict had been turned into a question of principle as to the authority of the King and the power of the parliament, Bismarck, appointed president of the cabinet in September, 1862, as the man for the situation, the man with the iron fist, undertook to actuate the reform and to carry on the administration without the passing of the budget, and thus won a victory for the King's will, no matter what it was, over that of the parliament. The Italian revolution had inspired in Bismarck no idea except that the new kingdom of Italy (as he had remarked in January of this very year) was "a creation than which nothing better could have been desired for the ends of Prussian politics," so much so that "if it had not been already good and done, it would have been necessary to invent it." But with the appearance of Bismarck on the scene, Prussian politics took on a different tone from that which others had tried to give to it in the "new era," and the liberal development of Prussia no less than that of the rest of Germany was interrupted and set aside.

In the Austrian Empire, the German element in particular, in which culture was more widely spread, disillusioned by the promise and then the withdrawal of a constitution, weighed down by the burden of the concordat and filled with shame by the unbridled insolence of the clergy, shared the common sentiment of Europe, and showed itself discontented with and intolerant of the unceasing paternal régime. Among the other nationalities, the Hungarian stood in the forefront, ever watching for the right moment to win back the independence that they had won in 1848. But that does not mean that the others were not pulling at the leash or that the Government was not worried by them, as had already happened with the Italians of Lombardy-Venetia, and as had been seen in 1858, when elections were held in Serbia for a national assembly and Austria, fearing the effect of the attraction that might be exerted on her subjects of Serbian nationality, did all that she could to prevent them, and did not succeed because of French opposition. The policy of centralization practised by the minister Bach, as is the case with all efforts that are against nature, had been built upon sand. Not a few who yet loved their country and desired her good were at this time brought to the pass of desiring a military defeat for her, as the only means to reopen the door to indispensable reforms and changes. And in fact when Austria had lost the war of 1859, the ruinous condition in which the finances of the state were struggling made it advisable to ask for collaboration and help from a popular assembly.

But the fear of such assemblies was still so great that it delayed all definite action, and first of all, in March, 1860, the plan was resorted to of enlarging the Imperial Council, adding elective members and giving periodicity but not publicity to its meetings. And since this patching-up of an organ depending on the Emperor was unable to satisfy anyone, least of all the Hungarians, in October of the same year a patent was issued which augmented this council by a hundred deputies from the provincial parliaments, gave back to Hungary her parliament in the form enjoyed by her before 1848, and established a more restricted Imperial Council for the affairs of the countries not belonging to the Hungarian crown. But even this was unable to give satisfaction, and gave none; the Germans showed their annoyance and the Hungarians were violently agitated, so that the whole thing ended in smoke. Nor were there more practical results from the real constitution of February, 1861, which established two chambers: that of the peers, partly hereditary, partly nominated by the Emperor; and that of the deputies, elected by the local parliaments, again with a duplex division, one for all the countries of the Empire, the other only for the non-Hungarian ones. Bohemia protested and manifested her discontent; Hungary did not send her deputies, nor did Venetia; and in 1865 the constitution and the parliament had to be suspended until the completion of the negotiations that were to be initiated with Hungary.

During those years the party of a "Big Germany" put in a new and brief appearance, and the minister Schmerling hoped by this means to compensate the Austrian Empire for the loss of Lombardy; but the new war, with the new defeat of 1866, which excluded Austria from Germany and also obliged her to give up Venetia once more, imposed the abandonment of the absolutist régime and for nationalities the adoption of the system of autonomies, which alone would be able to arrest or at least delay the dissolution of the empire, already begun by the loss of the Italian provinces. In 1867 the constitution and legislation of 1848 were restored in Hungary, and the other countries of the empire had a separate parliament; the two constitutional states thus formed were reunited under the name of Austro-Hungarian Empire, with a common cabinet for common affairs and an assembly of delegations which met alternately in Vienna and in Budapest. This compromise did not calm the other nationalities included in the Austrian part or united to the Hungarians, but created an agreement between the two most powerful groups, the German and the Magyar. After the constitutional life of the Austro-Hungarian monarchy had been thus initiated, the first evil that was shaken off, in 1868, was the concordat of 1855, annulled *de facto* by additional organic laws concerning matrimonial questions, control of the schools, and religious liberty; these were denounced two years later by the Pope—the usual conclusion of the indiscreet greed to which the Roman curia, whenever the right occasion appears, is wont to abandon itself.

In the most unlike points of Europe the progress of the national and liberal principle could be observed. In the Balkan countries the principality of Rumania, formed by the union of Moldavia and Walachia, passed through constitutions, *coups d'état*, and dictatorships under Alexander Cuza and at least received a constitution on the Belgian pattern with the dynasty of Hohenzollern-Sigmaringen. Serbia and Montenegro were slowly acquiring a greater independence, and Turkish domination over European lands was growing more and more limited and weakened. In the far north, in 1865 Sweden obtained, in the place of the old arrangement by classes, a more democratic parliament with two chambers founded on the varying amount of taxes paid and elected, the first by the provincial councils and by the corporation of the big cities, the second directly by the people. And if from there we go down to Spain, we find that in 1868 she rose, expelled Queen Isabella, and set off in search of a prince giving promise of order and liberty. Under this queen and under the cabinets of Narváez and González Bravo, Spain had undergone long periods of the most irksome and petty clericalism; the Government had announced that "the defence of the Holy See is the first duty of the country," and amid universal derision Pius IX had sent the Golden Rose to this queen who was proverbial for her immodesty. On the outburst of the revolution, the concordat of 1851 was burnt in front of the nuncio's residence. The Jesuits and all the other religious orders were suppressed and their property was confiscated. The people invaded and devastated convents that had risen illegally, and full religious tolerance was decreed. This country, which had delayed longer than any other in recognizing the kingdom of Italy, invited from the new Italy as its new

king the second son of the usurper of the Papal States, Prince
Amadeus of Savoy.

It also happened that Russia, like Austria, in consequence
of a military defeat, and because of the universal trend, addressed herself to the reform of her internal conditions and
the improvement of Poland's lot. This was afflicting all
Europe, especially the French and the Italians, for they
thought that they owed Poland and themselves as it were a
debt of honour. In 1861 Alexander II abolished serfdom
throughout Russia, so that forty-seven million peasants became free men, obtained the possession of their houses and a
small farm attached to them, the right to use a part of the
lands that belonged to the nobility, and the right to acquire
them by means of a system of payment facilitated by the
state. This was a great step, although indeed for the moment
it was not followed by adequate practical results in the improvement of their economic conditions. At the same time,
the Czar established the provincial councils, a first step
towards a parliamentary assembly; he granted a jury in the
law-courts; in the universities he re-established instruction in
philosophy, jurisprudence, and political science, which had
been suppressed, admitted a greater number of students,
needed to make magistrates and lawyers, the lack of whom
was deplored; he allowed private charity to open Sunday
schools for the people; he permitted a free press in St. Petersburg and Moscow; he started the construction of railways by
concessions to French and to several Polish companies, and
reopened the frontiers to such of his subjects as wished to
travel abroad. The minister Gorchakov, who hated Austria
and had therefore favoured the allies in the war of 1859,
threatening to occupy Galicia in the case of Prussian intervention, had begun to lean towards France, with whom he proceeded in agreement in Oriental and Balkan affairs. In Poland
Alexander II distributed amnesties and allowed the return of

the exiles, extended the reforms introduced in Russia, and prepared a sort of autonomy by the institution in Warsaw of a special section for religion and education and a council of state, and of elective councils in the cities, the provinces, and the governments. Notwithstanding tumults, attempts at assassination, and consequent repression, he actuated this new order and the corresponding reforms in education and in the universities, and the assignment of functions to local persons, the civil emancipation of the Hebrews, and similar measures, all acceptable to such Poles as did not reject union and good relations with Russia, if only in order to issue from the oppression that had lasted for thirty years.

None the less the insurrection against Russian domination broke out violently in 1863, directed by a vast secret society that resorted to terroristic means, but without the adhesion of a great part of the people and the peasants, with bands of volunteers (including Italians and Garibaldians); it was suppressed with much bloodshed. For the Western powers had been able to intervene only by means of diplomatic notes, which were unacceptable to the Russian Government and served only to offend its dignity and excite its pride, and Prussia, on her part, had closed her frontiers. After the victory, the Czar changed his method and, without withdrawing the concessions he had made, struck at the aristocracy and the Catholic clergy, which (whatever Europe may have preferred to see or rather not to see) were the real soul of the Polish insurrections, and with every means in his power undertook the Russianization of Poland, a plan that corresponded to the ideas of the Old Russian or Pan-Russian or Pan-Slav party. This party was opposed to all that came from the West, although its literary ideology, as we have seen, also had a Western origin; it was hostile to constitutions, the idea of which Alexander II was also gradually dropping in his disgust over the Polish insurrection, the attempt on his life in 1866, and the unreasonable attitude of the press. In no part of the Russian people could he find a firm support for a life of liberty. The great majority, composed of peasants at the bottom and government employés at the top, were completely indifferent to politics and in general shrank from all mental effort, and showed no inclination to or perseverance in study.

The intellectuals and revolutionaries, whose number was growing among the young, not only rejected these or those historical and present conditions, as was done in the other countries, but, armed with a certain knowledge of natural sciences and utterly void of classical and humanistic education, denied, with gross rationalization of argument, all history whatsoever, all the past, all beliefs, all customs, marriage, the family, society, property, the state, liberty, responsibility, the distinction between good and evil. And since in the place of what they rejected they did not place and were unable to place anything at all, the name arose for them at this time of "nihilists"; as is well known, this name appeared for the first time in the novel *Fathers and Sons* by Turgenev (1861). Tolstoy too, in *Anna Karénina* (1874), described them as without the necessary premise of a religious and moral education, and therefore as flinging themselves against society after the fashion of "savages." The ferment of this negation for negation's sake and of revolution for the sake of revolution; the frantic impetus towards the destruction of all civilization and all history, which already had an apostle in the older generation in the person of an emigrated Russian, Bakunin; the lack of a bourgeois and political class; the conditions of landed property among the peasants and their agrarian communities —these offered Russia no other choice but that between autocracy and anarchy, or rather, since anarchy is not a choice, between one form or another of autocracy, socially different, politically identical. And in truth, as political observers argued and as events proved, there were but faint hopes for a revolution in a liberal sense. Cavour remarked to the Russian envoy that a far greater danger threatened Europe from the communistic constitution of Russia's peasants than from her immense armies. With Alexander II's unsuccessful attempt the doctrine of Western liberalism, at its most vigorous and happy moment, had been applied with the greatest effort that was possible in Russia.

It was quite natural, on the other hand, that France, who had behind her centuries of civil development and rich culture, and the revolutions of 1789, 1830, and 1848, should, in spite of the abyss into which it seemed in 1851 as though liberty were sinking forever, and in spite of Louis Napoleon's boast that he had once more set up on its base the political pyramid that had been standing on its apex, and in spite of the doctrines that were then being compounded concerning the eternal absolutist form of government adapted to the French people and in general to the Neo-Latins and the Catholics—it was quite natural that France should gradually return to a liberal régime. As early as the elections of 1857 there had been a number of opposition votes, exiguous in regard to the total number but considerable in comparison with the preceding years; and three republican deputies had taken their place in the legislative body, who were increased in the supplementary elections of 1858 by another two and formed the so-called group of the Five. Orsini's attempt on the Emperor's life, which called for a renewal of severity expressed in the law of general safety, with arbitrary arrests for the purpose of intimidation and similar proceedings, was also the crucial factor that determined the war against Austria; and this war was the first incentive to the gradual dissolution of the authoritarian régime. How could the French remain in conditions of inferiority, under guardianship almost like minors, when the Italians, whom they had successfully helped to liberate from oppression and to encourage in revolution, had come of age? How was it possible to wage a war for the independence and liberty of one people against an authoritarian state, and keep under an authoritarian régime the nation that had fought that war? The means cannot conflict with the end, with which they form a unity, and when they seem to be in conflict, that signifies that a new end is rising in place of the first one. Upon the return of the army from the Italian campaign, an amnesty was granted for all political offences and the exiles were allowed to come back to France; and in November, 1860, an imperial decree restored to the senate and the legislative body the right to discuss and vote annually an address in answer to the speech from the throne, and also to discuss in secret committee the bills presented by the Government before nominating a committee to examine them; and it reinstated publicity of discussion with integral printing of speeches.

For several years books of various kinds had been multiplying, treatises, essays, histories devoted to liberty, such as Jules Simon's *De la liberté,* which came out in 1859. On the whole these were moderate and averse to Jacobin democracy. The first concessions, the first loosening of the reins, awoke in the French people the impressions and the emotions that convalescents undergo when they begin to move and to enjoy the sunshine and to breathe the open air. But the suavity of these feelings was not shared by the priests and the bishops, whom the Empire had cherished and economically and politically assisted, and who alone had enjoyed a liberty of their own, a privilege denied to other citizens. The Italian war and the occupation of papal lands and the threat to Rome made them furious; and Lamoricière, a man of valour, who had turned clerical and papal warrior, preached a crusade against the revolution, "the new Islamism," similar to that which he had fought with sword and fire in Africa; it must be killed without pity, "like a mad dog."

In the question of papal Rome, the French clericals continued to exert on the imperial Government a pressure that
was fatal to their country, because it played in the end into
Bismarck's hands, led to Mentana, prevented the alliance
with Italy and thus that with Austria, and left France isolated
in 1870. Meanwhile the clericals were losing ground in the
field of instruction and education under Duruy's ministry,
which promoted free and compulsory elementary education
and restored scientific liberty to the universities. In 1864 was
heard for the first time the motto: *"Le cléricalisme: voilà
l'ennemi,"* which was taken up later by Gambetta and became
a guiding force in French life. With the elections of 1863 the
electoral body was enriched by about thirty members of the
opposition, republicans and independents. It was felt that
the authoritarian system no longer "worked," that its men
were incapable of being renewed and rejuvenated, that its
organs no longer combined towards a single end, that faith
was lacking. Even the principal authors of the *Coup d'état*
lent their aid in trimming the sails in an opposite direction;
Morny advised the concessions of 1860, and in 1865, when
he was dying, exhorted the Emperor to restore liberty. Per-
signy, a few years later, spoke in the same sense and declared
that their rôle, that of the men of the Second of December,
was over. Prince Napoleon was so energetic in defending his
old convictions that he incurred the displeasure of his imperial cousin. Under the Rouher cabinet there was still some
hesitation, some delay, some show of resistance; but the laws
that were passed at last concerning newspapers and public
meetings set in motion a copious and vigorous opposition
press. With Rouher's resignation, with Ollivier's cabinet of
January 2, 1870 (he had been one of the Five), with the vote
of the senate on April 20 and the plebiscite of July 8, the authoritarian empire turned into a constitutional one. The Emperor kept the authority that came to him, over the head of

the chambers, from the plebiscites, and the responsibility of ministers exclusively to him, by whom they were nominated: this is what he called the "union of liberty with order." And it was the solution that was acceptable to the so-called Third party, which had been formed about this time, and which thought, in substance, with Prévost-Paradol that "liberty is a thing so holy and sweet that we should take it no matter what hand offers it, happy if we can receive it from a Washington, but glad to accept it even if it comes from a Stuart or actually from a Cromwell." Others did not think the same, for to them this dualism of parliament and universal suffrage, manipulated by the Emperor, offered no proofs of security.

England had aided the liberal cause even during the course of the events of 1859-60, when Palmerston upheld the principle of non-intervention in Italian affairs in a way that had been vainly desired thirty years before, namely, to allow Italian peoples, states, and individuals to intervene in favour of or against Italian states and individuals without the interference of any foreign power. Worthy of being recalled also is England's cession to Greece, in 1862, of the Ionian Islands occupied by her. In her internal life, with her greater economic and political development, she was in advance of the events that took place elsewhere several decades later. And the Manchesterian doctrine of free trade, which had celebrated its greatest triumphs there, was submitted to criticism, its limits were laid down, attempts began to be made to integrate it, bearing in mind the economic and also the political needs that could not be satisfied solely by means of free trade. This took at first, with Disraeli, the form of amorous interplay between the aristocracy and Toryism and the lower classes, who were supposed to come to a reciprocal understanding against the middle class—something like the attraction between grandparents and grandchildren and, in any case, an example of elective affinity of which other examples might be found in the history of other peoples and in other centuries. But in this particular and transitory form were comprised what later were known as "social measures," "state intervention," and, according to the intentions and the parties that proposed them, if requested by radicals, "social democracy," and, if proposed by conservatives or by conservative radicals, "state socialism," and so forth. The franchise was broadened in 1867, thirty years after the memorable reform, after a series of incidents and in the end after many requests and agitations; the new elections that caused the fall of the Disraeli cabinet marked another great step forward on the path of popular government.

Ireland, where the population was decreasing and poverty was increasing, took on a more terrifying aspect with the end of the American Civil War, when thousands of Irishmen who had taken part in it were left without pay. They formed the terroristic faction of Fenians, and attempted an attack on Canada as well. It became necessary to remove one of the most pungent and permanent motives of the rebellion, the injustice of the tithes that Irish Catholics had to pay to the Anglican clergy; and the champion that rose to defend this cause was Gladstone, vainly opposed by Disraeli, who, with his quaint romanticism, saw in this strange tyranny, in this hateful ecclesiastical exploitation, the "sacred union of Church and State, the fountain-head of English civilization and of England's religious and political liberty." In 1868 Gladstone passed the bill for the disestablishment of the Established Church in Ireland. The agrarian law for the acquisition by the state of big landed estates to be distributed among small owners was intended as a remedy for another cause of distress and rebellion in Ireland, but its effects were scanty. English prosperity, on the other hand, flourished; during the fifteen years between 1853 and 1868, the population had increased by three and a half millions, commerce had been doubled, the railways more than doubled, tonnage increased by one third; and an Atlantic cable united England with America. English industry was at the head of the world, and enjoyed almost a position of monopoly.

This is also the period of Europe's great expansion, when China was opened to her by the war conducted there by England and France (1858-60), and also Japan, who in 1868 accomplished a revolution that made her pass rapidly from a mediaeval to a modern country. England overcame the insurrection in India, completely suppressed the authority of the East India Company and brought the country under the Queen's Government (1857). Her colonies of Australia and South Africa were developed and enlarged; the cutting of the Isthmus of Suez became an accomplished fact; Russia spread into Turkestan. It was political and commercial expansion that was exalted in the consciousness of European civilization, spread of the power of her science and technical skill, of the duties and the rights that came to her towards all the other races to be gradually raised to the same form of civilization; and it comprised the forces, once distinct, of conquerors and missionaries, now gathered together in the modern state that represented these rights and these duties. Its procedure was often harsh and cruel, as in Algeria, in the wars to subdue and bend barbaric populations or such as were restive in their inferior civilization; but these were wont to derive their justification from the good that was to come, from the *timor domini principium sapientiae.* The aversion to slavery—which, as has been said, had been abolished by the states of Europe in almost all their colonial possessions—led to the bloody four years' war between the states of the North and those of the South of the American Union and ended in 1865 with the victory of the abolitionists. There was a living and general consciousness of progress, not only as a concept of historical interpretation, but as a certainty that the royal road had been entered upon at last, that the human race now had acquired the mastership over things and, what was more important, over itself, and that it would not again abandon or lose this road but would follow it forever.

During the two or three years that preceded 1870, there were some who still allowed themselves to believe that through wars they had almost ended war, since everywhere national states had been formed with free institutions, with Italy no longer a battle-field as it had been for centuries, Germany on the path to unification, Austria separated from Germany and in agreement with Hungary. And they hoped that a peaceful competition would be started among the nations that were henceforth equal and had no more reasons for grudges or hatred, now that the Italian words to the Germans during the years of the Risorgimento had become actuality: "Let them cross the Alps and we will be brothers once more." The magnificent world's fair at Paris in 1867 seemed to be a demonstration and an omen of this. And even a Congress of Peace met at Geneva in that year, through the efforts of the international democracy, attended, among others, by John Stuart Mill and Jules Simon, by Quinet and Victor Hugo, by Pierre Leroux and Herzen and, greeted by general expectation, Garibaldi.

However, even in these same years several disquieting signs appeared that contradicted these hopes or offered no good presage of their immediate fulfilment. In fact, the imperial régime in France, just as it was yielding to transformation at home and in this respect was denying its *raison d'être,* felt that it was deprived of authority in foreign politics, since it was unable, after the Italian war, to point to anything but a series of errors and failures: its inclination for and impotence in diplomatic action in Poland, its disastrous attempt to found an empire under French influence in Mexico, the absolute lack of advantages obtained in the territorial manipulations of Germany, its having unintentionally allowed a great state to be formed in Italy, which was not even friendly because it was opposed in the question of Rome, so vital to its interests. All this stimulated and agitated this empire to seize once more the rank that it had held after Sebastopol. And since the rival that had risen beside France on the Continent was Germany, elevated to new splendour by the Prussian victory of 1866 over Austria, and since it was Germany that French public spirit was watching with suspicion and jealousy, it was there that Louis Napoleon too was obliged to look, spurred on in spite of himself to seek for a field of action there from which to bring back the glory that the French people thirsted for and which was necessary to the empire. And, reciprocally, Germany was aware of this hostility and of the hindrance that it was raising or would raise to her political development, and she lived through in memory all the past of this rivalry, all the damage that the "hereditary enemy" had inflicted upon her, and she too dreamed of her glory in a victory that would be both revenge and the definitive termination of this damage and this menace. There was, therefore, the obscure danger of another war in preparation. But the war that broke out before long was fraught, because of the way in which it was conducted and closed, with grave consequences to the whole of Europe, and contributed to determine in her a state of mind very different from that which had been in the desires and the hopes of the generation that had accomplished its work from 1848 to 1870.

VIII. THE UNIFICATION OF GERMAN
POWER AND THE CHANGE IN THE PUBLIC
SPIRIT OF EUROPE
(1870)

THE formation of the German Empire and that of the kingdom of Italy are generally placed side by side as two
parallel cases of the general national movement, which with
these two new states was supposed to have reached its principal aim and to have rested there. This common judgment is
due to the consideration of certain generic and extrinsic resemblances and to the prevalence of the chronological vision
of contemporaneity over the truly historical vision, which on
the contrary discerns what is peculiar and characteristic in
the two events, and leads us to consider them as two distinct
forms or ideal epochs, the one closing, the other opening. Certainly, as has been noted, a more intimate affinity between
the two peoples and between their ideals was suggested in
1848 and outlined itself in the so-called new era about 1860;
and that explains why Italian patriots were stirred by a feeling of brotherhood for what the Germans were demanding
and seeking, and why they did not look too closely at the imperialistic tone of the Frankfort Parliament itself. But the
affinity was submerged in the process that actually developed
from 1862 to 1870 and which, diversely from the Italian, was
not a movement for liberty nor for independence from foreign
rule, and not even one for compact national unification. On
the contrary, it consisted in driving out of the union of Ger-

man states the state that throughout a long and venerable historical tradition had represented the entire Germanic nation
before the world, and in regrouping the others under one of
them of more recent origin and importance, thus constituting
the German Empire. It was, therefore, rightly speaking, the
formation of a power, or, which comes to the same thing, the
potentiation of powers scattered and feebly joined together
thanks to a unitary process of soldering, and the acquisition
in this way of the capacity to exert a political efficacy or preponderance in Europe by means of one great state placed at
the centre of this union.

The man who laboured at this task, diversely from Cavour,
was a purely political genius, caring nothing for ideals of any
kind, a "hard realist," "man of reality," "man of will-
power," "dominator," "titanic," as his compatriots hailed
him; a man prone to scoff and mock like one who always is
and always wants to be practical, with a sneer of contempt
and scorn on his lips like one who deals with arguments of
force: a physiognomy utterly different from that of Cavour,
who counted on the irresistible force of truth and liberty, and
who, with none of the "titanic" in his make-up, half man of
affairs, half gentleman, was none the less a great man. The
very devotion that Bismarck professed to monarchical authority, as we see if we look at it closely, did not express a
moral ideality but was the affection for his working instrument, for he found in the Prussians' attachment to their King,
in their disciplined readiness to fulfil their duties as subjects,
in the army that the first Frederick William and old Fritz had
prepared, the means that he needed and which would not fail
to serve his end. If it had been a moral ideality, it would have
manifested itself as it had in the romantic Frederick William
IV, or as in certain respects it still manifested itself in William I, as consciousness of divine grace, a religious link with

the historical tradition of the princes and of the German people, invincible revulsion from innovators and democrats and
revolutionaries and liberals, a pledge of chivalresque purity
that, upon occasion, might even disregard political utility.

Bismarck knew nothing but this utility, although he certainly understood it in no mean fashion—on the contrary,
with grandeur and far-sightedness. The name of Austria inspired him with no holy reverence, and he made the use of
Austria that suited him according to the times and the events;
now he maintained that German affairs should be regulated in
constant agreement with her, and now he called her an enemy
and treated her as one. He liked the feudal lordlings and they
liked him, but he also knew how to displease them and how
to be rid of their company. Now he disapproved of liberal institutions and assemblies and wanted to trample on them,
even going so far as to call the press and the newspapers
"arms of Antichrist," and now he came to terms with them
with compromises and half-way measures. He defined any
alliance whatsoever with democracy as "shameful," and gave
the German people universal suffrage and lent an ear to Lassalle's socialism; and he loathed rebels and revolutionaries,
but in no wise objected to conspiring with them, whether they
were Hungarian refugees or Garibaldian republicans from
Italy, or to instigating insurrections and upheavals against
the monarchical principle in Europe. He wanted to make an
end of the "dangerous idea of solidarity among all conservative interests"; and legitimate rights and treaties and sworn
oaths he deemed old rubbish of paper defences that could
offer no resistance to the onslaught of force.

From all this arose also the conflicts between him and his
King, who was moved by a sentiment different in origin and
quality from his own, often proposed plans of action that did
not agree with his, from time to time shrank from committing

certain acts and reluctantly consented to others, and wanted to go further than or not so far as his minister. Even the little consideration in which Bismarck held liberalism and parliamentary discussions and deliberations, and the intellectuals, and savants and men of letters, was due to nothing but his conviction of the tactical and political impotence of such procedure, of such assemblies and such men, principally because of his experience of the Frankfort Parliament, which had so ridiculously (so he said) fooled itself that its deliberations might preserve any efficacy in the face of the orders that the King of Prussia might issue to his subjects. But when by this liberal and revolutionary method a form was developed that created or transformed a state, he changed his judgment and remarked, of the kingdom of Italy for instance, that even revolutions can generate a state, and that the Italian state was there and was a fact. He did not understand how England could have given the Ionian Islands to Greece, and judged that she was an exhausted power "because she gave away instead of taking." For his part, he wanted to make and did make politics and nothing else but politics, just as Von Moltke made war and nothing else but war; and he carried on his politics with sure calculation, bold and cautious, knowing how to give up a lesser for a greater profit, what was momentary for what was lasting, profiting from all opportunities and changing with the changing of conditions, without ever losing sight of his goal, which was, as we have said, the creation of a centre of power. Not that he bore a clear design in his mind, one gradually carried out and completed in 1870, as some fancied, for that is contradicted by his words and by his acts and by historical documents. Such imagination of preconceived designs, however it may strike the fancy of the crowd, does not correspond to reality. For the poet has, to be sure, his inspiration but does not foresee the work it will lead up to and which comes even to him as something quite new and which he himself can contemplate; and the philosopher has a glimpse of truth and does not know whither it will lead him until he has reached the end of his research and his system is born and he is its first hearer and disciple; and in the same way the politician follows an incoercible tendency and through obstacles and pauses and deviations and concessions attains to the political achievement that incorporates this tendency.

The intimate impulse that Bismarck obeyed had as its instrument the force, as we have said, of the Prussian state of the Hohenzollerns, and as its immediate material the Austrian Empire, which he had to take apart and put together again in a different way, and France, against whom he had to defend his own political creation and, during the struggle, to augment and strengthen it. When he rose to power in 1862, he had for many years gone back to Frederick II's anti-Austrian line of politics, which the French Revolution, Napoleon, and the Restoration had interrupted. He saw clearly that the aggrandizement and rounding out of the Prussian state in Germany, and with it the new condition of the minor states and the establishment of a hegemony, could not be obtained and settled without Austria's resigning all interference in German affairs, and so, since such a renunciation was not in the field of possibilities, without a defeat of Austria. And he immediately expressed this conviction of his to the Austrian ambassador and when the latter objected, gave him the first hint of his idea that Austria would do best to transfer her centre of gravity to the East. Soon after he spoke of "blood and iron," by which alone, and not with parliaments, the problem of German unity would be solved. He therefore refused to let his King take part in the assembly, summoned by Austria, of German princes in Frankfort, and answered their plans with another, which also never became more than a plan, of a re-formation of the federal council with Prussia on a footing of absolute equality with Austria—the right to declare a federal war exclusively in the hands of these two powers—and with a parliament by direct popular election.

With such a state of parity, with Austria at his side, and excluding the military contingents of the German Confederation, he conducted the war of 1864 against Denmark, who, in defiance of the London Protocol of 1852, had annexed Schleswig. But even while he was waging the war and winning it with Austria as an ally, and occupying the two duchies in common, he meant to win them for Prussia in one way or another; and the final outcome of a long series of negotiations, provisional compromises, postponements, concealed provocations, menaces, was—amid the almost general opposition that Bismarck encountered in Prussia and even among the members of the royal family—the war of 1866. In this war Prussia was left quite alone in Germany, for the majority of the other states and the most important of them took sides with Austria. The German population was hostile to Prussianism because of affection for their old native dynasties and for their independent states, because of suspicion of Prussian tyranny, and also in part because of the repugnance of Catholics for the hegemony of a Protestant state and dynasty. But Bismarck had obtained, on the other hand, the alliance of that liberal kingdom of Italy which, as he had said, it would in the interests of Prussia have been necessary to invent if it had not already existed.

Austria beaten, he effectuated the North German Confederation with a parliament elected according to his wishes, and formed alliances with the South German states; but the attitude of France during this war, her threat of military intervention, the obstacles that she placed in the way of the South German states' entering the Confederation, the compensations

in the way of Rhenish territories and military assistance for
the annexation of Belgium that she asked for in return for
further unification and for a Franco-German alliance, the
excitement of French public opinion, which considered the
victory of Sadowa as a French defeat, made him foresee a war
with France as inevitable, and made him even consider it as
desirable because of the position that it would confer on the
new Germany in Europe. So that while he was making his
military preparations, he displayed consummate ability in
isolating the enemy politically. In Italy he aroused the Garibaldian expedition against papal Rome which ended in Mentana, setting Italian feeling against France, thereby rendering
impossible a triple alliance between her, Italy, and Austria.
As to the last, he entrusted her to the hostile vigilance of
Russia, with whose chancellor Gorchakov he cultivated a close
understanding, which permitted Russia to obtain the opening-
up of the Black Sea, forbidden by the Peace of Paris. The
war of 1870, which was an almost uninterrupted series of
military triumphs, effected the union of the North German
Confederation with the South German states under the new
title, covered with glory because of its mediaeval memories,
but not understood by Bismarck in its mediaeval sense, of
Empire.

Thus rose German power and, in the place of the French,
German leadership on the European continent; and since the
German Empire was a formation of power that aimed at leadership, Bismarck did not think it was worth while to show
any consideration for French feelings, which, as he explained
to the cabinets of Europe during the course of the war, would
always, in any case, be full of hatred and plans for revenge.
And so, not satisfied with having obtained a free hand for the
arrangement of German affairs without any further menaces
and chicanery on the part of the French, not satisfied with a

war indemnity of an amount unheard-of in the past, and all the other advantages he had obtained, he snatched two provinces from France, turning them into lands of the Empire, providing for a better defence of the frontier in conformity with the opinion of the military caste and to the satisfaction of German national pride, to which it seemed that in this fashion not only recent history but the history of centuries that was to Germany's detriment had been cancelled. If the Italian Risorgimento had been the masterpiece of the European liberal spirit, this rebirth of Germany was the masterpiece of political art in union with the military virtues: two masterpieces as different from one another, in general appearance, as a fine poem is from a powerful machine. And the Bismarckian creation, which was and wanted to be nothing but a demonstration of power, needed no other justification, and could not even gain anything from the legal fiction of a plebiscite, a symbol that might interpret the spirit of liberalism but was void of significance, even as a symbol, where the whole work had been carried out, and was meant to be continued, solely by the authority of princes and of the prince of princes, the King of Prussia, now German Emperor.

The impression awakened by this rapid and dazzling ascent of Germany was very great, equal to the clamour of her victories. Nor was it surrounded everywhere with admiration, for many, in all parts of the world, were saddened, not, to be sure, by the national unity attained by the honest and hard-working German people, but by the way in which it had been reached and by the effect that it brought with it of a reinvigorated authoritarian spirit. They felt in their hearts the shock of the violence and brutality that was crushing France; and they were unable to view with sympathy the jubilation, which appeared to be doubly fratricidal, of the German people and the contortions and bombast of its men of letters and historians, who sang the praises of Arminius and Alaric and the Ottos and Barbarossa, a spectacle that offended both human feelings and good taste. But in the majority, the admiration and applause that follow success prevailed, and, with them, the urge to imitate. If at the end of the war of 1866 the Prussian military system had been studied as a model, and with it the scholastic system (to which a greater part of the armies' victories were attributed, so that it was said that the conqueror of Sadowa had been the German schoolmaster), now admiration spread to the other aspects of German life and even to the qualities of the German mind and the German soul. Conservative castes of all sorts, and such temperaments as exerted authority, or worshipped it and were prone to serve it, were encouraged by facts and by big facts, and employed them as irresistible arguments in their polemics.

And it was natural, it was even useful, like everything that teaches us to know reality better, that democratic illusions concerning the magic power of certain words should be lost—such as the miracles of volunteers and of the nation rising to arms. Already the latest happenings in Poland and in Italy had been supplying lessons in this sense, and Gambetta's "national defence," which caused armies upon armies to spring from the soil of France and yet was ineffectual to drive out the highly disciplined and technically prepared invader, wiped out the legend of the invincibility of popular and patriotic impetus, born from a somewhat fanciful military history of the great Revolution. But even the liberals were distressed by doubts of their own faith, because they no longer beheld before them one of those old régimes in which authority—poorly supported by relics of clerical and aristocratic cliques, deserted by men of intellect and culture, incapable of progress, reactionary and backward—revealed so that all might read its inferiority in the historical struggle. Instead they saw a state that had rejected popular government, based itself on authority, taken its rules only from above, and was obtaining such triumphs as no other state in Europe had the ability or the audacity to challenge; a state perfect in its mechanism and in its administrative work, and a people that was the best taught and the richest in knowledge and learning of all the peoples of the world, and before whom there was unfolding as well a vast field of activity in economic production and commerce. The idea arose that, to say the least, men had not given enough weight to the forces of history and tradition, and that they had perhaps destroyed and rebuilt on an abstract rationalistic basis, had certainly relied too much on criticism and thought; and that enthusiasm and the moral virtues had caused them to overlook the vital instinct and the will to power and the prodigies which at times issue from them; and that the religion of humanity which inspires and leads history had blinded them to the moment, inherent in it, of force. At other times, the tooth of doubt penetrated even deeper, and attacked the very principle of liberalism, the concept of liberty, causing it to totter.

This distress and these doubts might have been, indeed, transitory and without any positive effects. They could have been readily overcome by a personal application of the reprimand that is addressed to men of little faith and limited vision, and also by making a reasonable allowance for forgotten and neglected aspects of life that were now claiming attention, and also by reflecting that all is not gold that glitters, by noticing certain deficiencies and rifts in the vaunted greatness of Germany, and by voicing discreet doubts as to her future. But the energy to repair, the capacity to reconcile, that were needed to this end began just at this time to diminish or to disappear at the very source where they should have been sought for, in the circle of the moral sciences or moral phi-

losophy, whichever one may choose to call it. All that had
been achieved by the liberal and national organization of European society, by the end of ecclesiastical and absolutist-
monarchical oppression, by the possibility to draw breath and
the faculty to move and work and act according to inspiration
and vocation, by progressive and orderly political development instead of ruinous and fearful quakes and upheavals—
all this had been in closest relation with the idealistic and
historical thought that had matured in the first decades of the
century, and which had now taken shape and was living in its
institutions. But if the waters had bathed and fertilized the
earth, which had been covered with a good harvest, the source
from which they had sprung had been gradually growing less
and was now almost dry. Where was the great philosophy and
the historiography that it inspired in Europe around 1870?
Of the first, no trace, or imitations at best; of the second, a
few last vigorous offshoots. The place held by philosophy and
historiography had been gradually taken by Science, who had
finally seated herself upon its throne as crowned queen. However, natural science, with its complement of mathematics
and mechanics, was still the daughter or at least the grand-
daughter of thought; and this usurpation by its methods of
the place that belonged rightfully to philosophico-historical
thought may have caused a distortion in the mind and directed it towards a sort of new illuminist abstractism, but did
not of itself give rise, practically, to any further harm than
a few Utopias or a few simplifying proposals and hopes, like
several that were seen and such as can still be met with today
in minds that reason in this fashion: as, for instance, in H. G.
Wells, when he writes in his widely diffused *Outline of History* that "all the diplomatic fussing, posturing and schem-
ing, all the intrigue and bloodshed of these years, all the
monstrous turmoil and waste of kings and armies, all the
wonderful attitudes, deeds, and schemes of the Cavours,

Bismarcks, Disraelis, Bonapartes and the like 'great men,' might very well have been avoided altogether had Europe but had the sense to instruct a small body of ordinarily honest ethnologists, geographers, and sociologists to draw out its proper boundaries and prescribe suitable forms of government in a reasonable manner."

The important fact that presented itself at this time was different and more complicated, and is to be attributed not to science but still to philosophy, not to natural science, but to naturalism, that is, to a hasty and poorly reasoned philosophy, and consisted of this: that science, as it is established, considers and should not consider anything but force or forces, without any moral or aesthetic or intellectual qualification, physical force or vital force, and must treat it deterministically in order to measure it and give it laws; and that the philosophy of this time transported this scientific concept of force to the summit of the life of the spirit and made it the fountain-head of it. From this followed the philosophical pseudo-theories, more or less mechanistic, and the pseudo-hermeneutics of history at the basis of these fanciful theories, and therefore, by a sort of sympathetic correspondence between theory and practice, the elevation to an ideal of simple and abstract energy and vitality as the law of the strongest and the value of action quâ action and of fact quâ fact. Darwinism at this time provided a conspicuous exemplification of this transition from a few simple observations and conjectures of natural science to a general interpretation of life, reality, and history, and in the end to a dictation of practical living and to a supreme rule of conduct. Another example is the theory of races, constructed at that time by Gobineau and others with him, which converted a few very empirical naturalistic classifications into real entities, and conferred upon one or the other of these entities the right to dominate society and history.

At this period, historiography was either gradually declining to simple erudition or philologism or else assuming the shape of historical determinism, from one cause or another or from a variety of naturalistic causes; even the history of literature, with Taine, was being resolved into the constant effects of "race" and "surroundings" and into the variable effects of "moment"; and the philosophy of art as spiritual creation no longer found room in the culture of the times or, if it put in an appearance, was received with mockery. Russian nihilism might have remained a manifestation of the particular and singular life of Russia, but took on European significance inasmuch as it was an extreme and mad form of the premises posited by European naturalism. It was incapable of understanding the spiritual life and the formations of history, and therefore in turn inclined to accept them all on the same footing and indifferently as inevitable and irremovable effects of given causes, or to deny them all because all of them, looked upon in this fashion—not as works born from within but as impositions coming from without—appeared to be unjustified and irrational and to invite to rebellion. Reactionaries and anarchists, because of this identity of mental premises, were able to join hands and sometimes did, without any offence to logic. "Ideas" and "ideals" were discredited (and this fact was often noted and seen as a motive for congratulation); and man, through the efficacy of the naturalistic philosophy that had prevailed, felt himself attached to facts, urged on by facts, but lowered in his feeling for liberty, enriched with scientific notions and laws but robbed of his own spiritual law, shut out from the knowledge of the meaning and value of human life. Liberty demands ideas and ideals, and the infinite sky, and the background of the universe, not as extraneous to man but as the very spirit that thinks and works within him and joyfully creates ever new forms of life. Naturalism and determinism and practical materialism are its enemies, just as they are the friends of absolutism and despotism of every kind.

Even European economic activity, the immense development of which we have noted, concurred in lowering in men's minds the moral life and with it this feeling for liberty; not indeed because, as is commonly said, it produces effeminacy and flabbiness by means of prosperity and comfort, but on the contrary because it hardens and creates the habit of so great unilateral tension as to hinder the harmonic development of all the faculties, that "harmony" in which the Greeks justly placed man's nobility and healthfulness. When the great political battles were over, the new generations, and even the old patriots and combatants, devoted themselves to business; and competition and the struggle for markets, in their turn, helped to suggest the primacy of energy, force, practical capacity, over ethical and rational motives. The great economic prosperity that was supposed to supply new and plentiful gifts to the work of human ideality seemed, on the contrary, ready to suffocate it; and what Marx had said of modern capitalism, that it would not be able to dominate the productive forces that it had let loose, did in a certain sense and to a certain measure come true, not in the economic but in the moral world.

And yet another one of Marx's previsions was verified, although in a manner different from what he had intended: namely, that all society would continue to divide itself with growing precision into capitalist nuclei and the working masses, into plutocracy and proletariat; because, in fact, the interests of the industrials and those of the working-class, the demands of the first and the needs of the second, and the conflicts between them and the expedients that were resorted to in order to compose them, began to come ever more into the foreground. On one side parliamentarians devoted more and more attention to economic questions, and on the other

what was known as the middle class—which is not, to begin
with, a class at all, but is drawn from and rises above all the
economic classes as the peculiar representative of spiritual
values, and therefore as mediator and harmonizer and inte-
grator of the battling economic classes whether they are at
war with one another or at peace—was growing poorer. And
it was the least evil that, as these politicians no longer were
endowed with the passion, the vocation, and the preparation
in which they had once been so rich, this class supplied for
the moment lawyers and other professional men who could
be sent into the parliaments. And yet, where were the forces
of resistance and equilibrium still to be found, if not in this
intellectual middle class? And what possibility was there
then, or will there ever be, of rekindling and strengthening
and increasing those forces, if not by means of that class?
There was not the slightest hope that these forces could come
from the old religions and their churches, because the Catholic Church, although still continuing to render certain services, was incapable of invention and renovation; and the
others still less. Of the Church of England it has been noted
that although it still showed at this time a certain familiarity
with questions of canon law and ecclesiastical property, it had
no part in the moral reforms of English society, nor in those
of the penal laws, nor in those others which provided for
hygiene and the education of the people, nor in those which
tempered the harshness of economic competition with laws
regulating labour.

Literature is also a good mirror here, because this was the
period when realism and naturalism, "verism," were born,
and the programme of an art as impersonal as natural science.
Novels and dramas were no longer patriotic or socialist or
humanitarian, but sociological and physiological and pathological, in flagrant opposition to the literature of the first half
of the century. Because of this opposition, it was said that

romanticism was finished; and finished it certainly was, and gone out of fashion, in its theoretic and positive acceptation, like that romanticism which is identical with philosophical and historical idealism and spiritualism, and which therefore follows their destinies, and rises again (for it cannot help rising again) in absolute unity with them. The natural sciences and the naturalistic conception had won the upper hand in literature and art, which expressed this triumph.

But the other romanticism, which we have distinguished from the first, the sentimental, practical, and moral (and in this respect unhealthy) one, which, especially after 1840, had in general calmed down and been chastened and changed into severer behaviour and into civil and political activity, received new life from this same naturalistic conception. This was the time when a philosophy came into vogue to which half a century before, when it had first appeared in the world, nobody had wanted to listen, considering it a not very profound rehash of things already thought by others, directed towards the non-philosophical end of a capricious and sterile negation of life—the philosophy of Schopenhauer. It created a school and aroused imitators and had its bards, for it was consonant with the times in its basis, which was in the blind unsaturable will. It offered a conclusion, welcome to less elevated minds, in the renunciation of willing, which was at the same time a renunciation of the duty of ceaseless seeking and unwearying activity, and a fictitious purification in the impurity of idle indifferentism, decorated with the name of asceticism and mysticism and Buddhism and Orientalism. Beside this pessimism, another form of reawakened romanticism, which came from the same naturalistic vision, turned with eagerness to sensual exasperation and ecstasy, in which it hoped to satisfy the unsated discontent by which it was spurred. This it idolized as Beauty, a beauty utterly different from that in which the smiling joy of life can be found, because the image in which it was pictured was, on the contrary, that of sad and bitter sensuality, of decay and death, and was tinged with Satanism and sadism. These men were very far both from the Faust-like impetus of the first romantics and from their dreams of sublimated love and the fusion of souls. And far from the day-dreams of the earlier romanticists of a life all art and poetry was their neurosis for words, for colour, for rhythm and verse taken for themselves, for the hermetic and esoteric forms, for the sophisticated daintiness that delighted and tormented several of the neo-romantics. And in all of them reigned supreme the disgust of politics, of party feeling, of social struggles, of parliamentary debates, of newspapers, of all the manifestations of practical activity. They no longer dreamed even of the ingenuous mediaeval and religious and chivalrous life, and Ruskin, who did, and who in opposition to industrialism adored craftsmanship, and in opposition to factories, cathedrals, and in opposition to railways, the adventurous voyages and the pilgrimages of times long gone, was a belated romantic of the first age.

The imagination of the neo-romantics looked to the Italy of the Borgias and the Byzantium of Theodora rather than to the legendary Rhine for symbols of the sensuality, the sadism, the Satanism, that raged in their souls. Turned thus back on themselves and torturing themselves, they felt no interest in the human memories of history or in the spectacles of consoling or religious or mysterious Nature. In the verses, the fragments, and the confessions of Baudelaire, the books and letters of Flaubert, the journals of the De Goncourts, and in other works not only of French literature in particular but in that of England as well, you will find such states of mind. In the greatest of these writers, men to whom the nobility of sorrow was not unknown, these sometimes had their poetic catharsis, and then the way was truly opened to Beauty. In

Italy similar but less intense manifestations were noted between 1860 and 1870, during the very years when Venice and Rome were being aimed at, and when Giosuè Carducci was flinging out his political iambics. And men then spoke once more, as they had spoken before and as later those who have nothing better to do and to think have spoken again, of the "decadence of Europe," with a feeling directly opposed to the general belief of the nineteenth century, the "century of progress." But it is more characteristic of the neo-romantics that decadence was very frequently transformed from a negative to a positive concept and from an anti-ideal to an ideal. They not only preferred those Latin poets of the decadence whom in the preceding generation Nisard had analyzed in order to set forth and to censure the romantic style and in whom they now enjoyed sensations and nerve-vibrations and corresponding images that were not to be found in the great and classical poets, but they adorned their own age with the name of "decadent," delighted to consider themselves as such, and gave this name to some of their schools of poetry; and so, through this quality of romanticism, the name of "decadence" has come into use.

This apparent arrest or regression with regard to the thought, the feelings, the ideals, and the political activity of the preceding fifty years will seem incomprehensible only to those who do not consider or do not keep clearly in mind that not even liberty is an *ergon* but an *energeia*, and, like thought, always has a new matter, often knotty and stubborn, with which it must struggle in order to overcome it and to mould it, and so it may often seem that it is dominated by it. What was this naturalism and positivism and materialism which followed on the idealism and spiritualism of the earlier philosophy? Not the destruction of the indestructible truths of that philosophy, but the alternations of the attempts that were made to solve the new problems born from these truths, and at the same time the remains of problems not well solved, which in this way took their revenge. And what was the politics of sheer force, which towered with an air of crushing superiority in front of the liberal conception, if it was not the reflection of the belated and incomplete liberal and political formation of a great people whose capacities and virtues had been historically directed and employed for this end and now occasioned this boast of superiority? And what was the tumultuous impetus of economic activity if it was not, on one hand, the product of European civilization, and on the other, the ill-regulated relation between this product and the other parts of this civilization, which had now grown overponderous, whence resulted the stimulus to regulate it and, above all, to oppose it with forces of another quality that might restrain its excesses and lead it back between the banks and to the bed in which it ought to flow? And in the deplored falling-off of moral enthusiasm and in the incipient disaffection for the ideal of liberty, was it not necessary to assign its part to the natural rhythm of effort and fatigue, to the "Church triumphant," which has less vigour than the "Church persecuted" and which therefore demands watchful solicitude in order to go back perpetually from the *ergon* to the *energeia*, from what is done to what is to be done?

And the fact was, meanwhile, that the national organization of the states, even if not entirely accomplished, and liberal institutions, even if they were variously graded, were by this time in almost all Europe an acquisition that had cost many labours, and an assured possession. If the spirit gave a few signs of weariness and trouble, the body, so to speak, was solidly built and continued on its path of growth and healthy physiological life. It is a conflict between spirit and flesh or, to drop the metaphor, a conflict at times latent and at times manifest between two different ideals, in which the history that follows unfolds itself, and which might in a certain sense be called the history of the varied interweaving of the Cavourian ideal with the Bismarckian, and of their complications and transmutations and, as they admitted new elements within themselves, their development into new phases.

IX. THE LIBERAL AGE (1871-1914)

DURING the period that followed 1870 Europe beheld no
more revivals of old absolute monarchies or explosions
of new Caesarisms. There were not many attempts at such
things and not even many who dreamed of them, and a few
threatening clouds that appeared were scattered, leaving the
skies clearer than before.

The country that, in common opinion and judged by the
facts of its last eighty years of history, was held to be that
of extreme happenings and incapable of the orderly life of
liberty, France, established and confirmed her republic, born
from military disasters, with firm resolution and supreme
shrewdness. From these eighty years, during which she had
experienced the most varying and opposed régimes and had
vainly sought for the point of equilibrium, France derived
not the final perdition that many feared and that her enemies
hoped, but the experience that placed her on the right path,
upon which she entered as though by force of events—another
sign that it was the right path. The Third Republic, the "conservative" republic or the republic "without republicans," as
Thiers (with the authority of his long and personal experience) defined it, that is, without that kind of republicans of
1848 who had led to the ruin of the Second, entered upon
the scene with all the appearance of being temporary, but in

fact proved that it was lasting and not to be replaced by any other form. During its first period, it had to overcome the insurrection of the Commune of Paris, a convulsive movement of men who were conquered but armed and not resigned, in which absurd federalistic ideas rose again to the surface, as well as tendencies towards a social republic that were in travail. Then it had to avoid the monarchical restoration, which would have brought back unstable and intolerable conditions and the repetition of evils already overcome. France was saved from this danger by the legitimist pretender, the Comte de Chambord, who through his obstinacy in demanding as a condition for his return to the throne of his fathers the white banner of the Bourbons, made it quite clear what such a return would have implied, and helped to measure the abyss that had opened between the past and the present.

But the Republic had also to overcome the other danger of becoming too conservative and rigid because of the fear of the "radicals," as they were called, and because of the over-hanging images of 1793, 1848, and 1871, and therefore constitutional and not parliamentary—to conquer it with monarchical authority conferred on its president and with power actually in the hands of the military and the clericals. That is how MacMahon tried more than once to establish it during his presidency and with the various cabinets that he called into the fray, until he himself gave way and left a free course to what could not be avoided, and at last resigned (1879). Great was the disappointment of all those who had hoped for a *coup d'état* from him; whereas the new president, Grévy, declared in his first message that he was "sincerely obedient to the great parliamentary law" and in order to prove that there was no longer any cause to fear radicalism or revolutions, transferred the parliament from Versailles back to Paris.

Twice again the danger of, or the tendency to, a reactionary *coup d'état* was renewed in France, and both times it was frustrated. The first was between 1886 and 1889, with Boulanger, the general who was acclaimed by the masses, who looked to his success for the *"revanche"* against Germany and for that redemption from political and all other evils that the crowd is always hoping for. In the uncertainty of his concepts and plans, it would seem that Boulanger more or less consciously, and pushed rather than pushing, tended to something not unlike the Second Empire; and the old philosopher and politician, Jules Simon, who remembered the disgrace of that Second Empire, was quick to remind the forgetful people of France in a book that he called *Souviens-toi du Deux Décembre* (1889). Although in 1888 Boulanger obtained a clamorous electoral success and in January of the following year was elected in Paris, the statesmen of France flung their disdain and contempt in his face, terming him a "music-hall Saint-Arnaud" (the general of the Second of December) and a "Bonaparte without the Italian campaign." He himself lacked the spirit to march with his fanatics against the seat of government, so that he ended by undergoing trials and convictions and was obliged to seek refuge in Belgium, where he took his own life. The second time was ten years later, in the long struggle over the case of Captain Dreyfus and the justice or injustice of his condemnation. This struggle, under the appearance of a juridical or moral question, included a new offensive and defensive of republican institutions. For the ranks of the anti-Dreyfusards and anti-Semites were strengthened, and their political party was supported, not only by Boulanger's old adherents, but also by reactionaries, royalists, and great numbers of priests and monks and all the clericals, who by cheering the army thought they could excite it against the Republic. But they were nobly opposed by the union of all the republican and socialist forces; and when Dreyfus had been freed from imprisonment and his

innocence had been recognized by law, the reactionary movement was repressed and the liberal order issued from the fight
not only intact but strengthened and combative, as could be
seen from the work to which the victorious party now set their
hands and which was not so much a labour of revenge for
the past as of wise precaution for the future.

In rival Germany, the abolition or restriction of liberty
was borne in mind by the very creator of the empire, Bismarck, who did not regard as definitive the constitution that
he had given her with a national parliament and universal
suffrage. These were political expedients to which he had resorted and not things in sympathy with his ideal, which was
still monarchical absolutism, with the addition of his own
omnipotence as chancellor. At every obstacle or hindrance or
annoyance that he encountered in the parliament, his mind
ran, as to its immediate remedy, to the extreme measure of a
coup d'état: this can be seen in his letters, especially in those
written between 1878 and 1882, in which he speaks of the
Germans who are unable to handle the "Nuremberg toy" that
has been given to them and are spoiling it, and in which he
says of the German constitution that the moment will come
when it will be necessary to apply the phrase uttered by
Schwarzenberg at Olmütz concerning the Austrian constitution of 1849, that it was "an institution that had not shown up
well." He is forever insisting that the one thing in Germany
that is substantial and able to stand firm is the German
princes, and that it will eventually be they who must one day
decide whether it is not better to make an end once and for
all and to return to the ancient federal diet, preserving the
customs and the military union, but getting rid of the parliament.

During the last years of his chancellorship, he placed his
hopes in the youth who was to become William II, who, diversely from his father, Prince Frederick, manifested an ex-

treme intolerance of parliamentary régimes, like a true "soldier of the Guards," the *"rocher de bronze"* of which Germany stood in need. But when this youth, the symbol of such great hopes, came to the throne, and when in 1890 Bismarck, once more irritated with the parliament, to his mind not sufficiently docile, set forth his ideas to the Emperor, namely, to present new demands to this assembly for army expenditures and a harsher law against the socialists, and, upon their easily foreseen refusal, to dissolve it two or three times, to deprive the socialists of electoral rights by abolishing the secret ballot, and in the last resort to turn to the cannon—he was not listened to by the new sovereign, who was at the time striving for the favour of the parliament and the people. And so Bismarck fell after thirty years of uninterrupted government. He had no party, no current of opinion, to support him; and this plan of his was the divagation of a solitary, capable of great things in diplomacy and war but not in the interpretation of the human soul and of the demands that it expresses according to the difference of the times. And when, in his retirement, hearing the words and studying the acts and gestures of the second William, he changed his opinion and his concept and took to saying and repeating that the path of salvation lay in "strengthening the efficacy of the parliament," that it was necessary that the parliament should "criticize, verify, admonish, and in certain cases guide the government," that in the past there had been "too much dictatorship" and too much repression of the national representation—with these belated reflections he showed what his robust mind had been lacking in and what had made him, the founder of the state, unadapted to the rôle of educator of peoples, and, first of all, of his own people, of which in this respect he was rather an un-educator.

For indeed, even if he did not get so far as to carry out his coup against universal suffrage and the parliament, he did succeed in keeping Germany in the constitutional phase, preventing her from passing into the parliamentary one. The liberal party, which during the first years of his ministry had got on its hind legs and attempted to withstand his domination, consented after the war of 1866 to support his foreign policy for national ends, hoping to obtain in return a different direction in his home policy. This support of the national liberals, who formed the strongest part of the parliament, continued after 1870, still encouraged by this hope, and allowed him to obtain the seven years' military service, to accomplish financial reform, and to combat the Catholic centre. Even Crown Prince Frederick did not hide his inclination towards the parliamentary method with ministerial responsibility, and judged that the present constitution of the Empire was "an artificially produced chaos." But when Bismarck turned to protective tariffs, and for these and for the repression of socialism counted on the support of the conservatives and made friends once more with the centre, his former allies were no longer of any use to him and stood in his way. He would not hear of the condition advanced by them for further collaboration, which was the entry into the Prussian cabinet of some of the liberal right and others of the left, or progressives, for he was irrevocably resolved not to take a step that might lead to party cabinets.

This would have been, moreover, impossible for him, since the old Prussia had not been merged in a liberal Germany, but on the contrary a more or less liberal Germany had been aggregated to Prussia, who preserved intact the character she had received in the reaction after 1848 of a monarchy that had merely granted a few constitutional concessions and of a parliament elected by the class system. This was the opposite process to what had happened in Italy, where a liberal Piedmont annexed an Italy that turned liberal and was fused with her. The base of the German Empire always remained

Prussia, and as late as 1898 one of Bismarck's successors, Chancellor von Hohenlohe, wrote in his diary that when he sat among the "Prussian Excellencies" he clearly discerned the contrast between South German liberalism and the feudalism of North Germany. The former was incapable of holding its own with the latter, "too numerous, too powerful, and having on its side the King, the army, and also the Catholic centre." In vain, and only by way of rhetorical vagueness, did some speak emotionally of the idyllic marriage or the friendly disagreement between the "two souls" of the Empire, that of Prussia and that of Germany, that of Potsdam and that of Weimar, whereas in fact only one soul was supreme, that of Prussia and Potsdam; and the statements of Bismarck, during the first years of the empire, that it was necessary not to "Prussianize" Germany but to "Germanize" Prussia, were simply fleeting fancies or expedients of the moment.

The detachment of the liberals from Bismarck, after the passage of the special laws against the socialists, marked the decadence of the party, which split into various fractions and was considerably reduced as to the number of its deputies. It did not, moreover, make up for its lack of numerical strength in the country by the vigour, the depth, the firmness, of its liberal faith. For not a few of its components were, rather than liberals in politics, free-traders, and expressed the needs of the German economy of their day; others among their more prominent representatives continued to assign the primacy to the state (that is, to one of the two terms of a single relation) and to conceive liberty in the form of rights granted or recognized by the state, and they exorcised parliamentarism as the Evil One, limiting the right of the chamber to administrative criticism and to opposition. Modest as the German parliament was in its activity, none the less Treitschke, one of the pre-1870 liberals who had gradually become more and more Bismarckian, feared that it might actually be guilty of an "excess of parliamentarism"! All German science and political writing, from Gneist and Laband to Jellinek, is affected by this sort of obtuseness in understanding what is proper and essential in the political concept of liberty; and it restricts itself in, and sometimes delights to toy with, juridical constructions of the "legal state," or tries to effectuate liberty formalistically in institutions such as those of so-called local autonomies, which were tried in Prussia in accordance with the ideas of Gneist. The outburst of liberty that had taken place in Germany in the year of revolutions, 1848, had passed away almost without a trace; and the Frankfort Parliament was so looked down upon and consigned to oblivion that no one remembered to celebrate its fiftieth anniversary in a country that had not neglected to erect a great monument to Arminius in the Teutoburger Wald. It is true that this parliament was to be remembered and again taken as a model in the days of misfortune.

In other nations the parliamentary system had either been formed long since, as in England, or had been introduced together with other liberal institutions, or had gradually in practice come to take the place of the more monarchical system of the original constitutions. When, for instance, in Italy between 1898 and 1900 the idea was conceived, and an attempt made to bring about, with the motto of a "return to the constitution," a certain reaction in the direction of the older form of government, the opposition that awoke was lively and universal. The parliament resorted to obstructionism, and the plan, dictated by the fear of movement or of too rapid movement, was thwarted, with the consequence (analogous to what at the same time, and amidst different circumstances, happened in France) of a more resolute tendency towards liberalism. European society was all leaning towards democracy, as the phrase went; it would have been better to say that it was issuing from the guardianship of restricted ruling groups, of the liberal aristocracy that had guided it through the revolutions and into the new state order, and was now forming a more varied and mobile political class of its own, such as was required by the great variety and mobility of interests that needed to be upheld and reconciled.

A manifestation, an instrument, of this ceaseless progression was the gradual extensions of the franchise, which in almost all the countries of Europe led up to universal suffrage. This in other times had been instituted or made use of from motives of conservation and reaction, and now served the opposite purpose, that of movement and progress. France had inherited it from the Second Republic and the Second Empire. After the reform of 1882, which quadrupled or quintupled the number of voters, Italy obtained it in 1912. Belgium, which still had the property system, adopted it in 1892, modified by the plural vote, and yet even with this multiplying tenfold the number of electors. Austria, who had already enlarged her franchise in 1896, resorted to universal suffrage in 1907, with the hope of putting down, together with the passions and the battles of the democracy and the working-class, the untamable conflicts between her manifold nationalities. And so on in the greater part of the other European states, including those of Germany (Baden in 1904, Bavaria and Württemberg in 1906), but not Prussia, who with the reform of 1893 had assured the predominance of the conservatives and the centre, and now contented herself with touching up the distribution of constituencies and with increasing by about ten the number of deputies. In Switzerland, the constitution was several times revised, and experiments were even made of direct government by the people, either as initiative or as referendum or as sanction. With the reform of 1885 England increased her electoral body by two and a half millions; but her greatest progress towards a popular régime was the preponderance, and even the absolute power, given to the House of Commons in relation to the House of Lords. This had been included in the programme announced in Gladstone's last speech, in 1894, and was the origin of a conflict that burst out on the occasion of an increased income-tax and lasted for about three years, from 1908 to 1911. In this the allies of the liberals were the working-men's representatives and the Irish, but they succeeded in their aim, for the House of Lords was deprived of the right to reject financial bills and all others that, after being rejected by them, the House of Commons should approve in three sessions in the course of two years.

Furthermore, more or less in every country salaries or indemnities for the representatives of the people were introduced. This was necessary, moreover, considering the transformation of the political class, which had formerly been drawn largely from the landowners and the upper middle class. The monarchies, which had survived in almost all the countries with parliamentary régimes, took on a very modest aspect, for the actual political impulse no longer came from that quarter; but they were surrounded with respect, inasmuch as they stood above the din of parties, custodians of common statutory liberties, and exerted a mediating and moderating function. Upon this tranquil scene of European monarchy Emperor William II's noisy entry, and the pomp with which he delighted to surround his regal power and his very person, awakened at first, because of their novelty, a mixed impression between a wonder that admired and a wonder that shook its head in doubt, which in the long run gave way to astonishment at a spectacle that smacked of carnival. Not without precedent, moreover, in Prussia, for as long as fifty years before Heine had satirized these parodies of the past and these mixtures *"von gothischem Wahn und modernem Lug"*—of Gothic folly and modern falsehood. But at last, although late, after repeated exaggerated gestures and dangerous utterances of this Emperor, and notably after the imprudent interview published in 1908 by the *Daily Telegraph*, even in Germany public opinion and the parliament underwent a revulsion of feeling; and he had to promise that he would observe more carefully the law of reserve and silence, which was the *lex regia* of latter times.

Since the form of liberal government, which had now become proper to the society of Europe, was considered a sign and condition of civilization, it was natural that the desire should be felt to see it put into force everywhere. And in the countries where it did not yet exist, the need for it was voiced; if it was not expressed spontaneously, it was imported or prompted by the example and political writings of Western and Central Europe. The great lacuna was still in Eastern Europe, in autocratic Russia and in oppressed Poland; and so European liberalism abhorred Czarism and did not cease to urge eagerly its fall or its reformation. Alexander II, as we have seen, had interrupted his labour of reform because of the Polish insurrection and also because of the political immaturity of the Russian people. This immaturity was manifested even in the behaviour of the Russian revolutionaries, who were imbued with the most extreme Occidental doctrines, which they carried to the delirium of universal destruction. They disdained and sneered at the few among their number who were not simply rationalizing but reasonable, and so they grew ever keener on the idea of leaping over the liberal or bourgeois era, as they called it, and carrying out in Russia either full communism or the paradise of anarchism: a leap that (to make its hidden meaning quite clear) was simply nothing but the wish to do without political and moral reform in order to achieve one that would be purely economic, with the moral and political problem solved only in so far as it would be submerged and denied in an economic or material-

istic mysticism. Women too had their fingers in this pie, of
whom many came from families of the nobility, fanciful and
overlogical, rebels, and, in the midst of all the instigation to
a mad hatred, not without outbursts of generosity and prepared for heroic sacrifice: women students who had been
abroad and perfected themselves in the councils of the *émigrés,* and now, obliged to return home, proposed to "go to
the people," to awaken the populace of the cities and still
more the peasants, and to arouse them to their plans of radical palingenesis—a task in which they reaped a scant harvest.

But at this time there were also founded among the revolutionaries secret societies for "propaganda through action,"
for terrorist attempts on the life of the Czar, the grand dukes,
the ministers, the governors, as justice and revenge for the
harshness and cruelty of the imperial police, as a protest
against the intolerable form of this state. This practice of
anarchical violence, which had begun even before 1870, grew
in frequency during the next decade, and some of these atrocities were famous, such as that of Vera Zasulich, which served
as example and stimulus to a series of others of like nature.
During the worst outbreak of these acts of terror, Loris-
Melikov, appointed governor of St. Petersburg and placed
at the head of a commission fitted out with dictatorial powers
for their repression, thought it might be possible to break
the chain of government terrorism and revolutionary terrorism; he advised the resumption of reform and, if not actually
a national parliament, a revival of the provincial parliaments,
a certain liberty of the press and political criticism, the con-
vocation of an assembly of notables, and the severest vigilance against the excesses and the caprices of those in power.

The Czar was accepting these proposals when on the very
day that he had received the report in which they were contained, March 13, 1881, he became the victim of a new at-

tempt added to all those that had been made on his person. Alexander III at once laid aside all idea of reform, reasserted rigid autocracy and Russophilism against all contamination of Western ideas, protected the Orthodox Church, opposing the others and persecuting the Jews, distrusted the universities and limited the number of students that might be admitted to them, purged the lists of jurors, and suffocated all life of the intellect, although he devoted great care to the economy of the country, which was replenished with loans obtained in Europe and especially in France, promoted commerce, which then began to flourish, and constructed the great Siberian Railway. The epidemic of terrorist attempts was gradually diminishing, from inner exhaustion, and might almost be said to be ended, since that method was replaced by the other now preached by Russian socialists who had passed from the school of Bakunin to that of Marx. Towards the end of the century there might be noted in Russia the rise of a new group, opposed to the ideas of the old Russians and with Western and liberal tendencies, and in the first years of the following century meetings and discussions were held even among the *émigrés*. At this period was outlined for the first time a democratic-constitutionalist party (or Cadets), whereas the socialists were divided into moderates and majoritarians (Bolsheviki).

But not even during the first decade of the new Czar, Nicholas II, were there any hints of a changed political direction, until the unfortunate war with Japan gave the impulse and, amidst acclamations and menaces, festivals and disorders, enthusiasm and crime, and other similar accompaniments of revolution, and with the no less customary hesitation and tergiversation on the part of the Government (which yielded bit by bit, and first promised reforms, and then consultative and at last legislative assemblies), in 1905 Russia had her first national parliament, or Duma, which opened in May,

1906. The danger lay in the contemporaneous concourse and interweaving of two movements of opposite nature, the political and the agrarian, destined to hamper one another in turn because, to mention nothing else, the most important and most capable group of the chosen deputies, the democratic-constitutionalist group, had included in its programme, in order not to be overwhelmed by the socialists, the expropriation of lands, but not without compensation. This prevented it from joining the other liberal but moderate groups. And the Government, which represented the régime of authority, declared itself in its turn the promoter of radical agrarian reforms, in order to increase the confusion of the parliament and weaken its authority. This resulted in two consecutive dissolutions of the Duma, followed by franchise laws of increasing limitations, which led to the third Duma, that of 1907, in which the conservatives had the upper hand, but which was not reactionary and accomplished the task of critizing the extremely dishonest public administration. The laws it voted were subject to the approval and amendment of the Imperial Council. On the other hand the minister Stolypin, opposed to the parliamentary but favourable to the constitutional system, put through the peasant bill, which dissolved still further the agricultural communities, facilitated the acquisition of lands on the part of individuals, and called into existence several millions of small landed peasant proprietors. And yet, notwithstanding the fundamental absolutism that still survived obstinately and the scanty respect for fundamental liberties, and the ever threatening danger of a withdrawal of the liberty that had been granted and of reaction, and the weak consistency of a truly liberal spirit in the Russian people, an embryo of free life had been formed even in Russia.

About the same time began, with the introduction no longer of military and other technical institutions alone but with

that of Western liberal forms, the new history of Turkey.
The Committee for Union and Progress was formed and demanded the effectuation of the constitution that had been announced by the Sultan thirty years before, in 1877, when
he wanted to hoodwink the powers and the peoples of Europe.
In 1908 the Young Turks imposed, by the force of revolt,
the opening of a parliament of the people of Turkey, including the various nationalities, with two hundred and fifty
deputies, of which about forty were Christians and a few were
Jews. This parliament too, amidst attempts at counter-revolu-
tion and *coups d'état* and violence of all sorts, endured substantially; a copious political press flourished in Turkey, and
a sort of separation of Church and State was begun, which
dissociated the political personality of the Turk from that of
the Islamite. And with regard to the efficacy that the dominating state-form of Europe had over the whole world, it
suffices to remember that Japan, obliged to come out of her
close isolation by the work of the United States and England,
and rapidly learning the new customs, passed in the space of
a few years from feudalism to administrative monarchy, and
from this, in 1890, to constitutional monarchy on the German
model, with the addition of an opposition that tended to urge
it further forward, from the German to the English model.

To be sure, the mere institutional and juridical form, although it has its importance, is not enough to mark a people's
grade of liberty and not even to ensure the real existence of
this liberty, because some forms are empty and others are so
little or so strangely filled as to give rise to the phrase "apparent parliamentarism," the definition that was at first given to
that of Russia and to the different variety, but similar in this
respect, of the Young Turks. Even more or less extended or
even universal suffrage tells us nothing about the breadth and
the depth of liberalism, since in certain cases there is a
greater degree of liberal feeling and habit and action in coun-

tries with a narrower franchise than in others where it is
broadest, and since, as we have mentioned, many times universal suffrage is very dear to the enemies of liberty, feudalists, priests, kings, and popular leaders or adventurers.
England had a more restricted suffrage than France or Italy
or even Germany, with conditions laid on voters of having
to own a house or to have a certain income represented by the
amount of rent paid, and other similar requisites; and yet her
life of liberty was not inferior to that of France and Italy,
and was certainly far superior to that of Germany. Spain had
a very broad franchise and none the less her politics were directed by the King, who leaned on the army and the clergy,
and not much difference was made by the alternation in power
of the Canovas and the Sagastas, the moderates and the progressives, while the world of culture had no authority or
strength and remained in great part academic and rhetorical.

In Austria, the parliamentary squabbles were related not
to the intensity of political activity but to the jealousies and
hates between the nations of the empire, and over all these
conflicts what really ruled was what was known as the Austrian spirit, that of the court nobility and functionaries, and
for long periods the government was, under the appearance
of parliamentarism, absolutist. In Hungary the Magyars
dominated, often in absolute fashion, with limitations of the
right of association and speech, restriction or corruption of
the press, royal commissaries in the municipalities, and so
forth, and when the electorate was reformed in 1913, provision was made to do it in such a manner that the power
should not slip from the hands of the Magyar minority. The
reality of the free life of a people really lies in the force
exerted by public opinion and in the quality of the political
class that directs the people. And how great was the love of
country and of state, how great the audacity in undertaking
or in accepting the innovations that were demanded for the

advancement of the people, how great the sagacity and prudence of the political class of England, of France, of Italy
from Cavour to Giolitti, would deserve to be particularly
illustrated, for use in instruction, as a duty of gratitude, and
also as an expiation for the unjust judgments that unbridled
party passion has often expressed concerning these men, the
contumely and the calumny with which they were assailed,
the superficiality with which, for various evils not always
avoided or avoidable and because of so-called scandals that
followed them (the Panama, the Banca Romana, and so
forth), a sort of distrust and discredit was thrown over whole
political classes that were nobly doing their own duty.

Singular in this respect was the condition of the German
people, perhaps the best educated and the most orderly and
hard-working in all Europe, which profited by the new unity
and power Germany had risen to in order to give a marvellous development to her industry, commerce, science, technique, doctrine, and culture of every kind. And yet, although
it was able to produce from its midst a class of capable and
upright administrators and bureaucrats and another of ex-
ceedingly valorous soldiers (according to the Prussian tradition of bureaucracy and militarism), it was unable to form
a real political class. The scarcity of political sense in the
Germans was noted at this time by Germans themselves, who
wondered at this curious lack amid the excellence of all the
rest. But only later was the gravity of this want understood
or any attempt made to submit it to adequate analysis and
aetiology. There were no end of savants and professors, with
that peculiar air of limitation and ingenuousness and often
of credulity and puerility in judging practical and public
things which is the characteristic of their intellect and of their
mode of life; they were delighted with the strong words and
gestures of Bismarck, and the *"Oderint dum metuant,"* the
"We Germans fear God and naught else in the world" of the

speech of 1888. In their histories they glorified the "hard men of blood" who had, according to them, tempered Germany; they contributed to cultivate on the lips of the German Philistine the so-called *Sedanlächeln*, the smile of Sedan, the sentiment of superiority over other peoples, the contempt for the decadent or decayed Latin races, for their moral corruption, for their miserable parliamentary battles, even for England, land of spurious Germanism, nation of shopkeepers and not of warriors. Their literature abounded in theories concerning the state, in contrast with the frugality in this respect of the English and the poverty of the Americans, who, as Bryce wrote, had no use for theories on the subject but were satisfied with founding their constitutional ideas on law and history.

Bismarck had no regard for the professors and made fun of them freely, reminding them ironically that "politics is not an exact science, as the Herren Professoren think"; but he had certainly not laboured to create or prepare another political class by means of parliamentary debates, party struggles, alternation in power, lively exchanges between the people and its representatives. Indeed, as Max Weber showed in an examination of conscience to which with lofty civic sense he subjected his people, Bismarck let politics descend from above, through the faithful and sedulous bureaucracy, the execution of the thought and will of a chancellor, be he very great or very small, and of an emperor, be he very wise or very unwise. Even the little group of politicians who had passed through the experiences of 1848, and through the more recent ones of the Prussian parliament after 1860, were set aside, and as their ranks were gradually reduced by retirement or death found no successors. And so a new generation of statesmen came upon the scene, whose figures have recently been shown to us in the memoirs of Von Bülow. He himself, the third successor of Bismarck in the chancellorship, was

typical of them in his peculiar unconsciousness of what constitutes the function of one who governs the destinies of a
people or of the responsibility that he assumes towards his
fellow-citizens and towards history. The only parties that in
any way preserved their political physiognomy were, fortunately, those that Bismarck persecuted and wished to extir-
pate, the Catholic centre and the socialists, who had a faith
and an idea of their own, did not obey the beck and call of
the Government, and did not relapse into mere representatives
in the parliament of the interests of agriculture and industry,
or of this or that branch of industry.

Bismarck's persecution of German Catholics has been con-
nected with the danger that he scented in them as the survivors of the Austrian and anti-Prussian party in Germany,
with the awkwardness that they could create or cause to be
created for him by means of the Catholic clergy in Posen,
with their relations with the Guelph or Hanoverian party,
and with their obedience to the extra-national power of the
Papacy, which led them, sooner even than the French legitimists, to put pressure on the new empire in favour of military intervention with a view to restoring the temporal power
in Rome. But perhaps none of these motives, and not even all
of them taken together, justify the form assumed by Bismarck's repression, unless we take somewhat into account
anger, which is an evil counsellor, and that inebriation which
accompanies omnipotence and ends by not seeing the limits
that this has in the very nature of things. In December, 1871,
he desired to have inserted in the penal code a special para-
graph dealing with the abuse of the pulpit for political ends;
he abolished the division of Catholic affairs in the Prussian
ministry; he presented a plan for a bill for supervision over
Catholic schools. In 1872 he dissolved the Jesuit houses and
congregations related to them and expelled non-German Jesuits. With the laws of May, 1873, he prescribed university

study for the preparation of Catholic ecclesiastics, and for their appointment, the presentation of their names to the presidents of the provinces; he created a royal tribunal for ecclesiastical affairs; he regulated the disciplinary and corrective law of the Church. In 1874, he made civil marriage obligatory, extended the Prussian law concerning civil status to the whole Empire, made legal provision for the internment or expulsion of ecclesiastics who had been deposed and were still carrying out the functions of their office. In 1875 he cancelled the articles of the Prussian constitution concerning the liberty of the Church, deprived bishops and parish priests of their subsidies if they did not submit to his laws and decrees, abolished all orders and congregations except those for the care of the sick; in 1876 he presented a bill concerning ecclesiastical property. But the Catholics, under this downpour of laws and provisions against their Church, gathered together around their clergy and bishops, who allowed themselves to be deposed and persecuted without ever giving way, and the Catholic societies increased and the Catholic press received a new impetus and greater diffusion; meanwhile the Pope, from Rome, inveighed and condemned. Bismarck lost his head to such a degree that he asked the Italian Government to account for the words and acts of the Pope, who in the liberty of the Vatican could not be bent by him and made to toe the mark, as he might have been in other times, by the threat of a battleship or of a landing at Civitavecchia. And he encountered not only the *fin de non recevoir* of the Italian statesmen, but their smiles at the rage and inexperience with which he had entered into a quarrel with priests, who have to be handled differently.

In fact, Bismarck himself gradually realized that he had got into a blind alley; and while reflection took the place of his anger and bullying, not only had his original causes for alarm at the Austriophile, Hanoverian, Polish, and papal

Catholics disappeared, but he began to feel the need of aid
from the Catholic centre to add to the German conservatives
for the detachment that he was planning from the national-
liberals, of whom he had made use so far. So that he who
had declared that he would never "go to Canossa," did go,
and in 1880 opened negotiations with the nuncio, and then
in 1882 recalled almost all of the deposed bishops and miti-
gated the laws he had emanated. After this, gradually, in the
course of a decade, all this war legislation disappeared, or
only a few fragments of it survived, such as the civil status
and the cancellation of the articles in the Prussian constitution of 1850 relating to the Catholics; and he thus offered
a clear proof of the uselessness and infeasibility of the end
towards which this persecution had been directed. Bismarck
then said that the question of principle remained unsolved
and that "the hoary question between priests and king had
not yet reached its final conclusion in Germany"; for he was
unable to conceive it in any other terms than in those antiquated terms of royal authority and ecclesiastical authority.
But he had allowed the complaisant Prussian professors to
decorate it, on the other hand, with the name of *Kulturkampf*
or "fight for civilization," a denomination that the Catholics
sarcastically turned into the other of "fight against civilization." And they were not altogether wrong, because to fight
conscience with violence is not civilization; nor, on the other
hand, in Germany, a country with many religions, in which
the Catholics are more than a third of the population, and a
country of flourishing culture where the authority of science
and criticism is great, was there any necessity for waging a
special and harsh warfare in favour of civilization.

A more genuine *Kulturkampf* was then being fought in
Catholic countries, a struggle begun more than a century before by their absolute monarchies, which gradually liberated
the state from subjection to theocratic bonds, and carried on

by liberal governments with the consciousness—which there could not have been in those monarchies—of the true nature of the conflict, which tended to substitute culture for culture, thought for thought, or, as we may say here, religion for religion. In this task of substitution violence was excluded, not only because of its recognized inefficacy and futility in spiritual things, but because of the accepted principle of liberty, which had to be preserved at all costs, even by temporary remissions in dealing with the adversary and temporary acceptance of his supremacy. Without doubt, free discussion and propaganda were not always enough, because the obstacles set up by social groups and by the alliances that the Church formed with the forces of uncouth ignorance often made it necessary to pass into the field of more directly practical and political action. Still, in all this great prudence and delicacy were required in order not to pluck up with the evil the good, or parts and germs of good. This can be clearly seen, to give a few examples, in difficulties concerning religious instruction in elementary schools, where, by introducing purely lay and illuministic instruction, the risk is run in certain cases of entering into strident conflict with the home and maternal education of the children and of upsetting the authority of the parents; or in other difficulties concerning divorce, where resistance of a religious character is joined to, or alternates with, other kinds due to reverence for the institution of the family and to a noble desire to bridle excessive or egoistic individualism even at the cost of sacrificing individual happiness. And the same thing may be repeated, in general, for all that concerns more or less superstitious and fanatical popular customs, which should be corrected or respected, prohibited or tolerated, as the case may be. Nor is, in certain particular cases, a rigorous and radical procedure to be excluded; but if it is to succeed in its purpose, the other side must have worked, with indiscretion and disregard for moral sentiments, to prepare the favourable conditions and to justify their employment.

This process, which was called secularization, is to be observed at that time in Italy, who, in her formation as a unitary and liberal state, had taken from the Pope the temporal power, no longer defended by the better elements of Catholicism and grown, because of the behaviour of the papal government, an object of universal execration, and had carried to accomplishment the reforms that had not yet been perfected by the old monarchies or before which they had paused: abolition of the ecclesiastical tribunal and other privileges of the clergy, suppression of convents and monasteries and confiscation of ecclesiastical property, exclusion of theological instruction from the universities, and so forth; and an increasing modernization of education and culture.

In all this Italy was aided by the resolution reached, half in spite and half in hope, by the Church to draw to one side, with her flock, out of Italian public life, prohibiting Catholics from being elected or from voting in political elections and allowing them to take part only in municipal and provincial elections and in local administration. This prevented the possibility of a Catholic or clerical party in the Italian chamber, a fact that may have influenced political calculations because of votes given or denied to ministries; and it allowed greater liberty in dealing with the Holy See, relations with whom remained under the law known as that of the Guarantees, as well as in all measures of an ecclesiastical nature or dealing with public education. Much later, after more than thirty years, when all hopes for the disintegration of the Italian state or for its humiliation by foreign armies had been lost—hopes long nourished by Pius IX and even more by Leo XIII—when the defeat of the Papacy in this respect was made definitive and evident by the visit paid by the president of the French Republic, Loubet, to Rome

(1904), the new Pope, Pius X, came to a semi-official agreement with the Italian Government and removed the veto laid on Catholics, several of whom made an appearance as deputies in the parliament, although without for the moment constituting a party. In the course of the last forty years, a great task had been accomplished and remained as a solid basis: the critical spirit had grown more robust and more widespread, and the superiority of lay thought and learning had grown so great that even the clergy frequented state universities in order to obtain the right preparation for science and teaching. With the decrease in clericalism, anticlericalism too no longer found a fruitful soil and was reduced to petty warfare with the lower elements of clericalism; and it seemed as though men might hope for the further extension of lay culture from the peaceful course of things, from the acts that were being performed, and from the books that were being written and which everyone was reading, which certainly were not those of the priests.

France had to carry on a much longer task and make a far greater effort, because the clericals, who during the Second Empire had for a long time been complete masters, during the first years of the Third Republic, when they thought a legitimist restoration was imminent, behaved as though they had already returned to the days of Charles X, celebrated an orgy of processions and pilgrimages, protested in favour of the Pope against Italy and its ecclesiastical legislation, and demanded a war to give Rome back to him. This was tolerated or encouraged under the presidency of MacMahon, when De Broglie repressed the converse anticlerical and antitemporal manifestations, and prohibited purely civil funerals as being "scenes of impiety." Many obstacles to the establishment of the parliamentary Republic came from the clericals, who spurred MacMahon on to a *coup d'état*, while Monsignor Dupanloup advised him in religious and ecclesiastical affairs.

Thus the solidification of the parliamentary Republic and the fight against clericalism went on hand in hand, and in 1875 Gambetta once more uttered the cry that had echoed ten years before—"clericalism which is the real enemy." The radicals demanded at that early date the separation of State and Church, and meanwhile in 1877 the parliament voted an imperative resolution against ultramontanist manifestations. There followed in 1879 the decrees for the dissolution and the dispersion of the Jesuits and of unauthorized congregations; in 1881, elementary instruction, which as a result of the Falloux law was still in the hands of friars and monks, was secularized and made obligatory and free, while at the same time lay instruction for girls was instituted; in 1882, the "neutrality" of the school was announced, which was doubtless (as Simon pointed out) a "myth," but a myth for the commemoration of the religion of thought and criticism, substituted for that of revelation and miracles; in 1886, it was prescribed that teachers should be secular.

Quite vain to prevent the pursuit of this path was Leo XIII's recognition, at the advice of Cardinal Lavigerie, of the Republic. Although the Pope gave up his old legitimist allies, he none the less did not succeed in his cherished purpose, "*accepter la constitution pour changer la législation.*" The catastrophe was precipitated by the attack on the Republic at the hands of the Catholics in the Dreyfus question and by the attitude displayed in it by the Roman curia. This ferocious hypocrisy, in which the words of Caiaphas seemed to be heard once more from the lips of priests: "*Expedit ut unus moriatur homo pro populo,*" infuriated the civilized world. This clerical rage under the mask of patriotism and nationalism opened the eyes of the republicans; so that after the defeat of the anti-Dreyfusards, the congregation of the Assumptionists, which, with their newspaper *La Croix,* had been among the most impudent in the campaign, was dissolved, and im-

mediately afterwards the law was proposed against the congregations, which, among other things, because of the educational methods they employed divided the French from the
French, set up the youth educated by them against those educated in state schools, the *"deux jeunesses,"* as Waldeck-Rousseau called them, and weakened the moral unity of the French
people. The law became gradually severer in the parliament
and was applied with severity; but a few years later, when
the troubles with the Holy See grew more acute and France
suppressed her embassy to the Vatican, the step was actually
reached (1905) of separation of Church and State, the concordat of 1801 was abolished, the state was declared non-
sectarian, all citizens were granted equal liberty of conscience
and religion, the subsidies from the state and the municipalities to a particular cult were stopped, ecclesiastical property
was assigned to local charitable institutions, and the cultural
associations that were to be set up were allowed the use of the
ecclesiastical buildings and the dwellings of bishops and
parish priests. The French Catholics, and in the end the
Church of Rome herself, bowed to the inevitable, which their
own acts had provoked and rendered acceptable; and all that
they succeeded in obtaining in the years that followed was
permission to set up not societies of the kind established by
the state, but others that were called canonico-legal, which, in
truth, were more consistent with the liberal concept of separation.

In France and in Italy the forces that favoured this movement for reform and legislation lay in the public spirit; but
not, or in far lesser degree, in Spain, where only in 1910 was
there a beginning of the conflict with the Vatican concerning
the concordat. Unlike Spain, Belgium went on in its public
life in a purely popular and parliamentary development,
except that the population was in majority Catholic and ready
to fight for its traditional faith, and that the liberals were

unable to change this state of things or to depart from the liberal method to take up that of the Jacobins, with which, moreover, they knew they would not succeed in making any effective changes. And so they succumbed for many years in the unequal struggle, especially concerning the question of the schools, which was the crucial point and at the same time the symbol of the whole situation. For a brief space, from 1878 to 1884, they had been able to hold the reins of government and give a secular direction to the schools, placing them under state control, excluding religious instruction from the curriculum and giving the preference to pupils educated in state schools over those from private and Catholic schools. But they thereby incurred the ire of the Church of Rome, and, what was graver, they encountered very strong resistance in the country itself, ceaselessly stirred up by the Catholics against the Government. So that when the Catholics returned to power, which they kept for a quarter of a century, they hastened at once to undo the labour of the liberals as to education. Nor were they shaken by the very ample extension of the franchise in 1893, for on the contrary the elections held on this basis returned them in greater numbers and strength, and the liberal party was almost annihilated. And in 1895 a new educational reform made religious instruction compulsory, provided methods of exerting pressure on heads of families, and caused the clerical schools to spread throughout the country. The spiritual atmosphere was then very heavy in Belgium, and it was impossible to lighten it, for at every new election the overwhelming Catholic majority issued intact and the very attempt of the liberals to ally themselves with the socialists only increased the number of votes given in the country districts to the Catholics. The introduction of the proportional system in 1899 somewhat improved the lot of the liberals; but only much later did the unwearying agitation for compulsory education, which they began in 1911 in union with the socialists, lead to a result, which was the education law of 1914.

This resistance by sectarian thought and habit, even in the atmosphere of the liberal state, was seen among other peoples, although not in the marked form and with the victories that it could boast of in Belgium. Would it some day be possible for the new and secular religion to penetrate into all the social strata, and even among the rural populace, by tradition so "pagan" and backward and old-fashioned? Or was it better to propose as sole aim, or as sole immediate aim, to penetrate into the ruling class, making it still more coherent and certain, firm and active, and to resign oneself to leaving the *plebs,* or the common people, which is often not plebeian, in their temporary or permanent paganism? The course of the hoped-for religious dissolution, purification, and recomposition proved to be far more laborious and slow than the illuminists and Jacobins had believed; and yet it was not advisable to hasten it or rush it impatiently, because by such Jacobin methods either nothing would be obtained or worse results would ensue. Modern civilization now had a free path ahead and its task was to potentiate its own forces in loyal competition with the old faith; nor was the danger of a Catholic reaction, similar to that of the Counter-Reformation, to be considered as anything else but fantastic, for all the real conditions for it were lacking, and in addition there was no Spain able to supply the support of her arms and policy as she had in the sixteenth century (although, to add an amusing anecdote here, the last king of Spain, Alfonso XIII, when he visited Rome, mindful of the past, offered his sword to the Pope in defence of the sacred cause). Even the concept that some had formed of the international power of the Papacy was to be judged exaggerated, for too many bonds attached the Catholics of the various countries to their states and to the parties that lived and operated in the sphere of those states.

It was clear that the German Catholics defended against Bismarck rather their own cause than that of the distant Pope. Those of Italy for some time and in some places observed the order to refrain from voting, but more generally, when laziness and indifference did not prevent them they did vote for the deputies who best answered to their interests and who enjoyed their friendship and admiration. Those of France, when Leo XIII had decided the *ralliement* to the Republic, were split and obeyed but poorly. The Irish did not listen to the Pope's admonitions and words of moderation concerning the acts of terror with which they accompanied their national protest. The Germans of Austria, when the Catholic clergy supported the Czech element against the German, reacted in 1897 with the cry of *"Los von Rom!"*—of separation from Rome—and left the Catholic Church by thousands. The great force of this church lay in the determinateness and immutability of her dogmas and of her discipline, which gave her the disadvantage but at the same time the advantage of the man who stands still over the man who is moving and, as he moves, does indeed go forward but now falls and now gets up again.

The attempts at reform in the very heart of Catholicism, such as that—which may stand for all of them because it was relatively the most important of all—of the Old Catholics in Germany, who did not recognize the new dogma of papal infallibility, proposed to return to the Church of the seventh century, and wanted to abolish the celibacy of priests and similar things, soon dried up and died like everything of a hybrid nature. And when, at the end of the nineteenth and the beginning of the twentieth century, under the influence of lay philosophy and historiography, there arose among the more cultured Catholics what was known as modernism, that is, the contradictory idea of opening Catholicism to historical criticism and at the same time preserving the unity and tradition of the Church and the authority of the pontiff, and dogmatic form, and shunning and professing to loathe Protestantism, the Church defended herself firmly and bravely in her old and well-guarded trenches, and ended by condemning modernism with the encyclical *Pascendi* (1907), rooting it out and casting it to the flames, although this defence and victory cost her the loss of many among the most learned and distinguished minds she possessed. But the loss was far less grave than the loss of her very *raison d'être*, which would have irremediably occurred if she had given way or ventured to compromise in any way.

As he had in the fight against the Catholics, Bismarck failed in the even more violent one that he undertook against the German socialists, demonstrating in this case too the inefficacy of authoritarian systems and methods and the scanty luck of his own policy when it was exerted in other fields than that of competition with foreign states. The socialist propaganda that was constantly spreading further among German working-men, the great number of its newspapers, the growing number of votes obtained by socialists in the elections—which in those of 1877 almost reached half a million—alarmed him and stimulated his natural disposition to resort to police or military methods. So that after having vainly tried to persuade the parliamentary assembly to accept the sharpening of several articles of the penal code, he took advantage of two attempts on the life of the Emperor in 1878, the importance of which he exaggerated and the political significance of which he altered, dissolved the parliament, proceeded to new elections, and put through the special law, previously rejected, by which societies, meetings, and newspapers of a socialistic or communistic character were prohibited, and the power was given to prevent from living in certain centres such persons as were considered agitators, to close public houses, book-shops, and similar places where socialists foregathered, and to promulgate the state of siege in places where the peace seemed to be menaced. Notwithstanding the dismay aroused in the beginning by these prohibitions and by the severity of the sanctions that accompanied them, and the fear and the apostasy and the cowardice of the denunciations that accompanied them, the socialists preserved their ranks practically intact, removing their newspapers to Switzerland; and their leaders went abroad. And although in 1881 the number of votes for the socialist candidates fell to little over three hundred thousand, in 1884 it was well over half a million, and in 1887 reached almost eight hundred thousand. The special law, valid for a year and a half, was prolonged for more than twelve; and Bismarck, who did not intend to upset his method of government, had no other choice but to make it more rigid and severe or even to resort to a *coup d'état* and deprive the socialists of the right to vote; and this desperate alternative, at which he finally snatched, was, as we have said, the occasion for his fall, so that it may be said that he disappeared from the political scene because of socialist activity. He did not bar the path but made it smooth for them, for from that moment their political representation in the German parliaments was constantly on the increase, and in 1912 had become the strongest element there, with one hundred and ten deputies; while several socialists even pierced into the semi-feudal Prussian chamber, thanks especially to the votes of the Berlin population.

After Bismarck no more real attempts were made to suffocate or disperse them, although William II, between 1893 and 1895, thought of carrying out himself the *coup d'état* that he had not allowed Bismarck to try, and spoke of it with his confidants. In 1894 he caused his chancellor, Von Hohenlohe, to present an *Umsturzvorlage*, a bill against the subversive forces, which was rejected by the parliament, and in

1899 another bill against strikes and the pressure brought to bear on non-strikers by strikers. Against the socialist movement Bismarck, who knew and practised the negative and repressive method but had no faith in and no experience of the positive one that was the method of liberty, adopted as his only positive method social laws, which were meant to deprive socialism itself of all its basis and stimulus by satisfying the legitimate needs of the working-class; and so in 1883 he created the fund for sick workmen; in 1884, insurance against labour accidents; in 1889, insurance against old age and disability. These laws gave an impulse to social legislation throughout Europe, but they were, under another aspect, a livelier resumption of what had been started fifty years earlier in England, not to go back to earlier examples— for laws of this kind were not unknown even under the absolute monarchies. And useful as they were, the conservative-authoritarian spirit that inspired them was not likely to awaken anything but mistrust among the working-men, as happens when one gives what has not been asked for in order not to give what has been asked for, and when one plans to satisfy various exigencies of the body in order to stultify the soul and weaken the will. And in addition it was felt that these provisions were in great part the effect of socialistic action itself, which had imposed them or had created the idea of them by its presence and by its express or tacit threat.

Socialism, if we leave out of consideration the Utopias that grow up around it of redemption or transhumanization of humanity by means of a purely economic and therefore material or materialistic upheaval, and if we look at it directly in its actual reality, is a movement of ascension or an impulse given to the ascension of those social strata, of those multitudes, which had remained rather passive than active in public life. Inasmuch as it is a movement of ascension, it is social and not antisocial, historical and not antihistorical, and therefore cannot be subdued or repressed, as though it were an animal rebellion, by the counter-attack of violence, nor softened and healed by charity and beneficence, as though it were an illness. And since this ascension implies that the number of citizens who share and take an interest in the state must grow and the ruling class be enriched and enlivened by new men, new passions, and new capacities, socialism has a noble political character. It is true that as soon as the misleading mirages have been dissipated and the corresponding false theorizings have been abandoned and socialism has been understood in its real efficacy as the creator of new citizens and the renewer of the ruling class, its action proves to be not intrinsically different from any other form of human advancement, from any other ethical and political activity, and, like all these others, to pertain to the world of liberty.

Socialism without liberty, or not effected by means of liberty, is not true socialism; and without speaking of that variety which sometimes donned its appearance at the bidding of absolute monarchs who flattered and instigated the populace in order to keep back the bourgeoisie—that is, the cultivated classes—which threatened them, that other which called itself Catholic was not real socialism either. Nor was that other which is called state socialism; or last of all, that which is related to it and which, after 1870, was formulated and flourished in Germany in the Verein für Sozialpolitik through the zeal of scientists and professors, who were derided under the name of socialists of the chair. This last socialism (to adopt a phrase used by Goethe for something utterly different) was good *"zu begleiten"* but not *"zu leiten,"* to accompany but not to lead, to study and propose technical resources and appropriate institutions, but not to awaken and educate the political mind of the working-men. And state socialism was of use towards this end only when it did not emanate from a conservative or reactionary state, but from one that answered the popular call. Catholic or Christian socialism was also out-side the political field, and obviously void of political thought was Leo XIII's famous encyclical *Rerum novarum* (1891), which flatterers called the Workmen's Christian Charter. The Catholic democrats, who in Belgium, earlier perhaps than in any other country, detached themselves from the older Cath-olic parties as Young Catholics, and who elsewhere and in the years that followed were known as "popular," repeated, with regard to socialism, the tactics that had been employed by the clericals with regard to liberalism, and appropriated a great part of the demands and even of the means of the latter in order to apply the effects towards the greater power or at least the conservation of the power of the Church; except for the case, which also occurred, of those who revealed a more direct and profound interest in socialism and for its implicit democracy or liberty in the face of the Church itself, and drew closer to the modernists, modernists themselves in the political field.

Now precisely because genuine and effective socialism be-longs to the world of liberty, the measure of its progress is given by its work on behalf of liberty, although it may not be conscious of it or becomes conscious of it later or only in a few of its disciples. What does it matter if Lassalle be-lieved in the conquest of power on the part of the working-men, which would have put an end to wage slavery, given everyone justice and prosperity, and deduced the correspond-ing political action from his hypothetical "law of bronze," which was an abstract economic scheme and not a historical and human reality? What does it matter if Marx (who in 1867 published the first volume of his laborious *Capital*) proposed an incorrect theory of surplus value and a still more incorrect law concerning the falling trend in the rate of profit, and an extravagant interpretation of human history?

In practice and in reality, it is certain that between 1862

and 1864 Lassalle gave impetus and direction to the working-men's movement in Germany and founded the General Work-men's Union, and at the same time demanded universal and secret suffrage, needed by the workmen for their progress. This suffrage was obtained later through Bismarck, who es-tablished it for his own ends and in imitation of Louis Bona-parte. But it was turned by them to their own ends and against Bismarck himself, nor was it possible to deprive them of it again. Marx, in his turn, by means of the International Work-ing Men's Association (the First International), founded in London in 1864 and lasting for ten years through many vicis-situdes, and especially by means of the doctrines that he in-troduced into it (although in the beginning he tempered them, in shrewd compromise, with the diverse concepts, which he despised as prejudices, of justice and liberty), raised a ban-ner around which another workmen's association gathered in Germany. And these two different associations, of Lassallians and Marxians, after clashing for many years and attempting in turn to take one another's place, were by the necessity of things led to unite in 1875, at the Congress of Gotha. They came to a compromise concerning their doctrinal theses, and combined those of Lassalle with those of Marx, but gave life to a compact German working-men's party, which began to send its deputies to the imperial parliament, two in 1871, nine in 1874, twelve in 1877; and it was this growing number of deputies and of votes given to socialist candidates that excited Bismarck's reaction. After this reaction, in the course of which socialism had also gained the social laws, had been overcome, it gained another moral victory, because the new Emperor, although he was soon to change his style, began by flattering the working-men and their claims, and solemnly affirmed before the world the gravity and urgency of the social question and the necessity of devoting oneself to it with fervour and of solving it "with a warm heart and a cool

head." He said that this would be "the second great feat of
Germany after the Reformation," and meanwhile he had summoned to Berlin an international conference on labour problems.

By this time the working-men's insurrections, such as the
battle in the streets of Paris in June, 1848, were becoming
a distant memory; the Commune of 1871 had not opened a
new era by showing how the dictatorship of the proletariat
over the middle class could be set up, as Marx liked to transfigure it for purposes of propaganda and as it was pictured
in the fearful imagination of the rich and of timid and quiet
people. The socialisms of the past had no propulsive force of
example or actual value as a premise, and gradually took
their place in the hagiography or golden legend of the party,
and its authors were venerated under the name of "precursors," from Plato and primitive Christianity, from the mediaeval socialism of Fra Dolcino and the semi-mediaeval socialism of Thomas Münzer and John of Leyden, to that of
Owen, Saint-Simon and Fourier, to whom the label still adhered that Marx had fastened on them, the name of "utopists." The new reality was now the electoral assemblies and
representation in parliament, with all the consequences that
this fact brought with it, although these were still developing
slowly and might not be discerned in advance.

In the congress held in Switzerland in 1880 German socialism separated itself permanently from the anarchists, who a
few years before, under the leadership of Bakunin, had been
the principal cause of the disintegration of the First International. And although this socialism still claimed to be revolutionary under the leadership of Liebknecht and Bebel, in
relation to anarchism it seemed and was termed moderate.
In fact, with the expulsion of anarchism, socialism was ex-
punging from its midst, unconsciously, communism itself.
For what else had been the anarchism of Bakunin and others

of his stamp if not the extreme opposite of abstract communism and of the oppressive state-intervention of Marx and his followers, the corresponding abstract individualism: the former, the negation and destruction of every form of state, the latter, under the formula of the end of the state, ultra-national and even dictatorial? The one conception was linked to the other and lived on the other; when the one was weakened, the other was ideally and substantially weakened and gradually forced to receive within itself and to satisfy so far as might be necessary the legitimate elements of individualism, and therefore to direct itself towards liberalism.

A further step towards the inevitable liberal conversion of socialism was the Congress of Erfurt of 1891, the first held after the cessation of the special laws, in which a programme in two parts was elaborated. The first criticized the foundations of existing civilization, set up against them the ideal of the future communistic society, and was ornamental in character; the second, later called the minimum programme, contained a series of practical reforms that could be carried out in existing society. The latter, it is clear, was the only part of a political and feasible character, that is, it could present and defend real and particular requests to the other parties. These were to accept some of them with modifications, and reject or postpone others, and in time were to receive them more generally and perhaps all of them, and so socialism would furnish a positive contribution to the common task of gradual social progress. German socialism was anxious to proclaim itself not only revolutionary but also, in agreement with the final peroration of the *Communist Manifesto* and with the idea of the association Marx had inspired and guided, "international"; and yet it was constantly growing more national, that is, "Lassallian." When William II, foiled in his expectations, changed his attitude towards the socialists and invited his people to the battle for religion, morality, and order against the party of disorder, he also threatened, in 1895, to call upon his faithful subjects to put in their right place those *"vaterlandslose Gesellen,"* those "fellows without a country," unworthy of the name of Germans. But the fact was that this socialism of the so-called expatriates was linking itself, by force of things and by force of logic, to the entirety of German economy and politics, so that later, in order to designate it, the phrase "social patriotism" had to be coined.

And although, with all the roughshod materialism of its theoretical premises, it looked askance at religion, and when it did not consider it a class lie of use to the middle class, reduced it, as in the Erfurt programme, to a *Privatsache*, a private affair, yet, unable to adhere to the old religion, it unconsciously fed in its depths on the new one, the religion of thought, criticism, and liberty. A certain consciousness of this began to make itself felt when, after 1895, the party realized the inner need of remeditating, discussing, correcting, or replacing the philosophical premises of Marxism, and recalled a diverse philosophical and ethical tradition, that of Kant. And in the end, with regard to the more properly political doctrine, the heresy broke out on the part of an old and for many years orthodox Marxian, Bernstein, who gave the slogan: "What is called the final purpose [the communistic society, doing away with the state] is nothing, but the movement is everything." The movement, that is, the concrete and progressive work of liberty, which in desiring any other particular end desires itself above all. What Marx meant by his alternating apocalyptic ideas and historical evolutionary ideas, oscillating between the cult of authority or power and that of liberty in human society, was given democratic and even historicizing interpretations. It was pointed out that he had never maintained the absolute superiority of socialism over capitalism and that he had always made the

superiority of an economic order depend on given circumstances.

The figure of the socialists, whose well-reasoned speeches
were heard in the debates of parliament and whose articles
were read in the newspapers and reviews, had grown familiar and no longer awoke shudders like the vague and
mysterious figure of the "internationalist" who had been
spoken of twenty years before and had been confused with
the "nihilist," the apostle of universal destruction armed with
bombs. Notwithstanding the theoretical intransigence that was
affirmed in their congresses, in practice collaboration and reformism had the upper hand. In 1913, in the opposite camp
Delbrück, as secretary of state, while admitting that unpleasant things might still happen in parliamentary life because
of universal suffrage and discord among the so-called bourgeois parties, openly recognized that socialism was "no longer
revolutionary, except among the extremists and in the hys-
terical members of the opposed parties." This "liberaliza-
tion," or "democratization," as people preferred to call it,
was confirmed by the formation here and there, on the mar-
gins, of new if not very important groups of revolutionary-
minded men, from whom later came the Spartacus Union,
whose chief was a son of old Liebknecht. But when the World
War broke out, these irreconcilables were overwhelmed by
the mass of the party, by the official party; and in Germany,
as in France and in Belgium, the socialists entered into what
were called "sacred unions" of all the parties. On August 4,
1914, the German socialists declared that they accompanied
with their warmest good wishes their brothers of every party
who were called to arms and that they would not be divided
from their country in the hour of danger.

Italian socialism more or less followed the development
of the German. After a first period, between 1870 and 1890,
during which the relics of Bakuninian insurrectionism and

anarchism smouldered, mingled with an evanescent working-men's Mazzinianism, the Marxian doctrines were at last imbibed and a party was formed which in 1892 also completed its separation from the anarchists, sent deputies to the parliament, announced its maximum and minimum programmes, and set off on legal paths. It was, however, unable to set itself against the working-men when they came into conflict with the police forces, or even against the disorders and uprisings, due to local conditions, of Sicily and its "*fasci* of workmen" in the years from 1892 to 1894. The new party had its period of persecution in consequence of the part played by some of its leaders in the Sicilian happenings, and later because of the Milanese movement of 1898; but this persecution soon stopped and gave way to amnesties, because Italian public opinion was opposed to it and, above all political divisions, manifested its sympathy for those who had been tried and sentenced. In 1900 the attempt to restrain the parliamentary régime was overcome, and there was ampler breathing-space. On the one hand, scientific criticism, which in a country of ancient culture and unprejudiced intelligence like Italy had rapidly corroded the philosophical, historical, and economic system of Marxism, and on the other hand, the influence of what was happening at the same moment in Germany, split the Italian socialist party into two "tendencies": the revolutionary and the reformist. These reached a compromise in the Bologna Congress of 1904, and another kind of compromise in that of Rome in 1906, until in the Bologna Congress of 1908 the reformist tendency prevailed altogether. Before Delbrück made a similar remark in Germany, Giolitti, the prime minister, said in the Italian parliament that the socialists had "put Marx away in the attic" and had become reasonable; and for his part he tried to draw their more capable elements into the government. Not even in Italy were the socialists able to remain international and "without a

country"; and they not only did their part in the warlike
preparation of Italian spirit against Austria, but their greatest theorist and writer, Antonio Labriola, was the champion
of colonial enterprises and of Italy's industrial and commercial expansion.

Revolutionary minds, scornful of accommodating reformism and impatient of the flabbiness into which orthodox socialism had fallen, devoted themselves in Italy also to seeking new formulas, better fitted to them; and one was supplied
by Sorel with his syndicalism. Sorel assimilated socialism, as
he conceived it, to primitive Christianity, assigned to it the
aim of renewing society from its moral foundations, and
therefore urged it to cultivate, like the first Christians, the
sentiment of "scission" from surrounding society, to avoid
all relations with politicians, to shut itself up in workmen's
syndicates and feed on the "myth" of the general strike. It
was the construction of a poet thirsting for moral austerity,
thirsting for sincerity, pessimistic with regard to the present
reality, stubbornly trying to find a hidden fount from which
the fresh pure stream would well forth; and tested by reality,
his poetry quickly vanished, even in his own eyes. But when
the World War broke out, the official Socialist party, which
had detached itself from reformism in the Congress of Reggio
Emilia in 1912, and had wavered irresolutely between moderate and revolutionary tendencies, did not show a spirit
equal to the occasion and, unable to and perhaps unwilling to
prevent Italy's taking part in the war, remained among those
who hung in the air, cutting themselves off from national and
even from international life.

Minor obstacles and hindrances to its junction with liberalism were encountered by socialism in France, because the
Marxian dialectics of history and of classes, the theory of
the structure and superstructure and of the ideal world as a
mask of economic interests, the total abstention that must

be observed from the concepts and sentiments of the other parties (all reprobates because "bourgeois"), the necessity at the same time to press to their extreme limits productive forces and bourgeois civilization with the intention of sending the latter along this path to destruction and to make way for a conversion to its opposite—because all these and similar things, adapted to a people like the Germans, who are very theoretical and fond of complicated theories, found little favour with the French. The revolutionary tradition of French socialism was that of Blanqui's insurrectionalism, which promised itself that by gaining possession of the seat of government it would reform society by reasonable legislation; but the military executions and deportations that followed the Commune, the state of siege that lasted for many years, the prohibition of the diffusion of the International, and at the same time the memory of the repeated defeats suffered, in the course of the century, by the working-men in their insurrections, had robbed this tradition of all hope and all impetus.

When the Republic was firmly established and the state of siege had been abolished, amnesties had been granted to the survivors of the Commune, and the problems concerning working-men could be taken up again, the republicans of the extreme left and the radicals had included in their political programme a special part called the social programme (legal recognition of trade-unions, legal restriction of working-hours, insurance for employés, and then also a progressive tax on income, nationalization of mines and railways, the nation in arms, elective judges, and so forth), something like what in Germany was called a minimum programme. So that the socialists found allies and co-operators in these republicans and radicals, on the condition that they did not insist on the future communistic society and other similar Marxian ideas. So about 1881 beside a Marxian group (Guesde-La-

fargue) that had founded a working-men's party, another was
formed, a more important one, of socialists (Allemane and
others) who were called possibilists because they proposed
to demand and obtain such reforms as were practically
possible in the present. Collaboration in parliament, and
eventually in the government, was implicit in such a programme, and Jaurès, when he was elected deputy in 1895,
outlined a parliamentary Socialist party, in agreement with
the radicals. If the chief of the Marxian group, Guesde, had
declared in the days of Boulanger, in the style of his school,
that the struggle between the two bourgeois parties left the
proletariat indifferent, the new socialists, on the contrary,
took part vivaciously, in union with the republicans, in the
Dreyfusard cause, that is, the liberal and secular cause,
against the clericals, the militarists, and the reactionaries.
After this crisis, in 1899 a socialist, Millerand, joined the
cabinet of Waldeck-Rousseau, taking over the portfolio of
industry and commerce; an event that troubled the calculations of the Marxian scholastics, was condemned by the congress or council of Dresden, and then, so as not to break (so
they said) the unity of the party, was blamed by other assemblies in France, and even by those who would gladly have
approved it as necessary for the defence of the menaced Republic and as a proof that the Socialist party was mature
enough to share in the government. It produced, in short, the
separation from the French Socialist party of the parliamentary socialist group and of the independents. In the elections
of 1902, which were fought over the question of the dissolution of the congregations and the religious policy, the socialists formed an alliance with the left, which won a clamorous
victory; in 1906 Briand left the Socialist party to participate
in the Sarrien cabinet, and the year after another socialist,
Viviani, became minister of labour.

Quite negligible was the influence of Marxism in England,

although it was there Marx elaborated his doctrine and from there he directed the International; the Marxian Social Democratic Federation, founded by Hyndman about 1884, found few followers. On the other hand, Henry George's ideas concerning the nationalization of land created great interest, as might have been expected in a country where a third of the soil belonged to the aristocracy, and was kept in great part as pasture-land, parks, hunting-grounds, and playing-fields. No attempt was ever made in England to persecute or to suppress socialism, nor were grave efforts and much trouble needed to gather it into liberalism, because from the very beginning the problems pertaining to labour were spontaneously incorporated into the framework of English society and politics, and liberals and conservatives busied themselves about them, and left little field to specific socialist activity. Liberal in spirit was also the socialism of the Fabians (1883), as the name itself implies; it barred unexpected and radical upheavals, and advised the practical encouragement of the natural development of things, which pointed away from unbridled freedom of competition and led towards a social organization of production. Equally reformistic and non-Marxian was the Independent Labour party (1893), and the trade-unions took care of what was needed and feasible. Bernstein, who lived many years in London, drew an example and a stimulus for the revision of Marxism and the reform of social democracy in Germany from what he saw in England, where, as he wrote in 1899, "no responsible socialist dreams any more of an imminent victory of socialism by means of a great catastrophe, or of a rapid conquest of Parliament by means of the revolutionary proletariat, and where on the contrary work is always being more and more transferred to the municipalities and other independent administrative organisms, and the habit has been lost of despising them, and here and there better relations have been entered into with the corporate movement."

Similar aspects and happenings, and an analogous course of things, might be shown with regard to socialism in Belgium, in Switzerland, in Austria-Hungary, in Holland, and in the Scandinavian countries. But after noting this important general feature of the ideal victory that liberalism gradually won over it by inviting it and inducing it to enter its circle, by persuading it to drop scission for collaboration, by clearing its imagination of millenarian expectations and turning it to the present, by turning its mind from materialistic and schematic into historical and humanist, it is necessary to consider as well the victory that socialism in its turn gained in this transformation, which seemed to be submission but was not. Socialism then became the principal subject for students of politics and statesmen; it attracted the finest among the youthful talents and generous hearts of that period; even literature, the novel, the drama, lyric poetry, became its mouthpiece. An English politician said: "Today we are all socialists." Extension of the franchise and universal suffrage were deliberately faced, in order that the needs of the working-men might obtain their representatives and take their place with the other needs of society, chastising the egoism of employers and of the rich, and in order that by discussing, voting, criticizing, this social class might educate its political sense and its sense of responsibility. The laws concerning compulsory education and against illiteracy and in favour of night-schools and Sunday schools, the people's universities, and such improvements, were real denials of the accusation that the "bourgeoisie" wished to keep the people in "ignorance." And such reactionaries, ridiculous rather than odious, as sighed for the lost protection of the good old times, were left to their vain grumblings.

There was a general tendency and goodwill toward pro-

posing, promoting, and accepting social measures, no longer
and not only for conservative purposes (worthy of praise,
however, if they were aimed at preserving the peace of society and at saving, as some said, the inheritance of a common civilization from disaster and barbarism), but also as a
serious recognition of what was right. The Bismarckian laws
for old-age, sickness, and accident insurance, which, after
Germany, all the other states came in the course of time to
adopt, and the numerous others of a sanitary character, were
followed, variously and with a varying rhythm, in Germany
and in all the other states by laws concerning the equality of
obligations between employés and employers, the prohibition
or limitation of night-work for children and women and its
regulation for other workers, the determination of the number of hours of work in the week and the obligations of rest,
and the reduction of the working-day. About 1890, the demand arose that this last should be limited to eight hours, and
the number certainly sank well below the fourteen that had
formerly been customary in many factories: in England in
Disraeli's time the number of weekly hours was fixed at fifty-
six and in France, in 1904, the day's work was limited to ten.
And other laws were passed concerning home labour, workmen's houses, the preference to be given to labour co-operative societies in engaging hands for public works, and so
forth. The trade-unions, the syndicates, the federations of
labour, the professional unions, received legal recognition;
labour councils and special divisions were instituted in the
ministries, and, last of all, even ministries of labour. So that
the other accusation also tottered, which might have been expressed in the saying of Sir Thomas More that the state is a
coniuratio divitum, or in that of Vico that the *patria* is a *res
patrum:* and the modern theorizing concerning "class warfare" and the ruling class as a "bourgeois class," intent only

on its own interests and closed to working-men, should also
have tottered and fallen.

This hypothetical antisocialist "bourgeoisie," which was
in reality an impartial culture, productive of new forms of
life since it—and not the proletariat nor the bourgeoisie, in
the economic sense of those words—had brought forth socialism, now went on to bring it up. As early as 1897 it had been
possible to get together a special *Bibliographie der Sozialpolitik*; in 1900 arose the international association for laws
protecting workmen, whose seat was in Basle; in 1904 France
proposed (and Italy was the first to accept the proposal) international labour legislation. Contributions were made to
this process of elevation of the people not only by political
socialism, but also by the non-political or less political forms,
state socialism, socialism of the chair, Catholic and Christian
and co-operative socialism, which were all carried along by
the current. The festival of May first, the working-men's festival, decided on in 1889 by an international congress on
behalf of the eight-hour day, which awakened suspicion and
fear almost as though it were a day for an international
rendez-vous for the universal revolution and in the first years
was opposed and gave occasion for demonstrations and conflicts, soon passed off quietly, and was opposed by no one;
it had become a habit. The new type of labourer designated
himself, and was designated, sometimes with a smile, as that
of the "advanced and conscious" working-man; but it was
also that of a working-man surrounded by all sorts of legal
guarantees, which were increasing from day to day. To those
who continued to place socialism in the future, in a remote
or an immediate future, and imagined it such that it might
be achieved all at once and once for all, and meanwhile did
not see or did not understand what was going on around them,
it would have been possible to answer that socialism was in
the present *in fieri*, and that it would always be the same,

in fieri, like all the mind and all the work of man, like the whole world, which is not, but is eternally becoming.

The socialist movement, and the social measures that were one of its most important effects, without intending to do so dissociated the too close relation, which was almost one of identity, posited half a century ago between liberalism and economic freedom, morals and economy, ethical institutions and economic institutions. It had seemed, during this first period, as though the way of salvation that liberty opened to the moral and political life of the nations ought to be opened in the economic sphere by free competition. This inference and this illusion were assisted by the industrial and commercial world of Europe, especially of England, and on this contingent experience was erected a doctrine of absolute value, one almost religious in accent; moreover, almost from its inception, it met with its sceptics and critics. But when this youthful era approached its decline, and the economic conditions had changed, and the hopes for a spontaneous disappearance of the "social question" through the prodigy operated by free competition had not been fulfilled, and when the monster of monopoly under the form of cartels and trusts was seen to issue from the very bosom of free trade, the same social problems had to be faced again, not only with the resources of free trade but with ethical and political skill, which bends these resources also to its own ends, and makes use of them when they are useful, modifying them or casting them off when they are not useful or are harmful. This change of mind and conversion can be observed particularly in the decadence of the Manchester school in England and in the resurrection of old opponents in new and modern garb, different from what they wore in the times of the battles over the Corn Laws, and having now their representative in Disraeli.

State intervention, formerly belittled, was rendered advisable not only by the necessity to protect the working-class, but also by the necessity that the states felt to preserve, in the ebb and flow of world economy, a certain economic autonomy in order to guarantee supplies of provisions and arms in case of war, to prevent the ruin of certain social classes whose functions could not be replaced in the life of the peoples; or to avoid too frequent and too powerful shocks to the social fabric, to support national industries in their beginnings; and also for more or less urgent financial reasons. Thus state intervention in favour of the working-class was accompanied in lesser or greater measure by protective tariffs, which sometimes opposed and sometimes favoured the interests of these classes (and always opposed or favoured the interests of one class or another), but which seemed to be of use to the collective good and the general tranquillity of the country. In this respect again Germany and Bismarck were the first or among the first to set the example, with the tariff of 1879, and they were followed by almost all the other states—excepting England, which was able more or less to stick to free trade. But protection was at this time tempered by commercial treaties, and in general it did not depress industry and commerce. It is obvious that the controversies as to the preference to be assigned to protection or free trade, and which of the two contains the absolute truth, are basically at fault, because free trade and protection are the two terms of one sole relationship, and whenever the one or the other is recommended, it is always done with formulas of a purely empirical value. The whole thing is to seize the right point, case by case, in practice, in the various and changing historical situations—and this right point will be that which is of the greatest economic utility, but will never be determined by purely abstract economic considerations.

The industrial power and wealth that Europe attained, with dizzy crescendo, during this period (notably after

1890), the technical discoveries made about this time and their applications, the variety in production, the extension of markets, the ever quicker means of transportation, are things well known and present in every one's memory, and may be taken for granted and passed over in this narrative, which takes for its field the intellectual, moral, and political life that offered the conditions for this marvellous activity and productivity and in its turn derived its strength and resources from it. Let us state as a symbol that the population of Europe, which had been a hundred and eighty millions at the beginning of the century, had grown to four hundred and fifty at the end, besides the millions of her sons sent to the Americas and other new countries, by which the United States of America alone rose from five million inhabitants in 1800 to seventy-seven millions in 1900. And whatever statistics are inspected, numbers are found that recall facts of this nature and can also serve as symbols: for instance, Belgium, where in 1850 industry employed a capital of three hundred millions and in 1913, seven billions, and in whose port of Antwerp the traffic in 1840 amounted to two hundred and forty thousand tons and in 1914, to fourteen millions; and the world production of anthracite, which was a hundred and thirty million tons in 1860 and rose to six hundred and fifty in the last years of the century.

Even the rhythm of colonial expansion underwent a rapid increase, especially after 1880, when the desire to own colonies seized almost all states, in emulation of England, who was at this time extending, solidifying, and regulating her colonial empire over a quarter of the habitable globe. France brought her realm from less than a million square kilometres to about twelve millions, with fifty million inhabitants. Germany, who had no colonies before 1884, soon reached the third place with accessions in Africa and Oceania and a few harbours in the Far East. Italy occupied Eritrea and later Tripolitania. Belgium, thanks to the activity of Leopold II, had the Congo State. Spain, which on the contrary lost with Cuba and the Philippines the remains of her old colonial dominions, clung to the coast of Morocco. Russia continued to enlarge in Asia. After 1896 the United States went imperialistic too. The feelings that led to these undertakings were very complex: economic advantages partly real and partly imaginary, power and political prestige, love of country that awakened the desire to extend one's own language and culture and customs to the other parts of the world—*"La France,"* said the colonialist Ferry in 1885, *"ne veut pas être seulement un pays libre mais un grand pays qui répand, partout où il peut les porter, ses mœurs, sa langue, ses armes, son drapeau, son génie"*—and, last of all, a greater love of humanity and civilization in general. England gave her empire a liberal character, allowing such portions of it as had risen to a higher civilization, which were known as the Dominions—Canada, Australia, New Zealand, and later South Africa—to have liberal and democratic institutions, their own laws and government, independent commercial relations, their own army (and some of them already asked for a navy of their own), and to remain attached to the mother-country spontaneously by their interests, community of language and tradition, and harmony of ideals. Economics acquired a true world-unity; Europe was fed with the grain that came from the other parts of the world, for her own production was insufficient, having been in part replaced by other crops and by other uses for the soil.

Hand in hand with the production of wealth went general prosperity, even if in some places or in some strata of the population want and misery were still undiminished and were rendered intolerable by the neighbourhood of prosperity, and if poverty was aggravated at times by the very rapidity of

economic changes. Everywhere might be observed a shift in
the proportions of city dwellers and country dwellers, the
centralization and growth of the industrial population with
the consequent diminution and almost the disappearance of
craftsmen and small businesses, and the formation of a numerous class of technicians and industrial employés. And in
all classes education increased, there was much reading and
generally in several languages; the newspapers, thanks to the
telegraph and the telephone, brought information concerning
life all over the world, every day and almost every hour.
Sometimes it would happen that a discussion, a controversy,
a question, that arose in one country would excite great interest in all countries, as was the case with the *affaire Dreyfus*.

None the less upon this age, so full of activity, and which
enjoyed a longer era of peace than Europe had ever known
before, has fallen the judgment, which has become permanently fixed even in the books of historians, of a "prosaic
age," and at the same time one "sceptical and dissatisfied":
a judgment that sounds strange and inexplicable unless it is
placed in relationship with the spiritual crisis begun in 1848
and grown to its full development after 1870, as it has
been delineated above. The practical activity that was encouraged and aided by the liberal spheres was no longer
joined to a lofty understanding of this activity, one capable
of appreciating its full meaning and of recognizing its in-
estimable value; and so the religious and ethical impulse was
weakened, the capacity for inventing and transforming the
requisite concepts was diminished, the inner life of the conscience was mortified, that life in which alone suffering and
sorrow and anguish can be gathered into purifying travail
and converted into consoling and revivifying forces. Towards
the end of the eighteenth and during the first decades of the
nineteenth century, Germany had been the philosophical
Athens of the modern age, and after two thousand years had

offered to all mankind a speculative harvest as original as
it was copious. But when it was believed that her rise as a
great national and political power would lead this speculation to new and greater fruit, she declined in quality, grew
mentally impoverished, lost the function that she had filled
of energetic knower and fertilizer of the thought and knowledge of all the peoples, and although the labour of her scientists went on assiduously and though their erudition was
great, she gave out no flashes of genius, and allowed the inheritance of her classical age to lie inert or forgotten and
even despised. In the country of Kant and Hegel might now
be observed, in the greatly narrowed field of thought, neo-
critics, psychologists, physiopsychologists, and other similar
worthy personages, full of honest intent, but without vigour
and without courage and of the earth, earthy. Elsewhere men
like Spencer and Ardigò met considerable success, and a hollow positivism and evolutionism stultified men's minds.

Even when liberty was defended and theorized over, the
defence and the theory were empirical and superficial, as they
were in the famous book on this argument by John Stuart
Mill. The central flame was extinguished, or smouldered only
in a few minds in which it gave out some sparks; and this
accounts for the subdued prosaic tone that was then customary. The regret was voiced that there were in the new generation no heroes of revolutions equal to the Mazzinis and the
Garibaldis, no political heroes equal to the Cavours and the
Lincolns; and these regrets were those of disappointed imaginations, which in periods of calm would have liked to admire
helmsmen guiding the ship into the harbour by powerful
effort amid the howling of the storm, and they were an injustice to the undeniably useful and upright labour of the
new men adapted to the new times. When French men of
letters were eager to deride and mock the annoyed and angry
politicians and statesmen of the Third Republic, Henry

Becque, in 1896, flung the answer in their face: Without those politicians and statesmen, these men of letters would have been servants or would have ended in prison, as under the Second Empire, and if he had had to choose between the political work and the literary work accomplished during the last twenty-five years, he would, in all conscience, have resolutely given the preference to the political work. But with all this, it must be recognized that at this time few indeed—and even these few but little heeded and with small results—were the poets, thinkers, seers, apostles, who introduce light and warmth into the war which in all times and under all conditions is perpetually fought in the minds and the hearts of men, and which has perpetual need of this aid and this guidance. Nor could the gap be filled by physicists, naturalists, sociologists, who at this time were indeed not wanting, but who from their very nature are of use to technique and not to what is above, or at the basis of, every technique.

The slight mental energy and the frequent loss of courage and consequent disposition towards pessimism were revealed by the way in which men generally received and interpreted the inevitable changes that the course of things brought into society and politics, and whenever it was necessary to choose and adopt decisions to be followed with a sure spirit. The Utopia of *laissez-faire, laissez-passer,* or of absolute free trade as the panacea of social evils, had been denied by facts; but instead of sifting in this doctrine what was Utopian from what was true, and understanding and appreciating this truth, and preserving it (as one should do with every truth) within its limits, which alone can guarantee it, tears were shed over this fallen faith and hope. There was no attempt to replace it with another, not even with that of state intervention and protection, the weak sides and dangers of which, on the other hand, were perceived; so that between the two rival theses no one knew what to do, and there was no way of bridging the gap. Furthermore, since the concept of free trade had been hazily associated with that of liberalism, the mistrust in the free-trade formula generated mistrust in the very truth of political liberty, which is a concept of another and a higher order. Equally, the other fact that the political battle no longer continued on the scheme of two parties, classically distinct and in opposition, the party of conservation and that of progress facing and fighting one another and succeeding one another in power, caused the parliamentary system to be considered organically sick and near to its death. For it had been supposed that these two parties, working in this schematic fashion, were a *sine quâ non* of this system, whereas it should have been noted that this clear distinction and contraposition answered to the times of the formation and foundation of liberty and its first growth, but could not be in absolute harmony with the situation when the things to be discussed and resolved presented themselves with greater variety and complexity, and when the very composition of parliamentary representation was more varied, and, in consequence, the variety of the political groups and combinations had to be more varied.

Nor was there in all this any ground for fearing that the reasons for conservation and progress, of the past and the future, of history and life, would ever be lacking, since these are two eternal moments that operate under the most different special forms. Nor did the disappearance of those "notables" of the liberal aristocracies who formerly directed the elections under limited suffrage by designating the candidates, and now were unable to survive and to exercise the same function under broader or universal suffrage, irremediably abandon the elections to chance and to demagogy, as many said, because in practice it was a question of finding new methods for new conditions, and these were already beginning to make their appearance and to turn out well. And one must have

overidealized the history of the past to wonder at it if in the
elections many frauds, deceits, and abuses were committed,
and one had to have no eyes not to see and consider what
much worse things were happening in the great American
republic, and yet were being corrected or rendered less harmful by the spontaneous forces of morality and by public opinion.

It was natural that when the franchise had been extended,
there should be a change in the parliaments with regard to
the quality of the men, modes of eloquence, behaviour and
customs, and not always in an agreeable fashion. But it would
have been well not to lose sight of the fact that even under
these forms or under these appearances, often so vulgar, there
was the guarantee of liberty for all, and that, no matter how
imperfect constitutional and liberal life may have been, for
instance, in the Spain of Alfonso XII or Alfonso XIII, it was
still a great deal better than political life in the days of Ferdinand VII or than what Carlism would have given her. So that
rather than draw the conclusion that it would be better to
abolish parliamentary institutions, here again the question
was how to proceed in order to guide and direct (as in practice happened) these assemblies in a good sense; for they
were not very different from the assemblies of all times, all
indocile, impressionable, confused, exposed to corruption,
and all of them looking for someone able to handle them.
It was agreeable to make great discoveries with great airs,
such as that of the "lie" of the electorate and the parliaments, where there was, indeed, no other lie but the difference
that always exists between the juridical form and the historical reality, with which that form may perhaps not coincide because it is made to regulate it, nor is it able to regulate it unless it employs rigidity and flexibility at the same
time. The same lack of reflection suggested supine admiration
of Germany, for her anti-parliamentarism, for her "strong

state," which made radicals and socialists toe the mark, for
her "ethical state," which seemed to carry out the idea that
German professors had conceived of it, attributing to the
merit of this political constitution the economic growth and
vigour of Germany, whereas it was her weak point. Antipar-
liamentarism, antidemocracy, antiliberalism, came into fashion and were an essential part of what was called everywhere,
by a word coined in England, snobbishness. In words at least
(but the worst of it was, that such words were pronounced)
one was often inclined to empty out the baby with the bath.

About 1890 there came into this sleepy European world
of thought and into its discoloured and inanimate political
literature the socialistic and Marxian doctrine of history and
the state. It boasted of being the daughter of German classical
philosophy, and so it was, although an illegitimate one, and
it preserved certain of its virtues in the positing of questions
and in its dialectico-historical method. Beyond a doubt it conferred not a little benefit in that people were called upon to
think over the very principles of human society and history,
and to formulate again the corresponding ethical and logical
problems; and on the other hand, in that an ideal, no matter
how deduced and conceived, once more lighted up the intellectual field and again attracted people to activity and apos-
tleship. But, as might have been expected, these Marxian doctrines were not able to maintain their positions, and had to
retreat in the economic field as regards theories of surplus
labour and surplus value, and in the philosophical field as
regards the metaphysics and dialectics of materialism. Yet
all the criticism that soon followed on the reception of this
doctrine, and which occupied a full decade, did not result
in an enlivened consciousness of human spirituality and of
history as the history of liberty. Indeed, one effect that remained from this long familiarity with Marxism and with
historical materialism (which Mazzini had loathed because

of its lack of humanity and kindliness) was the habit and the
mental inclination to think of the active forces of history as
"economic classes," feudalism, bourgeoisie, petty bourgeoisie, agrarians, industrials, bankers, working-men, peasants,
modified proletariat and ragged proletariat, and so forth, and
to treat political problems as a calculation of the interests and
forces of the various classes at odds, and a search for the economic class on which to lean. This meant closing one's mind
to a true understanding of history and of human life, and
losing the unity of the spirit that rules the whole and which
is beyond all these empirical schemes of abstract economics
and these calculations of shrewd people. It seemed to be a
great thing, and it certainly cost great efforts, to realize and
assert that over and above the economic classes there is always a "political class," moved by ideals that can be nothing
else but ethical. This observation ought to have led, but did
not, to a total change in the vision of reality, to a new philosophy, which failed to develop; and empiricism and naturalism continued to hold the stage.

If, then, the work of this age appeared to be prosaic and
narrow, that happened not because it actually was so, for in
reality the impulse of the great historical age that had preceded it was taking effect, but because narrowness and pro-
saicness were the attributes of the intellect that considered
it in its development, of the imagination that set it in a bad
light, and of the spirit that instead of embracing it and lend-
ing it warmth left it on the outside or despised it. A dangerous void of thoughts and ideals, which might remain thus for
some time without serious damage, but was close to the
mirage of false ideals. These had already shown their faces
in the literature of the baser romanticism, or decadence, and
now in the last decades of the nineteenth century and the first
of the twentieth they were rising everywhere and contaminating all political thinking. And even a certain awakening

and improvement in philosophy, which during this part of the century made crude naturalism and mean positivism intolerable, showed only partial signs of returning to the path of great philosophy, but on the whole lost itself in mysticism, pragmatism, and other forms of irrationalism. Nevertheless false ideals in practical life, irrationalism in the life of the intellect, spiritual enfeeblement and inner confusion, might have been overcome by criticism and education or worn themselves out like everything that has no intrinsic value or vigour, and given place to their opposites or to better things. But to this mental and sentimental danger was added another that was altogether practical and effective, which arose from the conditions of Europe in her international relations, for these offered matter to such dispositions of the spirit, nourished them, and ended by exciting them and precipitating them into action.

X. INTERNATIONAL POLITICS, ACTIVISM,
AND THE WORLD WAR
(1871-1914)

IF, in fact, the ideas of national individuality and political liberty had been firmly established in the territorial divisions and in the internal order of almost all the European states, and were put into practice in their laws and customs, far different had been the lot of another consequence of the principle of liberty, which had been deduced or divined from the very beginning of the movement: the hoped-for extension of this principle to international relations, in the form of an alliance of the free nations of the world, or, to stick to what was feasible, of an alliance of the nations of Europe, of the "United States of Europe." This goal had always been firmly held in view by that clear-sighted apostle, Giuseppe Mazzini; and there were moments when it almost seemed as though Europe might turn that way, as soon as she had removed the chief obstacles. Especially did this seem possible in 1859-60, under the impression of the independence, unity, and liberty of Italy; of what seemed to be in preparation in pre-Bismarckian Germany and what European liberalism was hastening with its wishes; of the defeat of Austria with the hoped-for ulterior disintegration of her Empire, to be replaced by national states; of the renewed hopes of independence for Poland; and of a modernization and Europeanization of Russia.

But then in this direction unexpected obstacles were encountered; there were pauses and digressions, and at last, after 1870, the renunciation of this idea, which passed among the Utopias, so that it was either no more spoken of among serious persons, or was smiled at, sometimes with melancholy as at an ingenuous youthful dream that has disappeared, sometimes mockingly as at a childish idea. Some perfection of states according to the principle of nationality was accomplished in the following decades; and as a result of the Russo-Turkish war of 1877-78, Serbia, Montenegro, Rumania, Bulgaria, and Greece became independent, or broke the last chains that still bound them to Turkey, or increased their territories. In 1905 the Norwegians, who also had their own nationalist or particularist movement, separated from Sweden, to whom they had been bound by the treaty of 1814, but not by community of political institutions and economic conditions. Autonomy, or Home Rule, was proposed and supported for Ireland by Gladstone, and after thirty years of rejection, counter-proposals, agitations, and rebellions, it finally passed the third reading in the House of Commons and thus received the force of law, although for the moment its execution remained in suspense. But the fate of Poland seemed to be irremediable and its recomposition as a nation ceased even to form an object of hope and a. theme of liberal writings, and in the end Finland lost her autonomy, while Prussia was making efforts to denationalize the Polish regions that were included within her frontiers.

In Austria, the German, Czech, Slovenian, Polish, and other nationalities were fighting one another without rest, after Taaffe's attempt to pacify them had failed in 1893; this rendered all parliamentary activity difficult and almost impossible. Nor was more than a breathing-space obtained with the electoral reform of 1907, by which the obstructionism in the imperial parliament was indeed overcome, but not that in the

local parliaments, and soon afterwards the irreconcilable conflicts were resumed with the same violence as before. In
Hungary, which on its part was trying to increase its autonomy in its relations with Austria, the Hungarian element was
still treating the other nationalities with harshness, suppressing ancient liberties, making the Magyar language compulsory in the people's schools, and holding them under such
complete domination that these oppressed nationalities, the
Slovaks, Rumanians, and Serbs, found in Europe a latter-day
Victor Hugo who became their champion and protector before all the civilized world in the person of the Norwegian
Björnson. Meanwhile the Croats were coming to an understanding with the Serbs in the kingdom of Serbia, and the
"trialism" that was spoken of by some seemed a desperate
idea, for it would have required a complete transformation of
feeling and of social and political relations in the Austro-
Hungarian monarchy, that is, in a political structure that was
a survival of other times, of the days of hereditary states.

Graver and more fundamental than this resistance by Austria-Hungary to the full actuation in Europe of the principle
of nationality was the renunciation of the hope of a free European union that was made impossible by the situation produced by the Franco-German war of 1870-71, which left
France wounded and offended by the loss of two ancient provinces and eager for revenge, and Germany, proud of her
booty, watchful for any threat to take it away again. Around
their implacable hostility the other European states were
grouped; so that in place of a union in which the nations
might find the most advantageous form for their labour and
their progress, the best and indeed the only expedient that
could be found to preserve peace was the old system of European balance of power by means of alliances and counter-
alliances and protective armaments.

All the same, peace was such a great good and so necessary

to Europe in the marvellous increase of her production in all
fields and of her civilization and culture that, thanks to this
balance of power, it was possible for a long time to prevent
a European war, which was feared by all, from breaking out.
Bismarck was the principal artificer of this policy of peace,
for he was very anxious not to risk losing what he had been
able to conquer for Germany and what formed his personal
glory, and was of the opinion that Germany, as he had fitted
her out with territories and power, had nothing else to desire and was, as he used to say, *"saturirt,"* saturated and sa-
tiated, so that another war, even if successful, could not bring
her any real gain. And so in 1878 in the Congress of Berlin,
which followed on the Russo-Turkish War—in which Russia
had thought she could solve the Oriental question in a purely
Russian sense and liberate her "Slav brothers," but which
had aroused the other powers to the protection of their interests and England before all the others—Bismarck boasted
that he had played the part of an "honest broker," whose
profit was the preservation of peace. And this redistribution
of booty among the belligerents and the non-belligerents
seemed at the time to be the best, or the least evil, that could
be accomplished towards that end. Meanwhile, Bismarck
allied Germany with Austria and drew Italy into the alliance.
Italy was worried by the possibility that further acts of aggrandizement might be accomplished to her disadvantage by
France in the Mediterranean and by that of a conflict with
Austria and a consequent reopening of the Roman question;
in this way the Triple Alliance was born. At the same time
Bismarck signed a Reinsurance Treaty with Russia and, by
means of Italy, linked England to the Triple Alliance. In this
field he was a past master, and since mastership is shown in
the ability to limit oneself, he also knew how to behave with
a broad mind and with moderation; and he allowed France,
from whom he shut out every possibility of revenge on the

Rhine, to expand elsewhere and to form undisturbed her great
colonial empire, provided she took care not to enter into competition with the German Empire. In the same way he avoided
laying obstacles in the way of England, who was now endeavouring by means of new occupations to ensure the path to
India and was adding to her empire. While he took no interest in the affairs of Russia and Turkey, and the dominion
of the Straits, and the so-called Oriental question, he helped
Austria to spread within certain limits in the Balkans, in conformity with his idea that Austria's mission lay in the East,
where she was the representative of Germanic culture, although he did not deem it advisable for the Germans of her
empire to be united to Germany, so giving preponderance to
the Catholic element, which he disliked and suspected.

In this fashion peace was maintained in Europe, that is,
in empirical and not in radical and constitutional fashion,
and was paid for not only by ceaseless efforts of vigilance
and diplomatic ability on the part of a genius of diplomacy,
but also by means of enormous and growing military expenditures in Germany and throughout Europe, with millions of
men under arms. Beneath this peace maintained by these
efforts and beneath the heavy burden of armies forever ready,
hostility and danger of war smouldered, however repressed.
Since the first years after 1870 France had been casting an
eye towards Russia, her probable future ally for defence
against her powerful neighbour and for the claims she was
nourishing. England and Russia were in conflict not only over
Constantinople but also over expansion in Asia, where the
two spheres of dominion touched. Italy considered that her
accounts had not been closed with Austria for the lands she
called *irredente.* Still, the peoples were resigned to postpone
the fulfilment of their desires until a more or less distant
future, for the sake of the observance of this balance which
constrained them to keep the peace, and still more for love of

330 International Politics, Activism, and the World War

this peace itself, for fear of the consequences that a war might have on their present territorial possessions as well as on their very political, social, and economic structure, and for the sake of human society, which seemed to be threatened by internationalism, anarchism, and revolutionary socialism.

The "European concert" was not equal to the European mission of civilization, and because of the discordant interests of its components proved itself, in kind, impotent towards Turkey, notwithstanding the horror aroused in Europe in 1876 by the atrocities in Bulgaria and in 1894 and 1896 by those in Armenia, and notwithstanding the fact that a statesman, Gladstone, had called the Sultan the "great assassin." In 1897 it scarcely succeeded in limiting, let alone preventing, the Graeco-Turkish War, and had still less effect on those in the Balkans. Only a few German historians dared to celebrate as an example of a general union "such as history had never before seen" of the principal states of the world, and therefore of capital importance, and *"welthistorisch,"* "a worthy close of the nineteenth century," the expedition decided by the powers in 1900 against China, which Emperor William II embellished with one of his fiery speeches of Attila-like tinge and which the military contingents of the various powers carried out with slaughter and rapine.

The internal beginning of disequilibrium in European equilibrium came from another conflict of far greater import than all the others that had existed so far, because it no longer concerned particular increases of power and dominion, but nothing less than the leadership of Europe and of the world: the conflict between Germany and England. Before it reached the spirit of the nations and the minds of statesmen, it started in the brains of theorists and professors, in whom, as we know, Germany was richer than any other country by way of dubious compensation for her deficiency in statesmen; and it may be observed how it began, not long after 1870, to

gain consistency in the Prussophile historian Treitschke. A
natural pride over the great military victories of 1866 and
1870, and over the European power to which Germany had
risen, was joined in these theorists to the visions they con-
jured up of the hegemony exerted by other peoples throughout the ages: by Greece, who was as it were a first Europe
against the East, by Rome in almost all the civilized world
then known, by Germany herself, who had held considerable
power with her Saxon and Swabian emperors from the tenth
to the thirteenth centuries. And, on the other hand, there was
added the odious spectacle of the leadership exerted by England at the present moment over a great part of the earth and
on the seas and the no less irksome memory of the way in
which she had ever been ready to cut short her competitors
on the Continent—Spain, Holland, France.

From these premises the conclusion was drawn that the
field was open to Germany, who would take up the glorious
task of her imperial heroes of the Middle Ages, thanks to
the Hohenzollerns, a new Greece against a new Persia, a new
Rome against a new Carthage, and that she would never meet
with the fate of Holland. Germany was verdant with youth,
military prowess, learning, ability in every field, civil virtues; England was quite faded, shrivelled, and decadent in
all these respects, a state that might be qualified as "reactionary," hypocritical like all those who feel themselves to
be old and weak, governed by statesmen of few and limited
ideas, enjoying a power that was obviously an anachronism,
acquired as though by theft in times when naval battles
and mercenary troops decided wars of world-wide importance
and when it was possible to seize forts and naval stations in
foreign countries, and which was therefore no longer admis-
sible in times of national states and great popular armies.
Now justice demanded that Germany should ask for a new
partition of the world, no longer accepting the present one,

which had been made when she was torn by internal warfare
and prevented by it from forming a great state; and equity
required that she should be entrusted with the hegemony that
England wrongly laid claim to and was no longer able to
hold, because Germany, instead, was ready to assume the
direction of the world with a more robust arm, with more
modern concepts, and with immense possibilities of development, perhaps even with the creation of a new synthesis of
East and West, of a new religion of Humanity. Thus did these
theorists and professors reason and reckon before swarms of
attentive students, basing their arguments on conventional
partitions and classifications and historical laws and on the
detritus of the old philosophy of history and biblical ideas
concerning the succession of the four monarchies, such as
the hegemony that belonged to each particular people, nation,
or state in turn, and the weary survival of those who had
exerted it and who now had to consider themselves permanently collapsed, no longer historically active, dragging out
their life in the train of the others, and supported or com-
manded by the one that is at present in power or the holder
of the hegemony; and on the virtue of certain tribes or races
born to command, such as the Germanic, and so forth. All
this is mere abstraction and mythology, treated as though it
were reality and substituted for the genuine and concrete
reality, which was at the same time far more simple and far
more complex, less theological or less naturalistic but more
human. Professorial pedantry, which lay at the bottom of
all such theories and opinions, was betrayed by the accusation, which summed up all the others, that was made against
England, that she had formed her empire little by little, im-
perceptibly and by theft, that is, that the British Empire had
risen spontaneously, *rebus ipsis dictantibus;* whereas the
other invoked by them would be constructed by philosophical
and historical deduction and by plan, and be achieved not

by occasional *coups de main* and guerilla warfare and simple
naval battles, but by great land battles between nations, like
those of Sadowa and Sedan.

There was, in this method of preparing politics, the same
defect that is generally to be noted in German literature and
art: the kind of criticism, that is, of theoretical formula,
which often precedes the fact and wishes to bring it forth in
its own manner; but in politics the consequences of this error
are far more pernicious. It was only very late, towards the
last years of the nineteenth century, that England raised the
vast empire that she had acquired in the course of a couple
of centuries to what was called imperial self-consciousness.
However, in international relations there are only two ways
of obtaining one's demands, either by negotiation or by force
of arms. It was quite out of the question that England would
ever be brought by negotiation to declare herself decadent,
aged, weakened, and ready to give up to Germany the sea,
her colonies, the Dominions, and the sceptre of government;
and there is no other way to find whether one nation is really
decadent or dead and another alive and vigorous except by
putting it to the test, which may furnish much matter for disappointment and surprise. For these reasons, if these theorists
had any practical intentions at all in the suit brought by them,
with the *actio popularis* of which they were the promoters in
the international field, it was clear that what they wanted,
sooner or later or at the right moment, was war. Thus were
sown in men's minds the first seeds of the world-struggle between Germany and England.

Bismarck, who did not believe that politics could be carried on with such historico-philosophical impedimenta and
mistrusted the professors, took good care not to encourage
these world-wide and warlike programmes. Furthermore, he
was not even very keen on colonies, and when in 1884 he
gave way to the pressure of the colonialists and began to

extend German protection over some territories of South Africa, he persisted in his conviction that this was not the path Germany ought to engage herself in. The year before his death, and after he had quite given up public business, when Admiral Tirpitz explained to him his naval programme, by which he proposed to guarantee Germany's commerce against England's control of the seas with a great navy, Bismarck could not conceal his anger at this dangerous political theorizing of technicians. But under another aspect, the German way of considering international relations, the familiarity with the idea of changing the appearance of the world by means of great blows of war, a certain wide-spread cynicism of speech due more than to anything else to the ideal of rough resoluteness or *Schneidigkeit* and which caused many good and honest persons of that good and honest people to contort their faces in fierce grimaces—all this sprang from his example, from his teachings, from the satisfied comments that he liked to make on his actions and on his successes over the enemies whom he had fooled, faced, and defeated, from his "Lombard sneer," as the old-fashioned Italian men of letters would have said. He strongly desired peace, because he thought that the needs of Germany were satisfied by the work he had accomplished; but what would happen when the first big meal was digested and a new hunger, a new desire for food—and already the first signs of it were visible—agitated this powerful body? How would it be possible, without discarding his example and his teachings, without deserving the sarcasm of his bitter realism, without abandoning the tradition of his sentiment and his attitude, to persuade her to choose a different goal, to follow in politics a different concept, a liberal and cosmopolitan or European concept? And what would happen, when he would no longer be steering the ship, or when he had been set aside as afflicted with senility and no longer equal to himself, and other men would follow

him, men not gifted with his sagacity, his prudence, his genius, but who remembered what he had done and said, and
were therefore disposed to imitate him materially, that is, to
give poor imitations of his work?

The new hunger, the new foreign policy, the new men,
came and the new age came, known as the "new course," with
Emperor William II. And soon the idea of the world-power
that Germany was to win towered over everything, was taught
and inculcated, entered into every German's mind, gave another turn to the relations with other states, and the web
woven by Bismarck was in great part destroyed. In 1890,
immediately after his retirement, the Reinsurance Treaty
with Russia was not renewed, so that this country, which was
already inclined to an understanding with France, was im-
pelled to approach her even more closely, and in 1894 a
formal alliance between the two was concluded. The danger
of an imminent war with Russia threatened for several years,
until Russia turned her attention to the Far East. 1896 saw
William II's famous telegram to President Kruger, an act of
open hostility towards the English and their South African
policy, and of encouragement to the Boers in the fight they
were starting and in which Germany then failed to support
them. In 1898 the same temerarious personage pronounced
the speech with the motto, "Our future lies on the sea," and
the next year repeated, "The great need is for a strong navy."
Work was begun on the construction of that navy, which
Tirpitz directed in the manner and with the intention that Bismarck had disapproved. And the Emperor travelled in the
Levant, in Damascus proclaimed himself "the friend of three
hundred millions of Mohammedans," and took Turkey under
his protection.

Already at this time aversion for England had become a
popular sentiment in Germany, and was answered, naturally,
by a like aversion, although one less laden with theoretical

arguments, on the other side. England was troubled by Germany's words and acts; there too one spoke of a *delenda Carthago*. Meanwhile the requisite precautions were taken; the "splendid isolation" was given up, and the English Government in 1904 concluded the Entente with France, while Delcassé was working on the policy that was known as the encirclement of Germany. In 1905 William made his unexpected appearance at Tangiers, and so in 1906 the conference of Algeciras on the affairs of Morocco was convoked, with the results of which Germany was dissatisfied because of the want of support from one of the powers of the Triple Alliance, Italy, who, without leaving the alliance, but preserving her ancient and steady relations with England, had initiated friendly relations with France. In 1908 Germany once more came to words with France over Morocco, and the treaties of settlement were not yet arranged when the Emperor committed another *coup de tête* with the interview published by the *Daily Telegraph*. In 1911, Germany sent a war-ship to Agadir, and war was on the point of breaking out—for England was quite ready for a break at that moment—when matters were patched up by a new agreement between France and Germany, which procured to the latter the acquisition of a big piece of the French Congo. England did not cease to prepare diplomatically and militarily, and in 1907 she entered into an agreement with Russia over Persia, Afghanistan, and Tibet, and also came to an understanding with Japan. Meanwhile Germany, allowing her relations with Italy to get on as best they might, bound herself more closely to Austria; that is, to the power that was least confident of her own future, and who because of the clashes of the nationalities that she enfolded in her bosom, and the others that were started in the Balkans, particularly on the part of Serbia, and because of rivalry with Russia, who protected the Slav populations, was with ever growing frequency imperilling the peace of Europe. This was seen in 1908 in the effect of her annexation, in defiance of the Treaty of Berlin, of Bosnia-Herzegovina, and during the Italo-Turkish War of 1911-12 and the Balkan Wars of 1912-13, and in the plan she conceived in 1913 of attacking Serbia, from which she was dissuaded for the moment by Italy's opposition. Military equipment was increasing in Germany, in France, in England, in all the states.

When today we re-read what was printed in German books, pamphlets, and newspapers between 1912 and 1914, we have the impression of being in the atmosphere of war. In 1913 General Bernhardi published his book *Deutschland und der nächste Krieg,* and his voice was echoed by other military writers and by many clubs and associations that had risen to promote land and sea armaments and which favoured education for and instigation to war. What amounted to an ultimatum was issued to England: she must give up world-supremacy, she must allow Germany a free hand on the Continent in such a way that she could become the centre of a union of all Central Europe, beat France and take away her colonies, annex Belgium and Holland, divide the French possessions in North Africa with Italy, and carry out without hindrance the economic penetration of the Near East. And the arguments were reiterated concerning Germany's prolificness, the two millions of Germans emigrated to America and lost to the fatherland, Germany's intellectual capacity, which was superior to that of the English; concerning France and England, who were decadent and dying, for whom Germany was certainly not meant to act as a charitable and insurance institution. Plans were made to add Turkey, Bulgaria, and Rumania to the Triple Alliance; and meanwhile, repeating the well-known words of Von Moltke in his letter to Bluntschli and the more recent words of General von der Goltz, the moralizing virtue of war and bloodshed was praised, and the se-

lection that it operates of the strongest and best, the regeneration of enfeebled mankind by means of this bath of blood, the
civilization that war alone can promote, the force that it alone
possesses to save humanity from stagnation, from *Domesti-
kation*—a new technical word that had come into use. From
time to time throughout 1913 and during the first months of
1914 the announcement and the alarm were heard that the
right moment for Germany had come and that she must not
let it escape her. In July, 1914, an officer published a pamphlet on what he called the Empire's fatal hour, which the
Crown Prince praised and recommended for dissemination.
In one of these years (February and March of 1913) the
historian Cramb gave a series of lectures in London on "Germany and England," with the intention of setting forth clearly
to the English, in its origin, its aspects, and also in its causes,
this violent passion and resolute will of the Germans, which
he did not make fun of and indeed considered as a serious
danger and a tragic struggle of supreme defence that England
would be called upon to face against a weighty and worthy
opponent.

   In such political plans and desires for war, men of noble
hearts and elevated minds took part, men like Stresemann
who in the years to come were summoned to the opposite task
of recognizing the common delirium from which they had
suffered and of trying to adapt the spirit of Germany and
all Europe to peace—Stresemann too at this time was asking
for a "place in the sun" for Germany and the conquest of
other colonies, and demanding land and sea armaments. But
there certainly were, even in Germany, some who tried to
gain a hearing for words of sense. Among these was Delbrück,
the master of military historiography, who had once been a
tutor in the house of Crown Prince Frederick, and who saw
the real peril to Germany's future not in the Socialist party
but in "Pan-Germanism," and saw that in the war many

wished to let loose "an unspeakable calamity for the Germans and for the whole civilized world, because it is useless, and, what is more, in the present condition of Europe victory is very doubtful." An Englishman, Norman (now Sir Norman) Angell, published in 1910, and reprinted with added arguments during the ensuing years, a book that was translated into all languages and was read in every country, *The Great Illusion.* Its thesis was that war, even if in other times it may have won lands and dominion for conquering peoples, was no longer adapted to the purpose, because the eventual winner of it would not be able either to seize the riches of another people—since, through the economic interdependence of the world these would evaporate as soon as they were touched and would cause those of the conqueror to evaporate as well—nor would he be able to impose his own language and customs, just as it was impossible even for the small foreign minorities in the existing states to do so; nor cause superior ideals to triumph, for there were no ideals in any country that another country did not enjoy as well, and in all of them there were the same clashes of ideals; nor would it be possible by this means to generate capacities and virtues suited to modern and civilized man. Since war is certainly, in one of its aspects, a utilitarian factor, this utilitarian calculation, the exactness of which has been proved by the event, was logical and convincing; but men do not always accept the results of arguments before they have verified them by experience, no matter how hard and bitter this may be.

And then, under another aspect and in another sphere, this war psychology was not a purely utilitarian fact, but was related to a moral disposition, which had to be examined and understood by itself, and which it was much more difficult to change by simple critical analysis, without bitter experience and provident misfortune. It has already been said that after

1870, in Europe, the active meditation of moral and political matters had diminished, as well as the faith that it alone produces and renews, and the warmth and enthusiasm that follow upon faith; it has been pointed out how dangerous this languor and this kind of spiritual emptiness were, and how the danger did not diminish but indeed grew graver when materialism, naturalism, and positivism were shaken off, a more cultivated philosophy was taken up, and the insidious paths of mysticism and irrationalism were willingly preferred. This danger was that of the formation and elevation of a false ideal. The conditions favourable to it already lay in the very forces of the modern world, in its indefatigable activity in commercial and industrial enterprises, in its technical discoveries, its ever more powerful machines, its geographical explorations, its colonization and economic exploitation, its tendency to confer primary importance on scientific and practical rather than on speculative and humanistic studies, even in the encouragement and development of recreation and social games—what is known as sport, from bicycles to automobiles, from canoes and yachts to air-ships, from boxing and football to skiing, which all in various ways conspired to give too large a part in habits and interests to physical development and skill, to the detriment of the part played by intelligence and feeling.

The same effect was obtained not only by the national armaments for defence and offence, but also by Marxian socialism, whose ideology, taken up by the very social classes that it was fighting, set in the foreground the fight of one class against the other, the general strike, the seizure of power, the violent overthrow of the existing social order, the dictatorship of the proletariat, and such things; so that no matter how individualistic and contemptuous of the people were those who opposed the socialists, they too devised similar means and, grown demagogues in their turn, looked eagerly to the "masses," that is, not to the people but to the swarm—blind and impulsive or sensitive to impulses—of the mob, a cheering and howling beast that any man of audacity can move to his own ends. Further contributions to the exaltation of violence were brought by the theories of ethnologists and pseudo-historians concerning the struggle of the races, and the artificial political consciousness that men were attempting to build on these of Germanic and Latin races, Slav or Scandinavian or Iberic or Hellenic races—as not only real facts but natural values to be asserted one against the others, and with the subjection or extermination of the others.

Warfare, bloodshed, slaughter, harshness, cruelty, were no longer objects of deprecation and repugnance and opprobrium, but were regarded as necessities for the ends to be achieved, and as acceptable and desirable. They were clothed with a certain poetic attraction, and even afforded a certain thrill like that of religious mystery, so that one spoke of the beauty that lies in war and bloodshed, and of the heroic intoxication that in this way alone man can extol and enjoy. This ideal may be designated by the word, which has already been uttered here and there, "activism": a generic term, which gathers together all its particular forms and therefore seems to be the most suitable. And although it has been called imperialism, we must point out that this name, which arose in England about 1890, did not in itself mean anything but a better, stronger, and more coherent development to be given to the British colonial policy, and that activism alone imprinted another character on it. And although it has also been called, and more commonly, nationalism, we must remember that this second name arose in France at the time of anti-Dreyfusism, and bore a connotation of anti-Semitism and at the same time of reaction or monarchical absolutism, but that the national idea in itself, and in the classical form that it received from Mazzini, was humanitarian and cosmopoli-

tan, and therefore the contrary of this nationalism which became activism and ran through the parabola already divined
by Grillparzer in the formula: "Humanity, through nationality, returns to bestiality."

What was, in its innermost nature, this ideal of activism
which was taking form and consistency in the soul of Europe?
Notwithstanding that above everything it fought and loathed
liberalism, the only element that—ready as it was to receive
all other elements and to enter into every alliance, including
that with Catholicism and the Church—it never received, and
with which it never allied itself; notwithstanding this, and indeed because of this, its original impulse was nothing other
than the principle of liberty, so intrinsic in the modern world
that it is not in any way possible to do without it. For if liberty is deprived of its moral soul, if it is detached from the
past and from its venerable tradition, if the continuous creation of new forms that it demands is deprived of the objective
value of this creation, if the struggles that it accepts and the
wars and the sacrifice and the heroism are deprived of the
purity of the end, if the internal discipline to which it spontaneously submits is replaced by external direction and commands—then nothing remains but action for action's sake,
innovation for the sake of innovation, and fighting for the
fight's sake; war and slaughter and death-dealing and suffering death are things to be sought for and desired for themselves, and obedience too, but the obedience that is customary
in war; and the upshot is activism. This is, accordingly, in this
translation and reduction and mournful parody that it
achieves of an ethical ideal, a substantial perversion of the
love of liberty, a devil-worship taking the place of that of
God, and yet still a religion, the celebration of a black mass,
but still a mass. And jf it hates liberalism, that is because the
devil is a *simia Dei*; if it still exerts a certain attraction, it is
similar to that of the fallen angel, or, to speak in less figura-

tive language, it is like that which Tacitus attributes to *malig-nitas*, in which *"falsa species libertatis inest."* It is not directly and properly reactionary, as it has been considered to be because of some of its fanciful additions, certain occasional decorations of the *ancien régime*, of monarchy *à la* Louis XIV, of the Counter-Reformation, and others; it lacks all support in previous history and bears full in its face the signs of contemporary industrialism and of the psychology that it favours—to such a degree that because of this aspect it is sometimes called Americanism. That this deviation of the impetus towards liberty leads to or tends to the opposite of liberty, and to modes of reaction, lies entirely within the logic of its procedure, for it leads to the domination of the individual over individuals, to the enslavement of others and therefore of itself, to the depression of personality, which in the beginning it had fooled itself into thinking it might potentiate, whereas by unbridling it and depriving it of moral consciousness, it deprives it of its inner life and sends it along the path to perdition.

Such is the moral and religious or (which amounts to the same thing) the irreligious and immoral nature of activism; we have seen what were the occasions that promoted it in Europe towards the end of the nineteenth century and the beginning of the next and provided it with matter and colour. But its deepest genesis still lies in morbid romanticism, which was never completely vanquished, although put to sleep for a while in the life of Europe (and to vanquish it altogether and eradicate it forever is certainly impossible, because it too is a perpetually recurring crisis of the human soul), that romanticism which had already put in a new appearance after 1860 under the form of aloofness from practice and politics and as "decadence," and which now, stripped of all the ideal and noble elements of its primitive epoch, was overflowing— and this was what counted—into the practical and political field. The result was the plethora of "dilettanti" of these things who were seen and heard and who filled old and expert statesmen with irritation and distrust. Literature, which was already feeding on erotic and pathological images, soon became imbued with this new romantic, pseudo-heroic, brutal and sanguinary tendency and confirmed it and introduced it into people's minds. Admiration for Napoleon started afresh, not as it had been in the *grognards*, in the surviving soldiers and officers of the Grande Armée and in the young men who listened to the narratives of that epic age, but rather in the form that Stendhal had given to it and that his contemporaries had neither understood nor felt, but which now found its right time (just as its author had foretold in 1880, specifying more or less the exact date when his fortunes would begin to mend). And a sort of *imitatio* was conceived of that man of action, audacious, resolute, clear-sighted, who cherished no hesitation or scruples, who took fortune by storm and conquered the world, and of other personages who resembled him in various ways or who were interpreted in the same fashion. A philosopher, too, who was more of a poet and who bore in his heart the yearning for purity and greatness, Nietzsche, was interpreted materially and turned into the prophet of activism. Men like D'Annunzio in Italy, Barrès in France, and many others libidinous and sadist like them turned, out of sensual delight or from the caprices of new stimuli and emotions, to this new romanticism. This, not content with inspiring the activistic ideal, after having on various occasions tried the hermetic style, lost even that modesty of style and became activistic or "dynamic" even in the artistic form itself, and called itself futurism.

The young men, naturally, were carried away by images of such grandiose appearance, and were stimulated by this instigation to throw away the past and with it all prudence and precaution, and in great numbers became "nationalists," "imperialists," "dynamists," "sportists," and "futurists," or all these things at once. And this happened in every part of Europe, and even outside of Europe; and not in Germany alone, which in this respect was neither more nor less morbidly affected than any other country, and cultivated no thoughts of this kind that were not cultivated elsewhere, although, in conformity with some of her traditions, she was particularly fond of ethnicism or racialism, and attributed activism to Germanism. This accounts for the interest and favour with which she received various literary products that made use of these tendencies and fancies to construct the philosophy of history and metaphysics. And this "activistic" state of mind really generated the European and soon World War, and made it impossible for the dangers of war that lay in the international situation to be thwarted, as they had been for many years when it was not yet dominant, but good sense and prose were still rife. And indeed, abstractly considered, it would still have been possible to thwart them on various occasions and, among others, in the often repeated attempts, such as those of 1908-09 and 1911-12, of a naval agreement with England, to which Tirpitz objected without finding anyone able to withstand him successfully. Opportunities are for those who know how to snatch them, and one man can do everything or nothing according to the degree to which the public spirit does or does not offer him the forces to use and help him in his good works and restrain and correct him in his errors; and little scope is left the peoples and the nations that obey the situations in which they have been placed by previous history and by the combination of events. All which goes to prove how hopeless is the inquiry as to the so-called responsibility for the war, which is imputed to individuals or to nations, all of whom can, by syllogizing, fling on to others the fault that others attempt to attribute to them,

and so from the first to the last lead it back to the author of
the world, who certainly is in this case really responsible,
because he and no one else arranged that European life, after
passing through so many trials and experiences, should still
pass through this experience of activistic romanticism and
blind and foolish nationalism.

And just as in Germany in the face of the Pan-Germanists
and the fomenters of war there were men who recommended
a more serious policy, so activism, under the various names
and in the various forms under which it appeared, likewise
found critics, satirists, advisers, and faultfinders. Much might
be said about the things that were written against instinctive
and animal fury, against speed become a passion in itself,
against mechanism that was a process of despiritualization or
Entseelung, against sport that was destroying "all higher culture," and against empty imperialism and empty nationalism
and their false and swollen rhetoric—none the less such because it wrapped itself in the words and images of energism
—and so forth. But the wind was blowing in that direction,
and many did not even realize in what direction they were
sailing; fate drew them on with its superindividual force.

And it drew them to the war, which, already in action in
the spirit of Europe, took fire, in the shape of a war fought
with arms, in that part of Europe where there was a simul-
taneous agitation of confused demands for national liberty
and nationalistic tendencies, where Austrian imperialism and
Russian imperialism were fighting for supremacy; and when
it had once been kindled, it spread until it became a universal holocaust. All, willing or unwilling, were drawn into
it, unable to withstand the forces let loose, obliged to draw
the conclusions of the premises they had posited, forced to
take part in the war because to keep out of it was impossible
or would have led to greater evils in the future. And the war

was envisaged as a war of supremacy between Germany and England, and (fulfilling a prophecy made in 1870 by the English statesman Otway) with a union or Entente of almost all Europe—and later even including that additional Europe which is the North American republic—against Germany, who remained with Austria-Hungary and drew Turkey and Bulgaria in with her.

The moral theme of the war was excellently conceived and proclaimed by the Entente as a defence of the liberty of the nations against the menace of a new empire like that of Charles V, a defence of the liberal system against the authoritarian system of Prussia and Austria-Hungary, of the Hohenzollerns and the Hapsburgs, a permanent liberation of those nations which were still oppressed or dependent, a redemption of the Germans themselves from the antiquated political régime that persisted among them (in contrast with Western Europe, all liberal and parliamentary), a permanent passage from the system of hegemonies and balance of power to the alliance of the nations. And the Germans, on the contrary, were extremely clumsy in the way in which they announced their reasons for war, because they were unable to put forward anything beyond the "sacred defence" of their people, which was something too generic, common to all the combatant nations for the very reason that they were fighting, and void of historical meaning; it did not settle what was the political ideal that was to be set up against that of the Entente. And when the German professors wanted to supply this precision that was lacking, they wrote such naïve things concerning the method that Germany would follow for the unification of Europe, like that which Prussia had followed for the unification of Germany, concerning the *pax Germanica* and the happiness and morality that the world would enjoy under the government of the Hohenzollerns and their bureaucracy, as to cause every free spirit to shudder or frown or

smile. After which, for good measure, they expressed amazement that the "war propaganda" (as the phrase was) of the
Entente was so much more efficacious or (as another phrase
had it) better "organized" than their own. In that hour the
mind of Cavour and that of Bismarck rose up against one another; and it was not to be wondered at if the first still radi-
ated that light over humanity, spread that warmth, kindled
that enthusiasm, which the second was unable to win.

Nevertheless, when the Germans cast the accusation of
hypocrisy at the system of ideas put forward by the Entente,
they were not altogether in the wrong. Not that it was all or
deliberately hypocrisy; this will never be admitted by the
writer of these pages, who, as an Italian, not only remembers
perfectly well the sentiments and the thoughts that at the
outburst of the war and during the months of Italian neutrality existed or were awakened among old liberals and
statesmen, and which were manifested in wide popular currents, but who also bears in mind the persons, the acts, the
writings, the letters, of so many of those young Italians who
went out to die on the Carso and in the Alps, sweetest flowers
of the Italian Risorgimento, educated by their fathers and
their teachers and by their poets, and by that last great Italian
poet, Giosuè Carducci, in the love of liberty and justice and
humanity. Similar thoughts and feelings were nourished elsewhere, and in England the liberals truly believed that the
war, which it was necessary to accept, was to be the last war,
and that after it international relations would be placed on
new foundations, and the system of balance of power and
alliances and counter-alliances and secret treaties would be
replaced by public treaties and guarantees of peace. And the
President of the United States of America no less seriously
conceived the famous fourteen points he proposed to the combatant peoples. But this accusation was true in so far as this

entire liberal ideology found no echo or answer in the psychology that we have described as being extremely powerful in Europe, just as much among the nations of the Entente as in Germany. And since this liberal ideology still preserved the power of persuasion in others or over the multitudes, the imperialists and nationalists and similar statesmen and publicists made use of it, hypocritically and unctuously, for political ends, treating it as they treated Catholicism, the latter as "Catholic atheists" and the former as liberals and humanitarians who despised liberty and humanity. They were shrewder, in any case, than the statesmen of Germany, who in feeble imitation of Bismarck declared that "treaties are scraps of paper" and that "necessity knows no law," and than her nationalists and racialists, who in Romano-Christian Europe, in the Europe of the Reformation and the French Revolution, dragged out Arminius and the Nibelungs and Teutonic mythology, and delighted in giving the names of Wodan or the Valkyrs, Siegfried or Hagen, to the lines of the German trenches.

In the ferocity of the long war, all respect for truth was banished from the mind, the tone of all the belligerents became inhuman, selfish, rapacious; other statesmen succeeded to those of the beginning or they themselves suffered a change of spirit and gave themselves over to the current of hatred and unbridled greed. And if German statesmen, in the partial victories won by their enemies, imposed the burdensome treaties of Brest Litovsk and Bucharest, when the war was won, those of the Entente instead of rising to a loftier sphere copied them with the Congress and Treaty of Versailles, where the conscience of humanity was grievously offended by the spectacle of the victors who were dragging to their tribunal the heroic adversary, dripping with the blood of a hundred battles, sitting over him as judges of morality and executors of justice, and obliging him to admit his guilt, when they too were guilty in their turn—if of guilt we must speak, and not rather, as it seems to us, of a common error that demanded a common expiation. The war, which had been announced to the peoples with the promise of a general catharsis, in its course and its end was completely untrue to this promise.

EPILOGUE

WHOEVER compares the political geography of before and after the World War, and sees the German Republic in the place of the Germany of the Hohenzollerns, the Austrian Empire disintegrated and in its place the new or enlarged national states with German Austria and Magyar Hungary restricted to narrow frontiers, and France with her provinces lost in 1870 restored to her, and Italy, who has gathered in her *irredente* lands and stretches out her frontiers to the Brenner, and Poland reconstructed, and Russia no longer Czarist but Soviet, and the United States of America risen to be one of the greatest factors in European politics, and so on through all the other great changes worked in territories and relationships of power; and whoever, on the other hand, remembers the orderly, rich Europe of other days, flourishing in commerce, full of comfort, with her agreeable life, bold and sure of herself, and considers her now, impoverished, troubled, mournful, all divided by customs barriers, the gay international society that used to gather in her capitals dispersed, each nation busied with its own cares and with the fear of worse, and therefore distracted from spiritual things, and the common life of thought, and art, and civilization extinguished—he is induced to see a profound difference between the two Europes and to mark the separation with the line, or rather with the abyss, of the war of 1914-18. But he who instead passes from what is external and secondary to what is intrinsic, and seeks for the passions and acts of the European soul, at once mentally sets up the continuity and homogeneity between the two Europes so diverse in appearance, and if he looks closely, without letting himself be put off by these superficial impressions, he finds in the two aspects the same features, even if after the war and what has followed it they are somewhat sharpened. In the altered political conditions he finds the same dispositions and the same spiritual conflicts, however aggravated by that heaviness and obtuseness that the war, killing millions of lives, creating the habit of violence and destroying the habit of the eager critical and constructive labour of the mind, was bound to produce along with the severer effects of its lofty tragedy.

Activism is developing with the same impulsiveness, and even with greater vehemence. The nationalist and imperialist outbursts inflame the victorious nations because they are victorious and the vanquished nations because they are vanquished. The new states that have arisen add new nationalisms and new imperialisms. The impatience for liberal institutions has given rise to open or masked dictatorships, and to the desire for dictatorships everywhere. Liberty, which before the war was a static faith or a practice with scant faith, has fallen from the minds of men even where it has not fallen from their institutions, and has been replaced by activistic libertarianism, which more than ever dreams of wars and upheavals and destruction, and bursts out into disordered movements and plans showy and arid works. It cares nothing for or despises such works as are built with meditation and love, with the pious sentiment of the past and with the ardent force that opens up the future: actions that come from the heart and speak to hearts; the speculations that speak words of truth; the histories that supply a knowledge of all that man has laboriously created by working and struggling; the poetry that is poetry and, as such, a thing of beauty.

Communism, which under the name of socialism had been inoculated into the life of politics and the state and into the course of history, has appeared once more in its scission and crudity, another bitter enemy of liberalism, which it derides and ingenuously calls moralistic. On a par with activism, with which it is often merged, this communism is sterile, and it suffocates all thought, religion, art, all these and other things that it would like to enslave and can only destroy. And once more we behold on the scene, almost as though they were ideas freshly born of youthful truth, all the distortions and decrepit sophisms of historical materialism, of which every man with a little knowledge of criticism and of the history of ideas well knows what to think, but which, none the less, have once more taken on an air of novelty and modernity simply because, transported from Europe to Russia, they have returned thence more simplified and more gross than they were before, and are successful once more in times of grossness, simplification, and credulity. On the other hand, Catholicism, which had attempted to regather strength from irrationalism and mysticism, has received and continues to receive, in great numbers, feeble or enfeebled souls and confused or turbid adventurers of the spirit. Even pessimism and the voices of decadence, which were heard in pre-war literature, are now heard once more, and are preaching the downfall of the West or even of the human race, which, after trying to rise from the animal to man, is about to relapse (according to the new philosophers and prophets) into the life of the beast.

All this is a fact, and it is useless to deny it and even to restrict it to a few persons and to this or that country, to this or that people, because, like the fact of which it is a continuation, it belongs to Europe and to the whole world. And since it is a fact, it has to fulfil a function in the development of the spirit, in social and human progress, if not as a direct creator of new values, at least as material and stimulus for the strengthening, deepening, and widening of ancient values. This function, whatever it is, that it fills will be known and described by the future historian, who will see before him, when it has reached the end of its period, the movement in which we are engaged and whatever it will have led to; but it cannot be known and judged by us for the very reason that we are engaged in the movement; as we live and move in its midst, many things can be and in fact are observed and understood by us, but not that one which has not yet occurred and the history of which it is in consequence not given us to conceive.

And what does it matter to each one of us, practically, that we cannot conceive this history? This matters: that we should take part in it not with contemplation of what cannot be contemplated, but with action according to the rôle that is incumbent upon each one of us and which conscience assigns and duty commands. Those who, contrary to the ancient warning of Solon, endeavour to understand and judge a life "before it is ended," and who are lost in conjectures and previsions, should beware lest this divagation into what it is impossible to know be not in fact the prompting of an evil demon, who is cradling them in indolence and distracting them from the task.

Not the "history of the future" (as the old writers used to define prophecy), but that of the past which is epitomized in the present, is necessary for work and for action—which would not be real action if it were not illumined by the light of truth. And from this necessity is born also this new meditation that we have gone through, and that we invite others to go through, of the history of the nineteenth century. And with regard to what is present and actual, it is necessary to examine, and in every case to re-examine, the ideals that today are accepted, or proposed or tested, to see whether they have the power to dissolve or overcome or correct our own ideal, and at the same time to change or modify it in consequence of the criticism through which it passes, and, in every case, to possess it again in firmer fashion.

That the ideal of a transcendent order of truth, of moral law and practice, and at the same time of government from above and from heaven, exercised on earth by a shepherd and represented by a Church, has not even yet been integrated by that intrinsic mental justification the lack of which, during the course of centuries, had been discovered in it, is obvious, and it is almost unpleasant to insist on it, as in all discussions dealing with the obvious and which may seem to be ungenerous. All the same, this is the substantial point; and the renewed cocksureness of the clergy in the years after the war, because of the difficulties that troubled the various governments and the concessions that they accordingly were led to make, may awaken anger, but has in itself no real importance and is a well-understood alternation and quite transitory. It may be worth while to refer here to what a German Catholic recently wrote: "It is only in appearance, and only on the surface of its natural existence, that Catholicism has made any gains during recent times, but the great idea that gave it unity is no longer alive, and has never been in such difficulties, never been so unstable and so entangled in material and incidental things." And truly, with regard to this last part, we may well doubt what force the Church can derive from the quality of the persons who have entered into her bosom in swarms. The spiritual motive, however, that has urged the best of these to take refuge in or to return to Catholicism (or to other similar refuges of less venerable and less constant authority) has been nothing but the need, in the tumult of clashing and changing ideas and feelings, for a fixed truth and an imposed rule: that is, mistrust and renunciation, weakness and childish fear in the face of the concept of the absoluteness and at the same time the relativity of all truth, and the necessity for continuous criticism and self-criticism by which the truth is every instant increased and renewed together with the life that grows and is renewed. But a moral ideal cannot conform to the needs of the weak, the discouraged, and the fearful.

Likewise, it cannot conform to the use of those who grow drunk on action for its own sake, which, experienced, conceived, and pursued in this fashion, leaves after it nausea and an indifference for everything that has aroused or that can arouse the enthusiasm of man, and inability for every objective labour. The human race has by this time become acquainted with all forms of nationalism and imperialism, and similar efforts and conquests, and has already uttered its verdict: *Inveni amariorem felle.* Activism still rages on all sides; but where is its tranquillity of mind, its confidence, its joy of life? Sadness is imprinted on the faces of these men—of the worthiest among them, because where even that is not found, there is worse still, there is uncouthness and stupidity. And perhaps even the excesses to which activism abandons itself, the passion by which it is rent, the upheavals that it menaces, are the symptoms of no distant recovery from the fever with which Europe and the world have been and are ailing: a fever, and not an ideal, unless one wishes to sublimate a fever to an ideal.

Communism, of which it is usually said that it has entered the reality of facts and been effectuated in Russia, has by no means been effectuated quâ communism, but in the manner indicated by its critics and permitted by its internal contradiction, that is, as a form of autocracy, which has deprived the Russian people of what little mental movement and liberty it enjoyed or obtained under the preceding Czarist autocracy. The abolition of the state, "the passage from the realm of necessity to that of liberty," over which Marx theorized not only has not taken place and communism has not abolished (and could not, nor will anyone ever be able to, abolish) the state, but by the irony of things, it has modelled the heaviest of states that it is possible to conceive. By which we do not in the least mean to belittle the necessity faced by the Russian revolutionaries to enter upon this path and upon no other; nor the greatness of the work that, under these conditions, they have undertaken and furthered, in their attempt to add to the fertility of their country's rich resources; nor the various lessons that may be learned from their various activities; nor the mystical enthusiasm, even if it be a materialistic enthusiasm, that animates them and alone can enable them to bear up under the immense weight they have shouldered and give them the courage to trample, as they do, on religion and speculation and poetry, on everything that we venerate as sacred, on everything that we cherish as amiable. But when we say that, we mean to emphasize that they have, so far, uttered a peremptory negation in words and by acts of violence and by methods of repression, but they have not solved, nor will they in this fashion ever be able to solve, the fundamental problem of human relations, which is that of liberty, in which alone human society flourishes and bears fruit, the only reason for the life of man on the earth and without which life would not be worth living: a problem that stands there and cannot be eliminated, that springs from the heart of things, and which they must feel vibrating in the very human material that they handle and which they are trying to mould according to their ideas. And if they ever in the future face it or others face it for them, it will ruin the materialistic foundation of their structure, and that structure will have to be differently supported and greatly modified; and just as today pure communism has not been put into practice, it will not be even then. Outside of Russia, this pseudo-communism appeals to the mind with the added weight expressed in the ancient adage concerning the *"major e longinquo reverentia,"* with the charm of what is distant in time and in space and therefore assumes outlines of fantastic fascination. But nevertheless it has so far not spread or has been suppressed as soon as it has made its appearance; and, in truth, in Western and Central Europe the two conditions are lacking that existed in Russia—the Czarist tradition and mysticism—so that it would seem that Miliukov was not wrong when, twelve years ago, he judged that Lenin "in Russia was building on the solid ground of the good ancient autocratic tradition, but that so far as other countries were concerned, he was projecting castles in the air." And even if experiments of this sort are made in other parts of Europe, it will happen either that this pseudo-communism, transferred to countries differing in religion, civilization, culture, customs, tradition, and in short having a different history, will become, under a like name and like appearances, something entirely different, or there will be a period of long and turbid travail, from the heart of which sooner or later liberty, that is, humanity, will spring forth once more.

Because this is the sole ideal that has the solidity once owned by Catholicism and the flexibility that this was never able to have, the only one that can always face the future and does not claim to determine it in any particular and contingent form, the only one that can resist criticism and represent for human society the point around which, in its frequent upheavals, in its continual oscillations, equilibrium is perpetually restored. So that when the question is heard whether liberty will enjoy what is known as the future, the answer must be that it has something better still: it has eternity. And today too, notwithstanding the coldness and the contempt and the scorn that liberty meets, it is in so many of our institutions and customs and our spiritual attitudes, and operates beneficently within them. What is more important, it lives in many noble intellects in all parts of the world, which, no matter how they are dispersed and isolated and reduced almost to an aristocratic but tiny *respublica literaria,* yet remain faithful to it and surround it with greater reverence and pursue it with more ardent love than in the times when there was no one to offend it or to question its absolute lordship, and the crowd surged around it hailing it by name, and in the very act contaminated its name with vulgarity, of which it has now been cleansed.

Nor does liberty live only in these men, nor does it exist and resist only in the government of many of the major states and in institutions and customs, but its virtue operates even in things themselves, it opens a path for itself with more or less slowness through the rudest difficulties. This can be seen principally in the sentiment and the idea that is arousing general solicitude, of a truce and a diminution of "preparedness" and armaments, of a peace and alliance between the states of Europe, of an agreement of intentions and efforts between her nations that shall save in the world and for the good of the world, if not their economic and political supremacy, at least their supremacy as creators and promoters of civilization, their acquired aptitude for this unceasing task. This is the only political project that, among all those formed since the war, has not been lost and dissipated but on the contrary gains ground from year to year and converts to itself minds that were hostile to it or displayed incredulity or would have liked to but did not dare to believe in it; and it is pleasant to hope that it will not be allowed to drop and that it will reach achievement, despite all opposition, overcoming and outflanking all obstacles, thanks to the arts of statesmen, thanks to the will of the nations. The World War—which perhaps future historians will consider as the *reductio ad absurdum* of all nationalism—may have embittered certain relations between states because of the iniquitous and stupid treaty of peace that ended it, but it has brought into intimate communion the nations who have felt themselves, and will always more and more feel themselves, equal in their virtues and their errors, in their strength and their weakness, subject to the same fate, troubled by the same loves, saddened by the same sorrows, proud of the same ideal heritage. Meanwhile, in all parts of Europe we are watching the growth of a new consciousness, of a new nationality (because, as we have already remarked, nations are not natural data, but historical states of consciousness and historical formations). And just as, seventy years ago, a Neapolitan of the old kingdom or a Piedmontese of the subalpine kingdom became an Italian without becoming false to his earlier quality but raising it and resolving it into this new quality, so the French and the Germans and the Italians and all the others will raise themselves into Europeans and their thoughts will be directed towards Europe and their hearts will beat for her as they once did for their smaller countries, not forgotten now but loved all the better.

This process of European union, which is directly opposed to nationalist competition and has already set itself up against it and one day will be able to liberate Europe from it altogether, tends at the same time to liberate her from the whole psychology that clings to this nationalism and supports it and generates kindred manners, habits, and actions. And if this thing happens, or when it happens, the liberal ideal will be fully restored in men's minds and will resume its rule. But we must not imagine the restoration of this ideal as a return to the conditions of another day, as one of those returns to the past which romanticism sometimes dreamed of, cradling itself in a sweet idyll. All that has happened, and all that will have happened in the meanwhile, cannot have happened in vain; several institutions of the old liberalism will have to be modified in greater or lesser measure, or replaced by others that are better adapted, and ruling and political classes of quite a different composition from the former ones will arise; and the experience of the past will produce other concepts and give a different direction to the will.

With this mental and moral disposition the problems will have to be taken up again that are called social, which certainly were not born today, over which thinkers and statesmen have laboured throughout the centuries, solving them from time to time according to the age, and which in the course of the nineteenth century formed the object of the most passionate attention and the most ardent care. And even then they were solved from time to time so far as they could be and with such results as greatly to change the conditions of the workers, to improve their tenor of life and elevate their juridical and moral status. Nor is "rationalized economy," as the phrase runs, which has now come into the forefront in discussion, anything intrinsically new, nor can the discussion turn on the replacement that it imposes of individual economics or of free initiative, which are indispensable to human life and even to economic progress, but only on the greater or lesser proportion to be attributed to the one with respect to the other, according to materials, places, times, and other circumstances. This is an argument for experts and statesmen, upon whom it is incumbent to solve it from time to time in such a way as may be most advantageous for the increase of production and most equitable for the distribution of wealth. But experts and statesmen will never be able to fulfil their function, nor to hope for an actuation of their proposals that is not fictitious, unless liberty prepares and maintains the intellectual and moral atmosphere necessary for so great a task, and guarantees the juridical order in which the actuation is to be accomplished.

All this, rapidly outlined, is not prophecy, for that is forbidden to us and to everyone for the simple reason that it would be vain, but a suggestion of what paths moral consciousness and the observation of the present may outline for those who in their guiding concepts and in their interpretation of the events of the nineteenth century agree with the narrative given of them in this history. Others, with a different mind, different concepts, a different quality of culture, and a different temperament, will choose other paths, and if they do so with a pure mind, in obedience to an inner command, they too will be preparing the future well. A history inspired by the liberal idea cannot, even in its practical and moral corollary, end with the absolute rejection and condemnation of those who feel and think differently. It simply says to those who agree with it: "Work according to the line that is here laid down for you, with your whole self, every day, every hour, in your every act; and trust in divine Providence, which knows more than we individuals do and works with us, inside us and over us." Words like these, which we have often heard and uttered in our Christian education and life, have their place, like others from the same source, in the "religion of liberty."

INDEX

Index

373

Reformation, 136
Reggio Calabria, 133
Reggio Emilia, Socialist congress of, 306
Reichstadt, Duke of, 113
Reinsurance Treaty (Germany-Russia), 335
religion, 18-19
Renan, 162
Rerum Novarum (encyclical), 299
Réunion, Tex., 148
Revolutions. *See* French, February, July; June insurrection.
Rheinische Zeitung, 127
Rhenish Bavaria, 107
Ricardo, 97
Ricasoli, 136
Richelieu, Duc de (1766-1822), 64, 70
Richelieu, Cardinal (1585-1642), 27
Rimini, Memorandum of, 120
Rinnovamento, 175, 206
Risorgimento, 225, 253
Robespierre, 149
Romagna, 106, 121
Roman Empire, Holy, 128-29
Roman question. *See* Guarantees, Law of.
Roman Republic, 173, 190, 200, 218
romanticism (*mal du siècle*), 42-57, 260-63; philosophic, 42-44, 261; political, 49-54
Rome, 25, 133, 225-27, 240. *See also* Papal States.
Rosmini, 121, 124, 136
Rossi, Pellegrino, 172
Rothschild, 138
Rotteck, 107
Rougier, 187
Rouher, 240
Rousseau, 32, 50

Royer-Collard, 98, 161
Rumania, 227, 234, 326
Ruskin, 262
Russell, Lord John, 192
Russia, 82-83, 108, 110, 113-14, 130, 188-90, 214-15, 235-38, 252, 276-79, 356-58
Russo-Japanese War, 278
Russo-Turkish War, 326, 328
Ruthenians, 110

Sadowa, 252
Sagasta, 281
Saint-Arnaud, 268
Saint-Simon, 59, 96, 118, 137, 140-43, 147, 207, 301
Sainte-Beuve, 88
Sanctis, de, 122
Sand, Georges, 146
Santa Fede, 26, 62, 166
Santarosa, Santorre di, 71
Sardinia, 115, 119-20, 133, 171-75, 209-13, 216-28
Sarrien, 308
Savigny, 85
Savoy, 121, 171, 223. *See also* Sardinia.
Saxony, 106, 181
Schiller, 13, 85
Schleswig-Holstein, 135, 182, 251
Schopenhauer, 261
Schwarzenberg, 182, 269
Sclopis, 210
Scott, 91, 109
Sebastopol, 216
Second Empire, 142. *See also* Napoleon III.
secret societies, 62
secularization, 287-88, 293
Sedanlächeln, 283
Serbia, 129-30, 232, 234, 326, 336-37
serfdom in Russia abolished, 235

GEORGE ALLEN & UNWIN LTD

London: 40 Museum Street, WC1

Auckland: 24 Wyndham Street
Bombay: 15 Graham Road, Ballard Estate, Bombay 1
Bridgetown: P.O. Box 222
Buenos Aires: Escritorio 454-459, Florida 165
Calcutta: 17 Chittaranjan Avenue, Calcutta 13
Cape Town: 68 Shortmarket Street
Hong Kong: 44 Mody Road, Kowloon
Ibadan: P.O. Box 62
Karachi: Karachi Chambers, McLeod Road
Lahore: Nawa-I-Waqt Building, 4 Queens Road
Madras: Mohan Mansions, 38c Mount Road, Madras 6
Mexico: Villalongin 32-10, Piso, Mexico 5, D.F.
Nairobi: P.O. Box 4536
New Delhi: 13-14 Asaf Ali Road, New Delhi 1
Ontario: 81 Curlew Drive, Don Mills
Phillippines: 7 Waling-Waling Street, Roxas District, Quezon City
Sao Paulo: Caixa Postal 8675
Singapore: 36c Prinsep Street, Singapore 7
Sydney, N.S.W.: Bradbury House, 55 York Street
Tokyo: 10 Kanda-Ogawamachi, 3-Chome, Chiyoda-Ku